BARRIE BENNETT • PETER SMILANICH

POWER PLAYS

Moving from Coping to Cooperation in Your Classroom

PEARSON

Feedback on this publication can be sent to editorialfeedback@pearsoned.com.

Pearson Canada Inc.
26 Prince Andrew Place
Don Mills, ON M3C 2T8
Customer Service: 1-800-361-6128

1 2 3 4 5 EBM 17 16 15 14 13

Vice-President, Publishing: Mark Cobham
Research and Communications Manager: Chris Allen
Managing Editor: Joanne Close
Developmental Editors: Gene Hayden, Sarah Mawson
Production Editors: Lisa Dimson, Debbie Lonergan
Copy Editor: Tilman Lewis
Proofreader: Kate Revington
Indexer: Noeline Bridge
Permissions Editor: Tara Smith
Manager, Project Management K–12: Alison Dale
Production Coordinator: Susan Wong
Cover and Interior Design: Alex Li
Composition: Aptara®, Inc.
Cover Image: Michael Hitoshi/Getty Images

ISBN: 978-0-13-287504-2

Jan and Ana (the wee Cairn)…you make life fun!–B. B.

To Lorraine, Jesse, Sarah, and my extended family.
Ultimately family is everything.–P. S.

Table of Contents

4 Key Factors to Minimize Conflict

The Teacher's Personality

INCLUDES
- being enthusiastic and wanting to teach
- having a sense of humour
- caring for students

The Teacher's Instructional Repertoire

IMPLIES BEING SKILLED AT
- designing meaningful lessons
- effectively structuring group work
- effectively framing questions
- effectively checking for understanding
- discussing the objective and purpose of the lesson
- using graphic organizers to present information
- differentiating instruction to meet diverse needs

The Teacher's Knowledge of the Curriculum

IMPLIES
- being committed to effectively and enthusiastically engaging students in learning the curriculum

The Teacher's Ability to Assess Student Learning

INCLUDES
- assessment *for, as,* and *of* learning

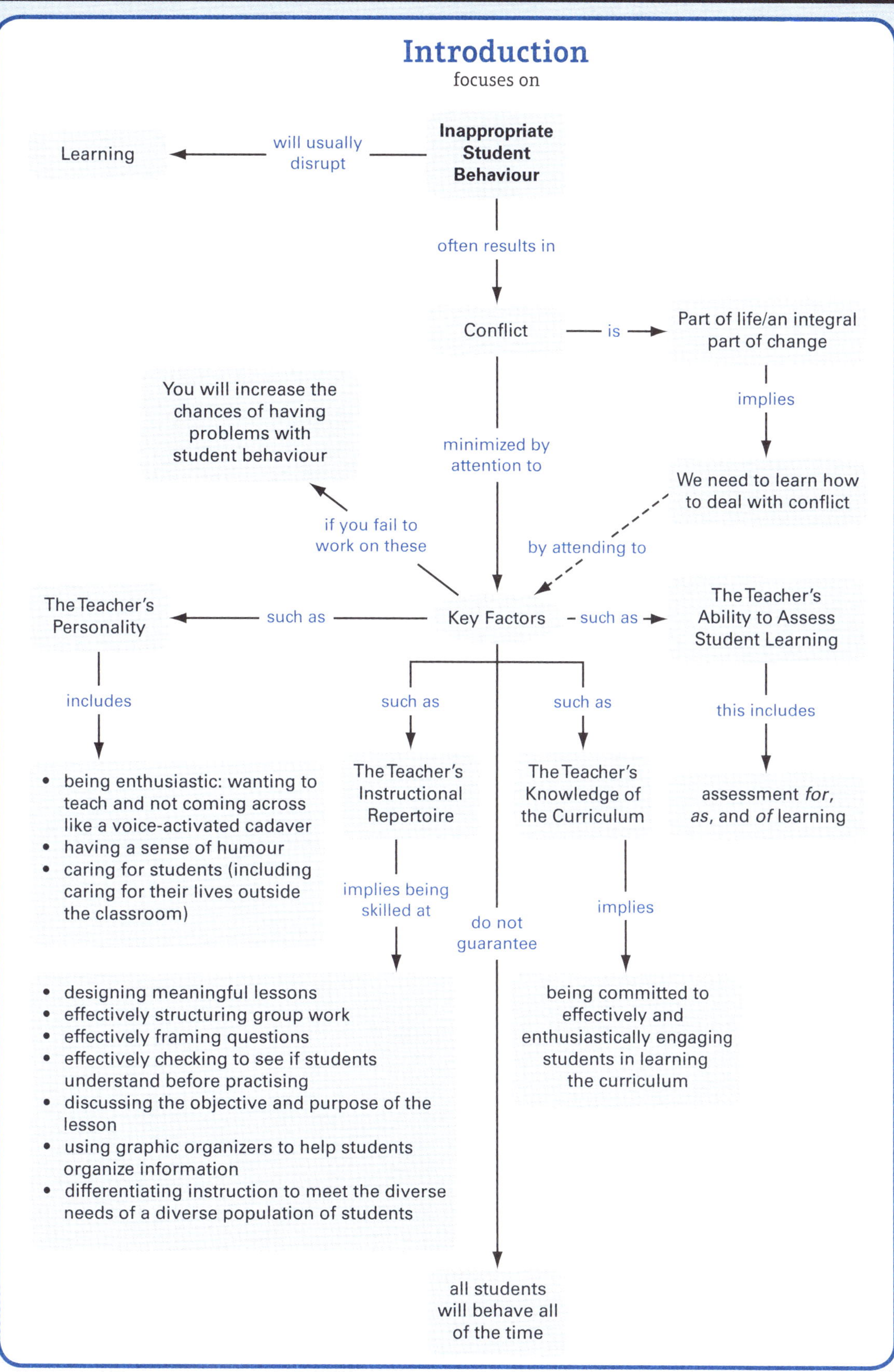
Introduction
focuses on
Inappropriate Student Behaviour
will usually disrupt
Learning
often results in
Conflict
is
Part of life/an integral part of change
implies
We need to learn how to deal with conflict
minimized by attention to
You will increase the chances of having problems with student behaviour
if you fail to work on these
by attending to
Key Factors
such as
The Teacher's Personality
such as
The Teacher's Ability to Assess Student Learning
includes
• being enthusiastic: wanting to teach and not coming across like a voice-activated cadaver
• having a sense of humour
• caring for students (including caring for their lives outside the classroom)
such as
The Teacher's Instructional Repertoire
implies being skilled at
• designing meaningful lessons
• effectively structuring group work
• effectively framing questions
• effectively checking to see if students understand before practising
• discussing the objective and purpose of the lesson
• using graphic organizers to help students organize information
• differentiating instruction to meet the diverse needs of a diverse population of students
such as
The Teacher's Knowledge of the Curriculum
implies
being committed to effectively and enthusiastically engaging students in learning the curriculum
this includes
assessment for, as, and of learning
do not guarantee
all students will behave all of the time

The purpose of this book is to explore and clarify power plays in the classroom.

As teachers, we are never so fragile as when we are expected to have control over a situation...and we don't. Situations involving conflict are daily realities for most teachers. For 200 days a year, six hours a day, while teaching some 300-odd outcomes, we face the possibility of behaviour issues and power plays erupting in our classrooms.

Earlier research on teacher retention (Johnson, Berg, & Donaldson, 2005; Rosenholtz, 1985) identified three key reasons teachers quit: (1) they don't know how to resolve classroom management issues; (2) they don't know how to motivate their students; and (3) they feel unsupported within their school. Current research by John Hattie (2012) shows that when newer teachers quit, the student achievement in the year the teacher decides to quit drops noticeably.

There is no doubt that school-wide discipline policies and school culture play important roles in preventing and resolving power plays. In this book, however, our primary focus is on sharing knowledge strategies that effective teachers use to prevent or respond to plays for power in their classrooms. We also illustrate why some teachers, working in the same school with the same students, get "caught up" in more classroom management issues and power plays than their peers.

Although no panacea exists for managing a classroom, there are actions you can take when students misbehave to increase the chance of restoring social order promptly so that learning can continue. In this book, we look at those actions and how to implement them in any classroom.

Key Considerations

The Ubiquity of Power Plays: Each of us experiences power plays as we move through life—as children, as students, as employees and employers, and as parents. We even get involved in conflict with those we love. Which parent has not been involved in a struggle for power with a child at some point?

A constant in teaching is that students will misbehave. Fortunately, methods exist to deal with those misbehaviours. An effective teacher's classroom has fewer incidents of misbehaviour. Furthermore, the

nature of the misbehaviour is less serious, and students respond more positively to requests to behave appropriately.

The Importance of Self-Control: Recent research indicates a major factor in children's future success is their ability to exercise self-control. Moffitt, Caspi, and Taylor (2010) followed 1000 children from birth to 32 years. They found that the more self-control children have, the higher their education level and their degree of success as they move through life. Children with strong self-control are less likely to have criminal convictions or experience substance abuse, and they have better physical health and better finances. The relevance of this finding to the book? Study authors and others in the field believe that we need to educate children and parents on the importance of self-control and find ways to foster growing self-control in the classroom.

Related to this finding is research on self-regulation. Conducted over the past several decades, this research, by both developmental and cognitive scientists, explores the relationship between a child's ability to self-regulate—to stay calmly focused and alert—and his or her ability to master the learning demands of our classrooms.

The difference between self-regulation and self-control is that self-regulation involves more than compliance. A child's ability to self-regulate correlates to his or her ability to respond to ever greater challenges and, as the child matures, to skills that relate to processing, assimilating, and mastering learning.

Shanker (2013) has written extensively on this subject and has identified six critical elements that can be seen in a child who is optimally self-regulated. She or he

- recognizes when feeling calmly focused and alert
- recognizes when feeling stressed, what is causing this state
- recognizes stressors in and out of the classroom
- has the desire to deal with these stressors
- develops strategies to cope with them
- recovers efficiently and effectively from stressors (p. xiii)

Self-Regulation

When teachers structure the classroom so that students share control and have influence over their learning, power plays become less likely. When we differentiate our instruction to respond to the ways in which students learn, students feel more in control of their learning and are less likely to misbehave. All students want to be successful, to feel safe and included, and to be interested and engaged in meaningful learning.

Teachers Who Struggle: Researchers Louis and Miles (1990) investigated a four-year effort by teachers at five schools struggling to improve their effectiveness as teachers. They found the key predictor of whether school staff would become, and stay, effective was their ability to confront and resolve conflict. They also found that the skill to confront and resolve conflict was learned—the staff worked at it.

Both authors of this book worked for six years on a project to support teachers who were experiencing conflict in the classroom and were at risk of losing their jobs. In addition, we were involved with Edmonton Public Schools in an initiative that asked highly effective teachers to design powerful learning environments. One of the authors, Peter Smilanich, was responsible for the design and initial implementation of the Edmonton Public Schools Teacher Effectiveness Program.

In our work, we found that although classroom management appeared to be the leading challenge for at-risk teachers, it wasn't the only challenge. Personality, instructional repertoire, organizational skills, assessment strategies, grouping abilities, questioning techniques, school culture, and more were all factors that could contribute to teachers being at risk of losing their position.

About This Book

Introduction to Power Plays Video

Section 1 focuses on power plays—their design and intent. By understanding the concept of these struggles in the classroom, we are more clearly positioned to understand the student who moves to power and the approaches that will de-escalate the situation and restore social order. Historically, Jürgen Habermas, who was described in the text *Fifty Modern Thinkers on Education* (Palmer, Bresler, & Cooper, 2001), focused on social justice—on responding to inequalities to give power to those operating in educational contexts. He identified four stages, which roughly parallel the key ideas in this section, for dealing with issues in educational contexts:

- Stage one: Describe and interpret the existing situation, to make sense of the current situation.
- Stage two: Penetrate the reasons that gave rise to the situation. Find how the actions and thinking have given rise to the current situation, which is working against a more progressive social order.

- Stage three: Design a plan to change things.
- Stage four: Evaluate the plan.

Section 2 connects teachers' instructional actions to classroom management. To illustrate that connection, we explain how the instructional skills of framing questions, checking for understanding, and structuring groups affect student behaviour. We also explore the impact of school culture and school-wide discipline policies on classroom management.

Section 1: Behaviour

Section 1 Video

Chapter 1: The Design of Power Plays. We clarify the "design" of power plays using four key questions from David Perkins's (1994) book, *Knowledge as Design*. The idea of "knowledge as design" may sound boring, but readers will discover it is essential to prevent or respond effectively to power situations. We also classify them into two types: (1) power situations that teachers can deal with in the classroom, and (2) power situations that require outside intervention or support from other teachers, school administrators, social workers, or parents.

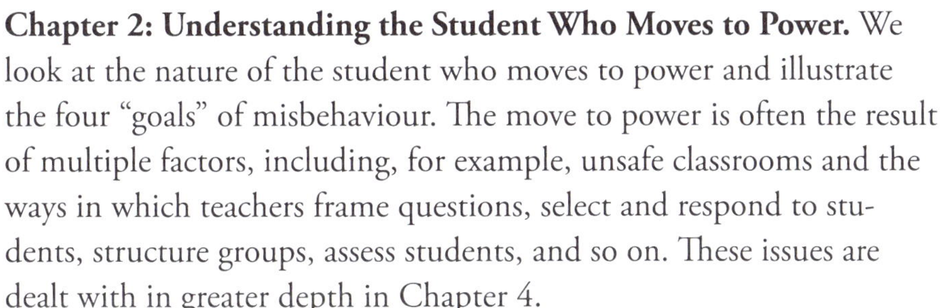

Chapter 2: Understanding the Student Who Moves to Power. We look at the nature of the student who moves to power and illustrate the four "goals" of misbehaviour. The move to power is often the result of multiple factors, including, for example, unsafe classrooms and the ways in which teachers frame questions, select and respond to students, structure groups, assess students, and so on. These issues are dealt with in greater depth in Chapter 4.

Chapter 3: Pre-Power Approaches: Our Theory of Bumps. We explain our theory of student misbehaviour through the concept of "bumps" or "escalations." This chapter covers the first four of six bumps detailed in the book. The chapter comprises an in-depth explanation of skills teachers employ to avert a potential power play. We illustrate how a situation escalates, or is "bumped up" in terms of complexity and stress. Interestingly, most teachers apply most or all of these pre-emptive skills on a consistent basis but are unaware they are using them. Moreover, teachers often integrate two or more of these skills simultaneously, unaware that their application involves a degree of art. By not being "artful" in how they apply these skills, teachers can unintentionally increase the chance that a play for power will emerge.

Chapter 4: Responding to Students Who Move to Power. An escalation of the four bumps covered in Chapter 3, this chapter clarifies Bump 5, Defusing a Power Play. We look at how effective teachers respond to power in the classroom. We illustrate a variety of situations that arise in classrooms and examine the options that increase the likelihood of de-escalating the situation and restoring social order.

Chapter 5: Power Responses: The Informal Chat. In this chapter, we look at Bump 6, The Informal Chat. We explore ways to co-plan with students effective solutions to resolve conflict and problems.

Section 2 Video

Section 2: Teacher Practice

Chapter 6: The Teacher Continuum: Moving Toward Effective Teaching Practices. What are the belief systems of effective teachers? of less effective teachers? The intent of this chapter is to assist teachers to reflect on whether we are contributing to a greater likelihood of power struggles in our classrooms. If we, as teachers, contribute to these struggles occurring or continuing to occur in our classrooms, then we are part of the problem, not the solution. The chapter then focuses on three key concepts—winning over, positive cohesive bonding, and inclusiveness—and how these concepts connect to empathy. These three concepts are key to a healthy classroom culture.

Chapter 7: How We Talk to Students: Questioning, Responding, and Checking for Understanding. In our daily dialogue with students, we can employ simple instructional methods to reduce tension and create a cohesive classroom environment. In this chapter, we detail techniques for questioning, responding, and checking for understanding that benefit all students.

Chapter 8: Cooperative Learning and the Inclusive Classroom. Here we detail the work of Jeanne Gibbs (Tribes), David and Roger Johnson (The Five Basic Elements), and Spencer Kagan. The contributions of these educators have done much to help teachers create the kinds of classroom conditions that are inclusive, safe, and conducive to learning. Brendtro, Brokenleg, and Van Bockern (1990) in their book *Reclaiming Youth at Risk: Our Hope for the Future* argue that cooperative learning in the classroom is key for reclaiming youth at risk.

Chapter 9: School-Wide Responsibility for Student Behaviour. We examine the role of the school administration, guidance personnel, and parents in supporting appropriate behaviour in the classrooms. We look at school-wide discipline policies and how these policies can assist in effectively dealing with students and teachers who end up in power struggle situations.

Chapter 10: Research into the Thinking and Actions of Effective Teachers: A Historical Perspective. As this chapter shows, power struggles are nothing new to educators. As we continue to strive for ways to make our classrooms safe, caring cultures where students can flourish, some historical thinking on behaviour is surprisingly current.

"I'll never forget the time you strapped me for talking in class."

Features of This Book and Companion Website

As you read, you will notice icons in the page margins.

- The professional learning community icon alerts you to activities in the book that provide opportunities for collegial learning.

The following icons alert you to resources available on the book's companion website: www.pearsoncanada.ca/powerplays

- The research icon alerts you to recommended books and links to online professional resources.

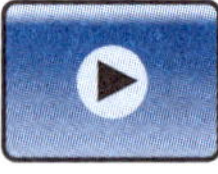

- The video icon indicates video clips where Barrie Bennett, one of the authors, introduces the book and provides some examples of classroom management techniques. (See pages 6, 7, 8, and 52.)

SECTION 1

BEHAVIOUR

The Design of Power Plays

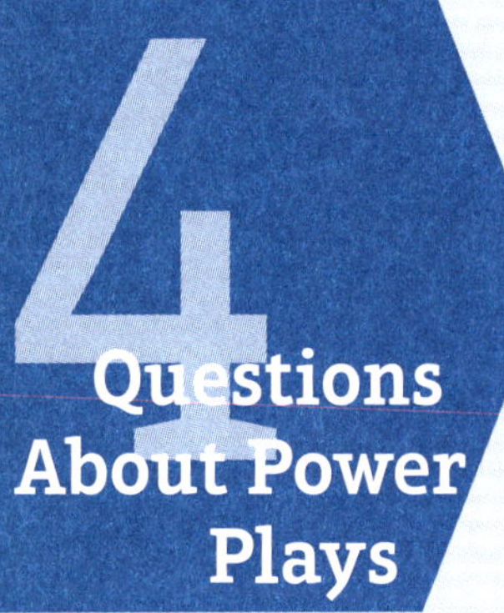

What Are the Critical or Essential Attributes of a Power Play?	• conflict between two or more people • one or more of the participants usually too emotional—pushing to anger • air of defiance
What Is the Purpose of a Power Play?	• need to have influence/control, usually over one's life
What Are Model Cases of Power Plays?	• continuing an action when asked to stop, or stopping momentarily but then continuing • actively refusing requests • passively refusing requests • challenging requests on one's own behalf or on behalf of others
What Is the Value of a Power Play?	• saving face • having some power or influence in one's life • payback for being mentally, emotionally, or physically hurt

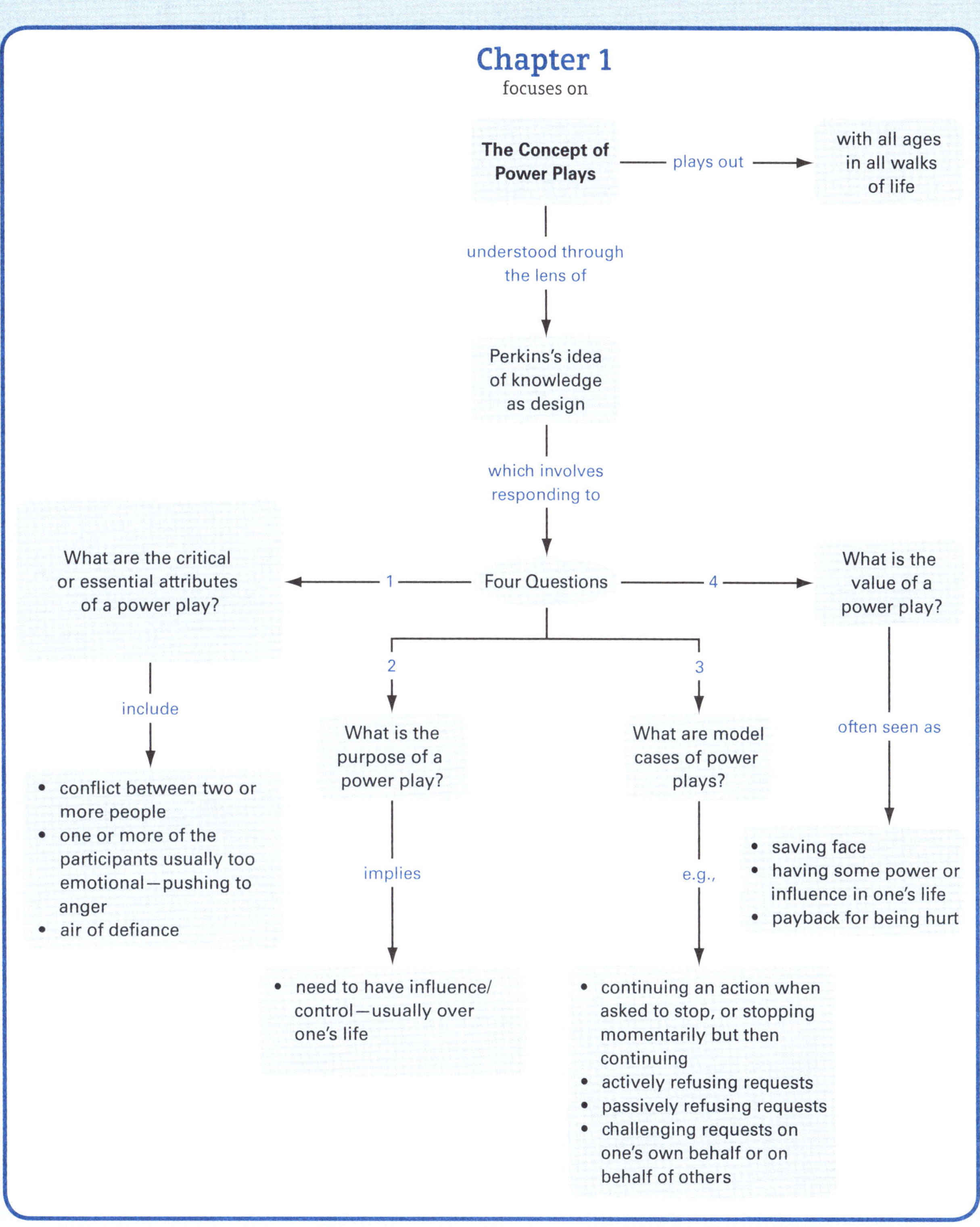
Chapter 1
focuses on
The Concept of Power Plays
plays out
with all ages in all walks of life
understood through the lens of
Perkins's idea of knowledge as design
which involves responding to
Four Questions
1
What are the critical or essential attributes of a power play?
include
• conflict between two or more people
• one or more of the participants usually too emotional—pushing to anger
• air of defiance
2
What is the purpose of a power play?
implies
• need to have influence/control—usually over one's life
3
What are model cases of power plays?
e.g.,
• continuing an action when asked to stop, or stopping momentarily but then continuing
• actively refusing requests
• passively refusing requests
• challenging requests on one's own behalf or on behalf of others
4
What is the value of a power play?
often seen as
• saving face
• having some power or influence in one's life
• payback for being hurt

The purpose of this chapter is to provide an in-depth understanding of power struggles—their critical elements, their purposes, their most common representations, and their value to the person who instigates the struggle. On the previous page is a concept map of the key ideas in this chapter.

Knowledge as Design

The Nature of Knowledge

A power struggle, like any concept, can be defined by its attributes, purpose, value, and so on. But David Perkins, in his book *Knowledge as Design: A Handbook for Critical and Creative Discussion Across the Curriculum* (1994), argues that true knowledge goes deeper than the facts and figures. To really understand a concept, we must also have a deep understanding of its *design*.

If we apply this argument to power struggles, we can truly understand the nature of the tension by exploring the design of power struggles. This will allow us to make predictions and take thoughtful actions to avert power struggles, or at least to defuse the tension appropriately. Without this level of understanding, the concept, in this case the power struggle, owns us—we cannot think and act on it effectively.

Perkins argues that students must answer four key questions to be able to "think" and "act" with a concept they have learned:

1. What are the critical or essential attributes of the concept?
2. What is the purpose of the concept?
3. What are model cases of the concept?
4. What is the value of the concept?

Let's use these four questions to explore the concept of power struggles.

1. What Are the Critical or Essential Attributes of a Power Play?

In general, a power play involves two opposing forces. English teachers, drawing an analogy with literary conflicts, might understand a power struggle as pitting one person against another, a person against herself, or self against nature. For students, a power struggle might be student against teacher, student against other student(s), student against parent(s), student against homework—or against any work at all.

Whatever its cause, a power play in the classroom will include one or more of these critical attributes:

- a noticeable manifestation of defiance—a challenge is made by word, intonation, or body language
- a conflict between two or more people—one or more believe they are right
- heightened emotions (which may not be visible) experienced by one, both, or all those involved

2. What Is the Purpose of a Power Play?

According to psychologist Alfred Adler (Adler, Ansbacher, & Ansbacher, 1967; Dreikurs, Grunwald, & Pepper, 1998) we all share the needs to belong and to have control over our lives. William Glasser (1985, 1999), a contemporary Adlerian, adds that we also have a need for fun and freedom. Adlerians argue that when these needs are not met, we take actions to achieve them. When we are not successful in fulfilling our needs in socially appropriate ways, we shift to socially inappropriate behaviours.

In essence, the purpose of the power play is often to fight or push back against what we sense is a lack of belonging or control in our lives. The struggle may also be prompted by our need to enjoy what we are doing, and to have some choice in what is happening to us.

More often than not, when we get into a power play, the actions we take in our attempt to get our needs met do not result in a socially acceptable resolution of the tension. This is true for both students and teachers. Students may believe their choice to be the "right" one, but the behaviour is not acceptable in an effective teacher's classroom and consequently, those students often end up outside the classroom.

A less effective teacher may act in a way that is also not acceptable, and still the student ends up outside the classroom. Now the school administration is forced to intervene and somehow resolve the tension between the ineffective teacher, who may have caused the situation to escalate, and the student, who may have behaved inappropriately.

3. What Are Model Cases of Power Plays?

Below are four genres of power struggles. What do they have in common?

1. Students who continue an action when asked to stop, or who stop momentarily but then continue.
2. Students who actively refuse requests.
3. Students who passively refuse requests.
4. Students who challenge requests on their own behalf or on behalf of others.

Below are examples of common classroom power struggle situations. Classify them into groups of your own choosing according to the nature of the struggle. (Note: This invokes concept formation, an inductive thinking strategy. See Appendix I for a description of this strategy.) You may create two, three, or four groups—the number is up to you; just be able to justify why you classified them the way you did. Once you have classified the examples, rank your groups from most difficult to least difficult to handle in a classroom or school. How do your classifications reflect the four genres outlined above?

a. A student has been asked to put away her cell phone twice within five minutes. She puts it away but when the teacher is not looking, takes it out again for the third time.

b. Two students (who are part of a group of four) are arguing about one of them not doing anything to help the group finish the task.

c. For the third day in one week, a student does not bring any pens or paper to class and so he simply sits and does nothing.

d. The teacher tells a student to stop talking. The student glares at the teacher.

e. The teacher asks a student to stop talking. The student replies, "Why do you always pick on me?" Another student adds: "Yeah, you always pick on her."

f. The teacher has asked a question, sees a student not paying attention, and says, "Jennifer, you seem to be thinking hard. Could you please give us the answer?"

g. The teacher writes out the student groups for a math task on the board. One student says, "I'm not working with him—he's a jerk!"

h. A teacher comes into class and finds students are far too loud and are not getting ready for the start of class. The teacher tries to get them to be quiet. Most continue to talk, ignoring the teacher's request.

i. A student gets up and heads to the back of room to sharpen a pencil while the teacher is talking; the teacher asks the student to sit down. The student replies, "Well, how am I supposed to take notes if my pencil is broken?" He keeps going toward the pencil sharpener, ignoring the teacher's request.

j. When asked not to call out answers, a student continues to call out answers.

k. The teacher asks a student to stop talking; the student stops for 10 seconds then starts talking again.

l. The teacher tells two students publicly that if what they have done is the best they can do, they might as well not come to school.

Which one of the above situations is somewhat different from the rest? The answer is at the bottom of page 19.

4. What Is the Value of a Power Play?

In the case of a power struggle, the value is similar to the purpose—to achieve a sense of belonging or control over our life, or to let people know that we are upset and will no longer accept what is happening to us. Note that this applies to both students and teachers.

Analyze the following classroom situations. Consider how your analysis connects to Perkins's four questions related to knowledge as design.

Classroom Situation 1: The teacher asks a student to remove his baseball cap (the school rule is no hats in school). The student says, with a pained, surprised look, "Why?"

Classroom Situation 2: One student says to another student: "If you're not going to do your part, go do it on your own." The other student says: "F—k you." (The teacher hears it.)

The Role of a Partner and an Audience

One of the most obvious ways to defuse a power play is to refuse to take part: it is difficult to have a power struggle if one person does not "want to play." This is akin to being asked to dance and saying, "No, thank you" and walking away. If the person still wants to dance, he will have to dance alone.

How often have you seen a child throw a tantrum when no one else is around? Almost never. An altercation needs a partner and in many cases an audience. One secondary school teacher of at-risk students begins the first day of school by informing her students that she loves teaching and will do her best to help each of them to learn. She also tells them that if they want to argue with her, they'll need to argue on their own—she won't take part. The teacher goes on to explain that if she is wrong in a situation, she will apologize and try to do better. This teacher earned a Teacher of the Year Award from Edmonton Public Schools for the artful way in which she teaches and her success with at-risk students. A Tribes trainer, she knows how to build safe, inclusive classrooms and understands the benefits of not providing an audience.

Here is an example of an after-school power struggle that would not have taken place without an audience.

> A teacher was leaving the school when he noticed a group of students just off the school grounds, clearly engaged in a scuffle. He went over and saw two Grade 6 girls pushing each other. Students surrounding the girls were asked to leave. All of them did, with the exception of one girl. When asked if she was involved, the girl said "no" and was asked to leave. The teacher asked the two Grade 6 girls why they were fighting. They said they didn't want to fight, but that the girl who had stayed told them if they didn't fight after school, she would beat them both up. They were best friends. The teacher thanked the girls, told them he was sorry that this had happened to them, and added he would talk to the girl tomorrow.

This situation is an example of bullying as it relates to power struggles—it required a spectator to play out. In Chapter 8, we examine how one school in the York Region District School Board dealt with bullying. Five years after implementing initiatives, the principal in this school reported that bullying had stopped. The students had developed the skills to deal with bullying: they were no longer willing to be the audience. One of the most recent and thoughtful books on bullying is titled *No Place for Bullying: Leadership for Schools That Care for Every Student* (Dillon, 2012).

Chapter 1 Conclusion

Power plays are complex; they range from passive to more aggressive forms of power, including bullying. The struggles can be between two students, between one student and a group of students, between the teacher and a student, or between a teacher and a group of students. They can be somewhat spontaneous or planned. They may be intentionally or unintentionally initiated by what we might deem an attention-seeking behaviour.

If teachers can better understand the elements of power plays—their purpose, types, and value—then they are in better position to understand how to resolve them.

Answer: (c) This student's behaviour does not prevent the teacher from teaching, or the other students from learning. Students who simply do not engage pose more of a motivational problem than a behavioural one. These students are also usually more complex to deal with. See Chapter 2, pages 29 to 30 for case studies of students who were unengaged.

Understanding the Student Who Moves to Power

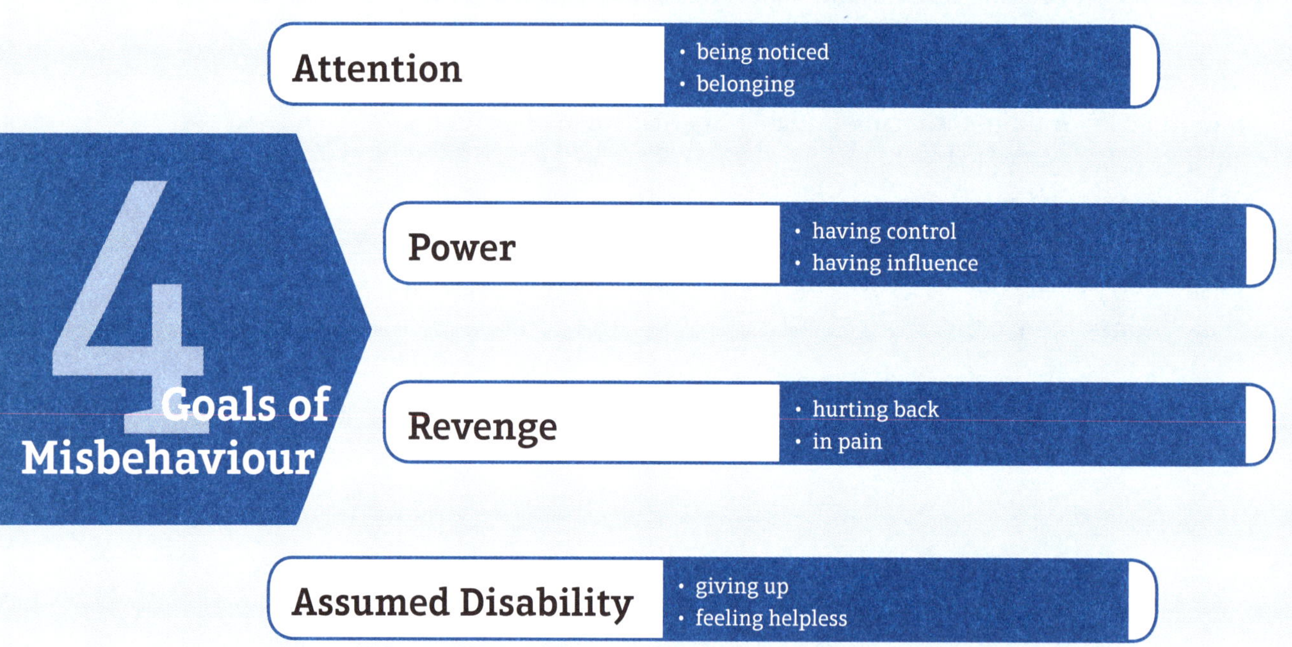
Attention
• being noticed
• belonging
4 Goals of Misbehaviour
Power
• having control
• having influence
Revenge
• hurting back
• in pain
Assumed Disability
• giving up
• feeling helpless

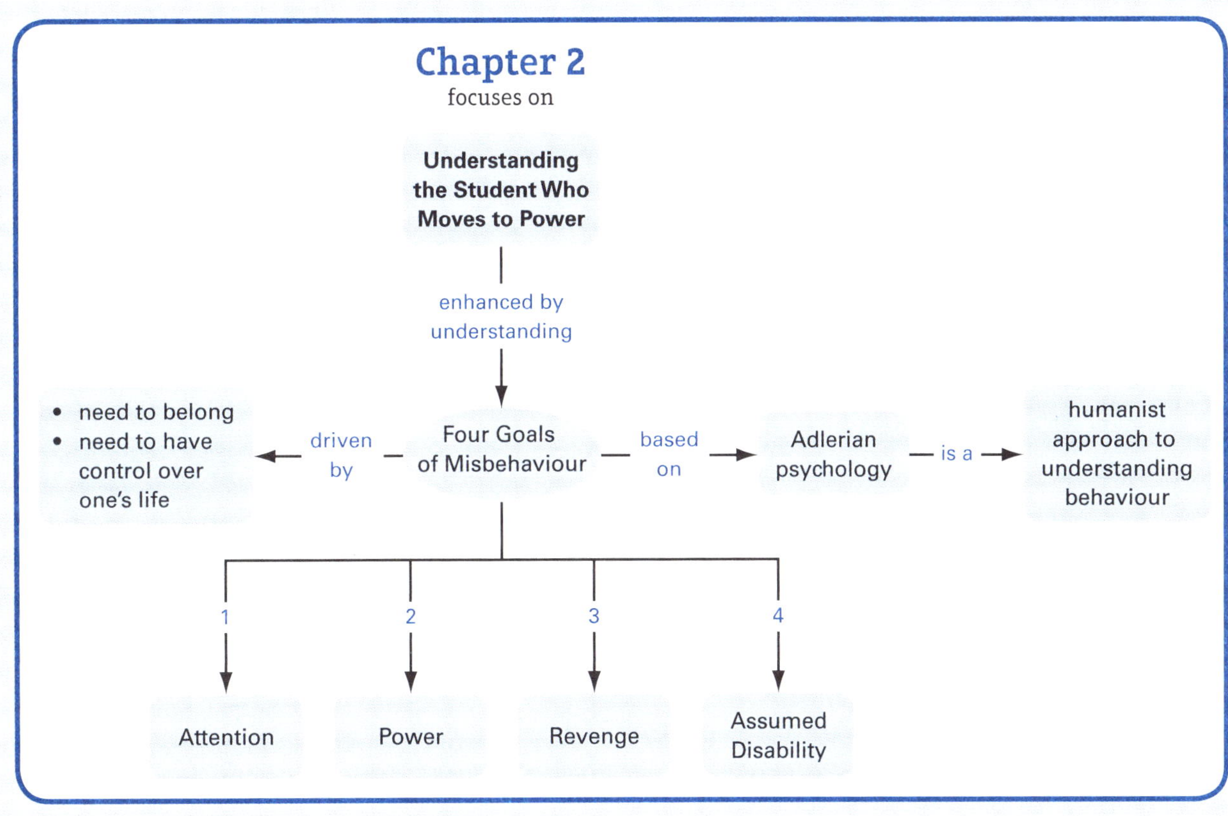
Chapter 2
focuses on
Understanding the Student Who Moves to Power
enhanced by understanding
Four Goals of Misbehaviour
driven by
• need to belong
• need to have control over one's life
based on
Adlerian psychology
is a
humanist approach to understanding behaviour
1
2
3
4
Attention
Power
Revenge
Assumed Disability

The purpose of this chapter is to provide greater understanding of students who move to power play situations. This is the first step to knowing when and how to best respond.

The diagram below shows two continuums and four quadrants. The vertical continuum represents the amount of disruption caused by the students' behaviour—from minimal to extensive. The horizontal continuum shows the frequency of disruptive behaviours. On one end of the continuum are students who rarely, if ever, get into power struggles at school. If they do, they are simply having a "bad moment" and the situation is usually easily resolved. On the other end of the continuum are students who frequently get into power struggles. These students operate with a perpetual chip on their shoulder; they set up situations that will escalate into power struggles. These students present difficult challenges for teachers.

A student in quadrant 2, for example, will cause frequent disruptions, but these disruptions will be minimal in nature.

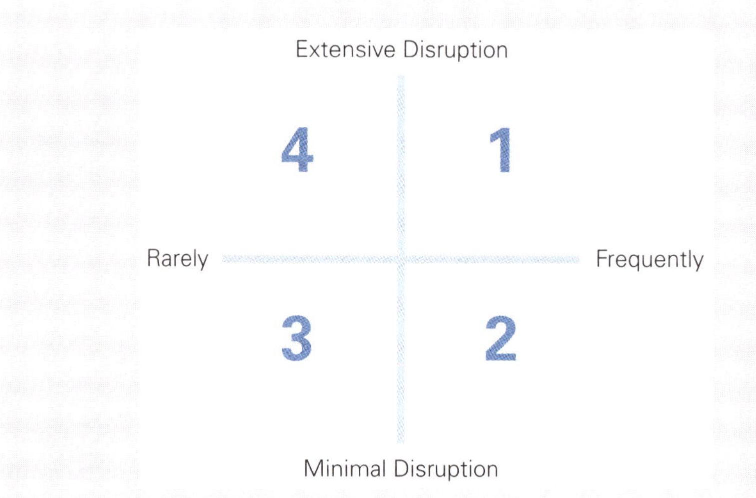

As teachers, we often fail to accurately understand the more complex students who move to power. For effective classroom management, it is essential to explore why power plays have become an integral part of the lifestyle of these students.

Goals of Misbehaviour

Rudolf Dreikurs (1968) identified four major goals of misbehaviour: attention, power, revenge, and assumed disability.

These goals are not meant as an exact, or exclusive, explanation of why power-oriented students behave the way they do. Rather, the goals provide insight to help teachers understand why students, and possibly teachers, misbehave. The more insight we have, the better equipped we are to create safe environments that encourage student learning.

Note that just because a student misbehaves does not mean that the student has a *goal* of misbehaviour. Anyone can have moments when they act inappropriately. However, a student has a goal of misbehaviour when the behaviour has become part of the student's lifestyle and prevents the student from interacting in a socially acceptable way.

Four Goals of Misbehaviour

Attention Goal: These students feel they are not getting the attention they believe they require. The students' mistaken belief is that they belong only when others are paying attention to them and they seek acceptance through the attention of others. They want the teacher or other students to provide them with additional recognition. They are not attempting to hurt or to control; they simply want others to attend to their needs. These students usually attain their goal through annoying or disruptive behaviours. Their effect is much like that of a mosquito's whine—it persists without end.

When you hear yourself saying, "How many times do I have to tell you?" or "If I've told you once I've told you a million times…" or "That's the last time…," a strong possibility exists that the student may have attention-seeking as a reason for misbehaving.

A teacher's feelings of frustration, irritation, and annoyance are indicators that the student is seeking attention. When these students get attention, they stop misbehaving, but only temporarily. Before long, they are once again buzzing and irritating. Unfortunately, the teacher is being conditioned by the student to continue to respond. The brief stoppage in return for attention gives the teacher relief, but only in the short term. A friend who is a teacher was a bit irritated by a student and stated, "I'm getting tired of always having to tell you not to call out answers." A very sharp student with autism quickly said to the teacher, "Then stop telling him." This student got it; we sometimes don't because we are too caught up in the moment.

Power Goal: These students' behaviour oozes defiance. The students have the mistaken belief that they are important only when they are in control of a situation or of others. Their defiance usually takes the form of temper tantrums, crying, or arrogance. It is expressed in tone and body language when talking back, contradicting, or challenging the teacher or other students. Another telltale sign: when asked to stop, these students continue to misbehave. That failure to stop gives the message that the teacher will have to *make* the student stop. These power situations are stressful.

Power-seeking behaviour is commonly perceived by teachers as an attack on their authority. As a result, the teacher feels threatened or embarrassed. Typically, anger quickly follows. Teachers' verbal response to a student can mirror their emotional state. They may threaten, "Keep that up and you're going to the office" or seek to embarrass: "Act your age." The display of anger indicates that the teacher's repertoire of responses is exhausted or being ignored. This use of anger is an attempt to overpower the student and make the student submit to the teacher's will.

Revenge Goal: These students hurt others physically or emotionally to help balance the fact that they are also hurting. This type of behaviour becomes cyclical. Students who are motivated by revenge set themselves up to be punished, and the hurt that comes from being punished renews their cause to seek revenge.

If these students are successful in achieving their goal, the teacher feels hurt and humiliation. When the student misbehaviour is severe enough, teachers are likely to experience feelings of repulsion and revulsion—once again their actions mirror the student's emotions. The less effective teacher may say something designed to hurt, such as "Only an animal would do that!" These students are often suspended, and denied privileges for extended periods of time.

Assumed Disability Goal: This misbehaviour reflects the students' feelings of helplessness and their mistaken belief that they have no ability. Such a student is an all but invisible presence who makes no, or minimal, effort. Students who seek this goal do not stop you from teaching, or stop other students from learning, unless they are expected to contribute to a group. Even then, the group ends up working around them.

Why Does My Mother Want to Die?

Miss, my mom tried to kill herself last night
She just took a lot of pills, she gave up, and she lost the fight
The fight, to live, to try another day
No matter what I did, no matter what words I could say

She just looked at me like I wasn't there
Lifted the bottle and said no one really cares
She said, you don't know what I have been through
Treated like a tramp, dirty, you don't have a clue

You didn't grow up in my home
Hardly any laughter, but surely a lot of gloom
I had you when I was barely eighteen
I feel like a failure, I don't want to be so mean

Miss, I kept her up all night
No way was I going to give up the fight
I love her so much and I wish she understood
How much prayer I sent up last night, I knew it was for the good

It was like something helped me get through the night
I know that suicide isn't right
It's love, compassion and a lot of tender loving care, you say
That will get us through, and find us a better way

I know that I may not understand all about life
We will go through a lot of storms, a lot of strife
It is like her past won't stop bothering her mind
If only she could understand, look up above and find

That true peace comes from heaven above
He was in our room, hovering over us like a dove
I will never forget this night
And my mom made it out all right

Miss, I didn't have time to study my spelling words
I was so amazed at the heavenly birds
Miss, my mom isn't going to die
She woke up this morning and is going to give it another try.

—by Vera Tourangeau, from *Miss, It Hurts*

If the student is successful in achieving this goal of misbehaviour, the teacher feels defeated. Again, teachers' actions mirror their emotions. Teachers who give up on these students will decrease their expectations to a minimum. The students are usually ignored, forgotten, or treated with indifference. Expressions that less effective teachers use with students evidencing this type of misbehaviour include "If you don't try, why should I?" and "When you're ready to work, let me know."

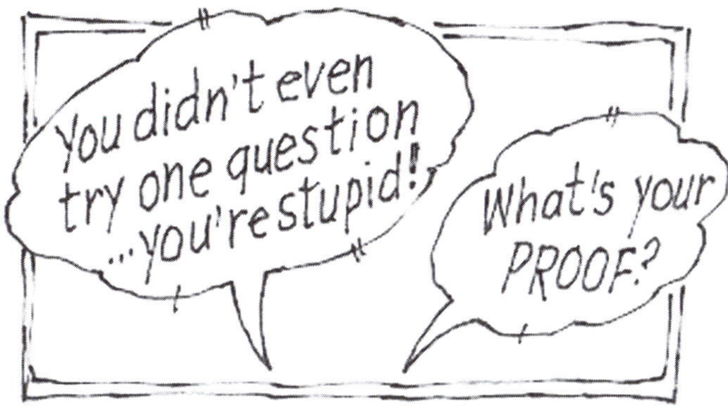

Students who hold any of these four goals of misbehaviour typically arrive in a teacher's classroom after a few years of being unsuccessful in home life and school life. The challenge for teachers is to determine how to motivate these children to learn, and how to make them feel worthy and safe in the classroom.

For additional information on goals of misbehaviour, see Dinkmeyer, McKay, and Dinkmeyer's (1997) book *The Parent's Handbook: Systematic Training for Effective Parenting*. Although this is an older book, the information is very applicable to today's home and school situations.

The Nature of Students Who Consistently Engage in Power Plays

To develop appropriate responses to power-oriented students, we must understand their key characteristics and the varied ways in which students engage in power situations.

1. **Power-oriented students are often natural leaders.** Unfortunately, they use their considerable capacity to influence others for personal interests. They are not concerned about the classroom running smoothly. They can behave appropriately when they want to.

2. **They often have few good friends.** Power-oriented students may move through the entire class list, bringing other students into their sphere of influence at different times. These students will often draw in pairs of others, manipulating the relationship between the two friends and prompting them to compete for the power-oriented student's attention. Often one friend is rejected as another is favoured.

3. **They are usually intelligent, but behind academically.** Often, academic failure is a function of too little application combined with missing school and a dysfunctional family. These students will, at times, produce a superior piece of work just to let you know they can do it but won't.

4. **They are frequently advanced verbally.** Most of these students have been unintentionally training from an early age to oppose what people expect from them. They often come across like classroom lawyers and can seldom be defeated verbally; they precisely recall previous situations to be used as precedents. "Why didn't Matthew have to leave when he talked back to you last week?" Expect everything you say or have said to be used in the heat of the battle. In upper elementary and beyond, their voices contain a perpetual lilt of arrogance.

5. **They appear to have a master's degree in group dynamics.** Power-oriented students are highly tuned to negative and positive cohesiveness between students, and between students and the teacher, and they will use their insights to meet their goals.

6. **They are acutely observant and file away information on what buttons to push.** Combined with their sensitivity to interpersonal relationships, these students are particularly adept at knowing which buttons to push and when to push them to draw others (including teachers) into a power struggle.

7. **Often, they compete with the teacher for control of the room.** If they can, they will lead the class to negative cohesiveness.

8. **They generate anger easily.** They do this inconsistently, and so in any exchange you are never sure whether they will escalate or stop the misbehaviour. This quick fuse, which is intermittently lit, generates anxiety in those around them.

Students Who Move to Power in Non-aggressive Ways

The following examples illustrate students who also engage in power plays, albeit in a more subtle, less obtrusive fashion.

Tina: The Class Clown (Attention Goal)

Tina, a Grade 6 student, had an infectious smile and could make anyone laugh at will. If the teacher was upset with her, she would feign surprise and respond with a big smile that would catch on with the other students. Exasperated, the teacher placed Tina at the front of the room, at the back of the room, and in a carrel. Nothing worked. She put her in the hall and continued to ask her class questions. The teacher said, "Hands up if you…" Then she started to laugh; Tina's hand shot through the door into the room as though looking around the room. The children also laughed. The teacher, still laughing, said, "Tina, come back in here." She continued, "I give up, Tina, you are the best I've ever seen; I even laugh now. You win. I lose. The problem is that we get behind in learning because I have to spend so much time trying to keep you focused. So think about it until lunchtime. After lunch let me know if you want to work, be funny when it is appropriate, and stay in my class, or be transferred to Mrs. H's class. It's up to you." Tina returned after lunch and said she had decided to stay, and that she would behave and only be funny sometimes. And that is what she did. Her disruptive behaviour came to an end. The key here is that this teacher was popular—the students had bonded with the teacher.

Ron: The Passive Resister (Assumed Disability Goal)

Ron was a Grade 9 special education student who never missed a class; he just sat there and did nothing. Or if he did do something, he would do it begrudgingly and with constant coaxing. With a small smile, he would comment, "This is stupid," "I did this last year," or "This is for babies." If the teacher left him alone, he would leave the teacher alone, and he did not disrupt teaching or stop others from learning.

Ron was not a classroom management problem, in that he did not interrupt teaching or student learning. The issue with Ron was his lack of motivation to learn—the solution was to "hook" him. The hook proved to be rabbits. He had rabbits at home and convinced the teacher that he be allowed to bring a rabbit to class. The rabbit he brought turned out to be pregnant and had babies, which sparked much conversation. Ron became engaged and proved to be better suited to a regular program. He had been misplaced in a special education class because of his refusal to work. Once he was returned to a regular classroom, he became socially and academically successful.

Russell: The Abdicator (Assumed Disability Goal)

Like Ron, Russell used passive power. Quiet, with big soulful eyes, Russell never bothered anyone. But you always had to find a pencil or book for him, and he inevitably left his (undone) homework at home. The school policy required students to return home to collect their forgotten homework, and they had to make up the lost time after class (they all walked to school). On one occasion, Russell was sent home for homework and did not return to school for three days. In conversation with his mother (he did not have a father at home), it was discovered that Russell had come home, stuck his finger down his throat, thrown up, and said he was sick. Later in the year, the teacher had to leave the room for several minutes only to return to a classroom in which students were coughing and opening the windows. Russell had scattered pieces of mothballs all over the floor. In an after-school discussion, he was asked why he did it. He cried and said, "I just wanted the other kids to laugh at me."

Russell was not a classroom management problem. Like Ron, he did not stop the teacher from teaching or others from learning. He had poor organizational skills and very little support at home, so over the years he had fallen behind. He needed to be successful; he needed to feel he belonged and for others to pay some attention to him. The four teachers who taught the special education program were extremely dedicated to the success of their students, who were behind by two or more years with accompanying behavioural issues. Unfortunately, the teachers did not know how to effectively structure groups and intentionally create safe classrooms. The students sat in rows. The teachers acknowledged that they lacked the understanding to manage the class more effectively.

All classroom situations are different, and that is what makes them so complex to resolve. That said, in most cases it comes down to one essential aspect: the creation of a safe, inclusive, interesting classroom that will form the necessary base on which to begin resolving student issues and needs.

The Missing Think

Read through the following examples of common classroom, school, and out-of-school occurrences. They share a common element that is not immediately apparent.

Classroom/School Examples

- You randomly call on a student to publicly respond to a question.
- You ask a student from each group to come up and get materials for their group.
- You put students into small cooperative groups to work on a task.
- You get your students ready to go from the classroom to the gym.
- Students are transitioning from their seats to their science stations.
- Students are transitioning from their centres back to their desks.
- You ask students for their attention as you are about to start the class.
- You have a school-wide discipline policy—students have to arrive at school on time.
- The bell rings and students start entering the school.
- You assign homework that is due the next day.
- A staffroom sign tells teachers to clean up their dishes.

Examples from Adult Life/Outside the Classroom

- You run into a store to get a paper and don't put money in the parking meter.
- You are late coming home for supper.
- You are taking your three children out to a restaurant for lunch.
- The sign says Handicapped Parking Only.

Answer: All of the above are normal activities that have the potential to involve conflict. Conflict to life is like ice cream to the cone. If you want to be successful in life, you must learn to deal with conflict. Can you identify one aspect of life that is free of conflict to you or to others? As authors, we can't. The only option is to learn how to manage conflict.

Classifying Student Misbehaviour

For better or worse, misbehaviour happens. But not all misbehaviours are equal. There is a continuum of inappropriate behaviour. On one end are inappropriate behaviours that are easy to deal with, and at the other end are misbehaviours that are more complex to resolve.

Easy ____ More Complex

Below is a list of common misbehaviours. Where would you put each of them on the continuum? Place the numbers on the line. Would a colleague agree with your assessment?

1. call-outs
2. racial slurs
3. sitting doing nothing
4. little drummer boy
5. hitting others
6. texting (first time you see it)
7. playing with toys
8. won't do homework
9. playing with Velcro
10. talking while you are talking
11. making funny noises
12. texting (despite requests to stop)
13. spitting on others
14. always using the washroom
15. name calling
16. never ready to start
17. blaming everything on another
18. doing the opposite of what you ask
19. always getting the last word
20. pushing
21. tattling
22. getting up and walking around
23. rocking in chair
24. wrecking other students' things
25. class clown burping
26. talking back
27. put-downs (e.g., "you jerk")
28. ignoring you
29. passing notes
30. hiding other students' things
31. fighting
32. forgetting work
33. tantrums
34. won't get started
35. biting
36. statements like "you can't make me" or "this class is boring"

You do not need to have a different response for each inappropriate behaviour. Instead, it is useful to group types of behaviours so that you can choose responses that are appropriate for a particular class of actions.

Below, you will see how teachers typically group these misbehaviours. When overlaying the variables of frequency, severity, time and place, and so on, a specific misbehaviour may fit into more than one category. The fact that an inappropriate action can fit into several categories is an important point. It illustrates why having only one approach as a response to a specific misbehaviour limits the teacher's ability to react appropriately.

1. Call-outs, little drummer boy, playing with toys, playing with Velcro, tattling, talking while I'm talking, making funny noises, texting (first time), passing notes, rocking in chair, class clown burping, getting up and walking around, constantly using the washroom
2. Talking back, tantrums, always getting the last word, ignoring you, doing the opposite of what you ask, statements like "you can't make me" or "this class is boring," texting (third time in five minutes)
3. Racial slurs, hitting others, tattling, spitting on others, name calling, fighting, put-downs ("you jerk"), wrecking other students' things, biting, pushing
4. Forgetting work, won't get started, never ready to start, sitting doing nothing, won't do homework, blaming everything on another

The following misbehaviours are particularly difficult to categorize: cheating, stealing, threatening to commit suicide, and bringing drugs, alcohol, or knives to school. Responses to these behaviours usually require the involvement of others, such as parents, guidance counsellors, social workers, school administration, and colleagues.

In the following chapter, we will discuss effective responses to the student behaviours identified above. As a bridge between these two chapters, consider the following two case studies.

The Value of a Repertoire of Responses

The following examples of power plays show how difficult it is for teachers to know how to react appropriately when they don't have a repertoire of responses for de-escalating conflict.

Darryl: Mr. L. walks into his Grade 8 classroom and finds Darryl ripping up the book of a quiet, smaller student. With the class watching, Mr. L. asks Darryl why he is tearing up a student's book. Darryl responds, "I'm teaching him to be a man." Mr. L. replies, "Oh, so if you want someone to be a man, you rip their books in half?" Darryl says, "Yeah." The teacher then asks, "Would you rip anyone's book in half to make them a man?" Darryl responds defiantly again, "Yeah." This teacher isn't aware that he has made a strategic error. Darryl, by default, has an audience that makes it difficult for him to back down. And it also makes it harder for Mr. L. to back down.

For the most part, Darryl's behaviour is acceptable, but at times he can be a bit of a bully. His home life is difficult. Darryl needs to feel he has more power or influence in his life; he also needs to feel he belongs, and to be perceived as having a position in the class. The teacher simply does not have the skills to know this. He has his class sit in rows. He works hard, is dedicated, and genuinely likes his students. However, he doesn't know how to promote effective social communication and a sense of belonging, two critical elements for learning.

Margie: Margie, a Grade 6 student, lives in an at-risk home environment. In Canada, one in six students lives in at-risk environments (on average, that is four to six students per class of 30). That means these students experience one or more of the following:

- emotional abuse
- physical abuse
- sexual abuse
- witnessing violence
- drug and/or alcohol abuse
- living with a single parent, in poverty, on welfare, in subsidized housing

Margie never appears to get upset or angry in class. When a teacher responds to her inappropriate behaviour, she just smiles and looks around, and soon continues to misbehave. Wherever she is put in the class, she controls it.

She has an extremely difficult home life. She was removed from her parents because of their alcohol and abuse issues and placed with her grandmother, where she was beaten with an electrical cord and had boiling water poured on her hands. She was then returned to her father, who had made an effort to improve. Margie now slept on the couch in the front room, as the daughters of her father's girlfriend were given the only other bedroom. Margie could look 18, and could be found on the streets on weekend nights.

When asked by her teacher where she would like to sit in the classroom, she says she would like to sit right in the middle of the class. Asked why, she replies, "Because then I can touch everybody." Clearly, sending her to the office or calling her parents would not result in changed behaviour.

Margie is not successful in Math class. The teacher puts students into groups of four with a high-performing student, two average-performing students, and one struggling student (Margie). Margie believes, or knows, that when they do the Place Mat on a math question, the other three students will think she is stupid. If you were Margie, would you want to work in groups? If not, but you were forced to work in groups, what would you do? Act out? This teacher has not been trained in creating a safe classroom. Remember that even though Place Mat is a useful small group structure, it can also be very unsafe because the student's work is visible for all group members to see. A better approach is to cut up the Place Mat and have students work on their own first, then have them get together to complete the Place Mat.

What happens to students who, as early as kindergarten, fail to achieve academic or social success? For these children, the classroom and school become conditioned stimuli for failure, places where they do not belong and do not feel safe. Deci and Ryan (2008) discuss the importance of students feeling they belong and are safe. Their research has shown that interpersonal environments that nurture the basic psychological needs for competence, autonomy, and relatedness enhance the motivation to learn. Students who are motivated to learn are less likely to be off task.

From brain research we have learned that the emotional part of the brain can override the cognitive part of the brain. Joseph LeDoux's research, described in his book *The Emotional Brain* (1996), focuses on the role of emotion in our lives. If students are in stressful situations for sustained periods of time, that stress can permanently damage their long-term memory. The study of stress has been around for a long time. Dr. Hans Selye's research in the late 1970s showed the physical damage of prolonged stress. He noticed that when people came to him with a sprained ankle, they *looked* sick. He asked, Why does their face look sick if it is their ankle that hurts? Selye called this distributive effect of a specific injury on the organism *stress*.

In Section 2, we will explore how our instructional actions affect class safety (e.g., how we frame questions, how we provide time to think before sharing publicly, how we select students to answer, and how we structure groups). At some point, most of those students who don't feel safe or feel that they belong will actively push back by getting into arguments and fights, or passively push back by refusing to do work or show up to class.

Chapter 2 Conclusion

When students decide to behave inappropriately, they are not necessarily enacting a goal of misbehaviour. Nonetheless, the behaviour disrupts the teaching and learning process. When students consistently behave inappropriately, they are most likely caught up in a lifestyle that situates their behaviour in one or more of the goals of misbehaviour. As a result, attention, power, revenge, and assumed disability make sense to these students.

Power-oriented students mistakenly believe that action is their only option—it is how they will belong, be noticed, have some control in their lives, make other people hurt for their pain, and so on. Of course, when others are in some way being hurt, they are also into revenge. If it does not work, they will disappear, buy out, stop trying—why try doing something you know you won't be successful at?

Student behaviour is affected by numerous factors, including circumstances at home, the effectiveness of the teacher and the school staff, learning disabilities, fetal alcohol syndrome (FAS), special needs, social challenges, and so on. As teachers, we must recognize that students' inappropriate behaviour is likely understandable given their life experiences.

Behaviour almost always has a reason. It is intentionally or unintentionally designed to achieve a goal or a purpose. Ultimately, all students need to feel they belong and are safe in their classroom. As teachers, we are responsible for learning to structure groups effectively, learning to frame questions effectively, letting students share with a partner first before having them share with the class, giving children enough time to think before we select them to respond, extending our repertoire of skills related to responding, creating a supportive learning environment, and learning how to check for understanding effectively.

Pre-Power Approaches: Our Theory of Bumps

4 Levels of Escalation

BUMP 1
Low-Key Responses

COMMON ATTRIBUTES
- fast: they don't stop the flow of the lesson
- use few words, if any
- don't invite an escalation

BUMP 2
Squaring Off

STEPS
- the teacher turns and faces the student
- the teacher provides a message to stop
- the teacher finishes by saying thank you

BUMP 3
The Choice

COMMON ATTRIBUTES
- related to the behaviour
- not felt as punishment
- done as immediately as possible
- not an ultimatum
- neutral tone
- you can follow through on the choice

BUMP 4
The Follow-Through (Implied Choice)

CONDITIONS
- done in a positive or neutral tone
- student, it is hoped, sees the logic in the implied choice
- applied consistently

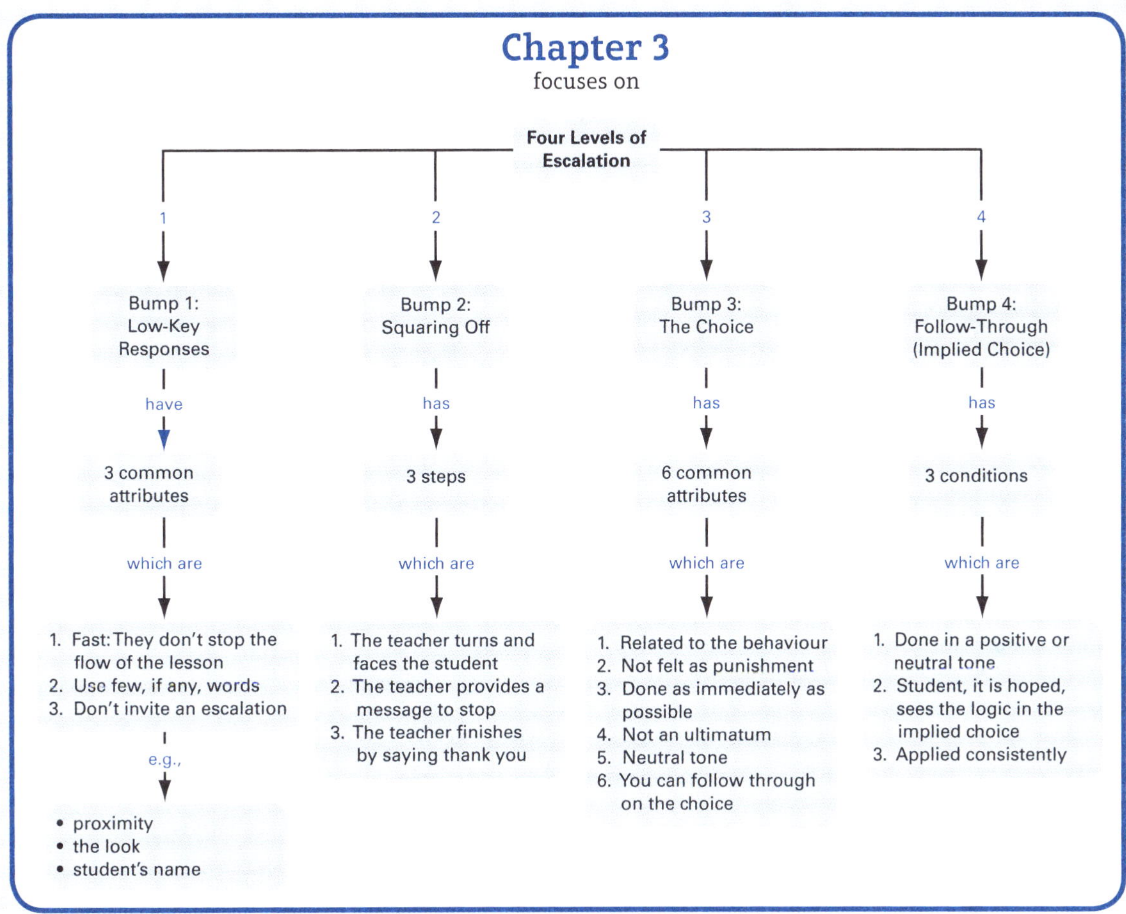
Chapter 3
focuses on
Four Levels of Escalation
1
2
3
4
Bump 1: Low-Key Responses
have
3 common attributes
which are
1. Fast: They don't stop the flow of the lesson
2. Use few, if any, words
3. Don't invite an escalation
e.g.,
• proximity
• the look
• student's name
Bump 2: Squaring Off
has
3 steps
which are
1. The teacher turns and faces the student
2. The teacher provides a message to stop
3. The teacher finishes by saying thank you
Bump 3: The Choice
has
6 common attributes
which are
1. Related to the behaviour
2. Not felt as punishment
3. Done as immediately as possible
4. Not an ultimatum
5. Neutral tone
6. You can follow through on the choice
Bump 4: Follow-Through (Implied Choice)
has
3 conditions
which are
1. Done in a positive or neutral tone
2. Student, it is hoped, sees the logic in the implied choice
3. Applied consistently

The effective teacher's response to the escalation of inappropriate student behaviour is similar to a doctor's responses to a patient's ailment that worsens. When a patient has a wound to the arm, the doctor will wash and dress it. If the cut is deep, the doctor will stitch it. If the arm is broken, the doctor will apply a splint or cast. If infection sets in, the doctor will give the patient antibiotics. However, doctors don't have a separate response for every single ailment. Instead, they have a group, or genre, of responses for a group of ailments.

"I'm sure you'll agree, we don't want an epidemic."

Teachers, too, have genres of responses to the four goals of misbehaviour: attention, power, revenge, and assumed disability (see Chapter 2, pages 23 to 27). Most teachers apply most of these responses, but they may not always do so with deliberate awareness. Effective teachers, though, make conscious decisions to respond effectively to escalations of inappropriate behaviour. We have classified these responses into six types, which we refer to as "bumps." The purpose of this chapter is to provide examples of how teachers enact the skills of the first four bumps.

What Are the Bumps?

The six bumps illustrate how teachers think and respond as a misbehaviour progresses from least to most disruptive. (In another of our books, *Classroom Management: A Thinking and Caring Approach*, we describe ten bumps, the last four of which happen outside the classroom and involve other individuals such as the principal, parents, a guidance counsellor, or a social worker. See Appendix A for an overview of those last four bumps.)

Our theory of bumps explains how effective and less effective teachers think and act when student behaviour escalates in power plays. According to our theory, effective teachers match their responses appropriately to student behaviour. The bumps are logical and they often play out in an orderly sequence, but classrooms are not always logical places. For example, if a student has been consistently misbehaving, your first response might be to offer the student a choice (Bump 3) rather than to say the student's name (Bump 1). To use an extreme example, if a student pulls out a gun, you don't start with a Bump 1, "David, please," or a Bump 2, "Are you finished?" Nor would you employ a Bump 3, "You have a choice, David, put the gun away or put it on my desk," or a Bump 4, "You've made the decision to put the gun on my desk." You would more likely go to Bump 34, "Run!"

Keep in mind that the student's behaviour may be partially or completely due to appropriate or inappropriate teacher behaviour. The student's reaction may be caused by how the teacher frames questions, structures groups, assesses students and provides feedback, and spends time making the classroom more inclusive and safe. See Section 2 of this text for more on effective teaching practices.

For the teacher, the key is to understand why the student is choosing to behave in a certain way and to use the best responses to restore social order efficiently so that learning can continue. Critical to success is the relationship that the teacher has with the student, as is the manner in which the teacher enacts the response, including the timing and place. Effective teachers recognize the nature of student misbehaviour, its severity, its frequency, the extent to which other students are affected, and how the student has responded in the past when asked to rethink the behaviour. The teacher usually knows about the student's life at home, learning struggles, and strengths.

All of this information factors into how the teacher will engage with the student, and it is precisely because of this wealth of information that classroom management is an art informed by experience and science (research). Effective teachers select a response (the science) to a misbehaviour and apply it effectively (the art). Even when the teacher's response is assertive, it is never disrespectful to the student. A choice may work with one student but not with another; it may not even work the next day with a student with whom it worked the day before. Don't blame the choice. There are no guarantees and no panacea for effective responses—there are only more precise possibilities of restoring social order.

Ultimately, much of your success depends on the extent to which the student has bonded with you or against you. Your mean score between 1 (least effective) and 100 (most effective) will, in the end, make your selection of responses and application acceptable or not. For more on mean scores, see Chapter 6, page 134.

Essential Low-Key Preventive Techniques

The following four factors will affect a teacher's effectiveness. Successful implementation of these techniques can help to avoid and defuse conflict situations, reducing the need to respond to inappropriate behaviour. When a response is required, these techniques can also help to improve the effectiveness of the low-key responses (Bump 1), as well as other skills presented in this book.

1. Transitions
2. Rules
3. Dealing with Allies
4. Winning Over

1. Transitions

A sequence of instructions or directions that is essential for keeping the classroom under control.

What: A sequence of teacher behaviours that increases the chances that student behaviour will remain orderly and efficient. The transition involves three components: *when, what, who,* usually presented in this order. For example: (1) Can I have your attention, please. (2) Don't move until I ask you to move. (3) Please put away all your books, and then letter off into your groups A, B, and C. (4) When I say *move,* A will get the information sheet, B will take out a calculator, and C will get out a pen. (5) Okay, move.

The Transition Sequence	The Rationale
1. a signal to attend	The transition must begin from a sense of order.
2. a statement of when the students will move	Start with *when,* because if you start with *who* or *what,* you'll get student movement before you want it.
3. a statement of what is expected of them	Given that *what* is the essence of the transition, if you say *who* first, the students will look around for who they will work with and miss the directions.
4. a statement of who will move	The *who* statement completes the information required for the transition.
5. the statement to move	Now that they have all the instructions, this is the signal for the students to implement them.
6. monitor movement and use proximity—be where the action is likely to be	If anything will happen, this is a dandy place for every attention-seeker to have 15 seconds on stage—be preventive.
7. provide specific and positive feedback	You want to maintain and enhance appropriate transition behaviour.

Why: Over the year, effective transitions can add an incredible amount of time for learning. In addition, effective transitions reduce teacher stress, so you'll remain healthy and psychologically able to take advantage of your retirement years.

When: Transitions occur any time student movement is required. As the year progresses, students should tap into their ability to move independently from activity to activity without much direction from the teacher.

Artful Nuance: Please note that transitions range from simple to complex. A simple transition may involve students putting away one set of materials and taking out another without having to move from their desks. A more complex activity might occur as students move from a large class lecture into cooperative learning groups for a laboratory experiment. The more complex the transition, the more the transition must be thought out and clearly explained to the students.

For visual learners, it's wise to post the more complex transitions. Writing the steps of the transition on the board or on chart paper will help them remember what they are to do, and cut down on superfluous questions. This is especially important for students with autism and FAS.

Remember: Transitions are breeding grounds for inappropriate behaviour. The wise teacher knows that all students will at some time misbehave. With that principle in mind, take steps to prevent inappropriate behaviour from occurring.

2. Rules

This is your one opportunity to set yourself up for a year of happiness or a year of grief—the decision is yours.

Overview: In discussions about classroom discipline, the importance of rules is frequently overstated. Rules seldom solve discipline problems and, contrary to popular belief, seldom prevent discipline problems from occurring. If they did, most classrooms would have few discipline problems, as most teachers spend time discussing expected behaviour. Rules do, however, set guidelines, and they are the first step in establishing classroom order. It is the teacher's ability to *act* on the rules that will determine whether they make a difference.

No one right way exists to establish rules for a class. Some teachers do it through discussion and democratic process. Others assert rules through explanation. Although these techniques seem diametrically opposed, they both appear to work when used with the following constraints:

1. Rules are few in number—five seems to be a common upper limit.
2. A rationale is established for each rule.
3. Ambiguous terms are explained.
4. Roles and responsibilities are learned.
5. The rules are stated positively rather than negatively. For example, "Treat each other with respect" rather than "Don't put each other down."

Our preference is for a class discussion of rules and for using some form of consensual process to arrive at acceptance.

Suggested Approaches to Establish Rules
(to be adapted for different grades)

Dialogue and Question: A Student-Centred Approach

Engage the students in a discussion of the need for order and how order is usually obtained. For example, have students look around their community for instances of rules (such as stop signs or stoplights and no smoking signs). Discuss why a community creates these rules. Then turn the discussion to where they find rules in school.

A useful technique is to include a story that explores why rules are essential—for example, the book *John Brown, Rose and the Midnight Cat*, by Jenny Wagner, has students decide on the rules under which the cat can live in the house. (If you don't have this book, just set up the situation where John Brown (the dog) and Rose have lived together for years and take care of each other. One day Rose sees a black cat and wants the cat to join the family. John Brown does not want the cat in the house.)

Place the students in groups of three. One person is John Brown (the dog), one is Rose, and one, the Midnight Cat. (If you want to use groups of four, add in the author.) Have students move to the four corners of the room and form temporary groups of three to four students (works like a Jigsaw). Allow the groups five minutes to come up with rules or conditions under which the cat can come into the house. Next, ask the students to return to their home groups and arrive at a consensus regarding those rules or conditions. From that exercise, they decide on the rules that would be appropriate in their class. For high school, read clips from *Lord of the Flies* by William Golding in which everything is falling apart and Piggy identifies the need to establish rules. Use the books as a starter activity, and then turn the discussion back to the classroom.

Ask students which rules they would like for their class. Accept whatever they say and write those rules on the board. Almost without fail, they will recite an endless list of don'ts. Allow this process to continue for a while, then ask if having rules like this has worked before. Typically, their answer is "no." Now start the process of establishing a limited number of positive rules together.

Concept Attainment Lesson on Rules

Bruner's Concept Attainment strategy can be used to structure a lesson on rules, as set up below. This process can be woven into whatever piece of literature you are using to spark a discussion on rules. (See Appendix I for an explanation of Concept Attainment.)

Focus Statement: Say to the students

"Below is a list of rules. On your own, please compare the greens and contrast them with the blues. When you think you have an idea of how the greens are similar and why they are different from the blues, share your thinking with a partner. Then decide together whether the testers below are greens or blues."

Present Data Set: Below are the examples

Greens	Blues
Treat each other with respect.	Don't throw things.
Please listen when asked.	Don't talk while others are talking.
Put up your hand if you need something.	Please don't get up and walk around.
Come into the room quietly and get ready for the start of class.	After recess, don't ask if you can leave the room.

Which of the following testers are greens? blues?

- Please do not bring knives or other dangerous objects to school.
- Please make sure your assignments are done on time.

- No put-downs.
- When working in groups, give each person equal opportunity to share.

Have students share their hypotheses about how the greens are different from the blues. Discuss whether students prefer the way the greens or blues work, and why. Greens are worded in a more positive way and set a different tone in the class. The blues are more oppressive. (You can usually use the students' responses from the *John Brown, Rose and the Midnight Cat* activity as green and blue examples.)

The next step is to begin a discussion on the meaning of key words within the rules. Below is a list of key words. If key words are important, you should have a process to assist students to understand those words.

- Quiet (being quiet)
- Listening
- Raising your hand
- Respect

Quiet means different things to different people. For kindergarten students, it may mean nothing. For some students, the words "Be quiet" are only important when yelled for the fifth time. We also know that "being quiet" varies from situation to situation. The quiet expected in an Art class or a Phys Ed class, for example, is not the same quiet as that expected during an exam or when an assignment is being completed in class.

Being quiet means being appropriate for a particular time and place. Other variables include the loudness of an interruption, the duration of an interruption, and the frequency of interruptions. For example, if students are working individually, it is usually acceptable—even while the teacher is explaining something—for one student to turn to another and quickly whisper something, as long as this is not repeated within the next couple of minutes. Even in this scenario, however, what is meant by a whisper should be defined and modelled by the teacher.

Listening is a more difficult term to define. For example, a student can doodle and quite possibly still be listening to the teacher. One attribute of "listening" is that the students can repeat in their own words what was said. Most teachers would appreciate at least periodic eye contact from students while the teacher is talking—this is called "attentive listening." Please note that whole-class listening is different from the behaviour expected in one-on-one listening. One-on-one

listening requires additional attentive listening behaviours such as nodding, more constant eye contact, and paraphrasing.

The idea of **raising your hand** when a student wants something may seem appropriate to some and too restrictive to others. Once again, it is important to teach definitions. First, teach what is meant by raising a hand. Demonstrate how you expect it to look. It may be worthwhile to also include some negative examples. It might be fun to model the "monkey," for example—the student who throws an arm up in a convulsive motion while making the "oh, oh, oh" sound of a jungle buddy. Of course, there is the inevitable guiltless call-out—students who raise their hand and call out the answer to the question at the same time—and these students can be relentless. This is why some teachers prefer the rule "No call-outs, no hands, please; just think to yourself and I will randomly call on you."

Explain that you would like students to request permission before they get out of their desks, move away from their group, or speak. The rationale is that call-outs and unregulated student movement are frequently disruptive to other students unless they are an accepted norm in the class. As students become more responsible and independent in a class, they do not have to raise their hands. In actual classroom practice, the need for this rule frequently withers away as the students learn expectations. Nonetheless, the rule is useful to have in reserve in the event that problems arise. (Where as adults do we have to raise our hands to leave the room?)

Respect usually means doing unto others as you would have them do unto you. Demonstrate this by example. When having a classroom discussion around an issue, consider both sides of the issue. For example, if students don't like being pushed, then don't push others; if you like being treated fairly, then treat others fairly; if you don't like someone interrupting you, then don't interrupt others; if you don't like being embarrassed, then don't embarrass others.

Explain that, in most cases, students know what kind of behaviour is expected and that you will rely on their common sense and cooperation to guide them. For younger students, using children's literature can be a great way to launch discussions about what it means to be respectful. Two classic books to consider are *Maxine's Tree* by Diane Carmel Léger and *The Deliverance of Dancing Bears* by Elizabeth Stanley. The first is about being respectful to trees and nature, the second about being respectful to bears and nature. Following a discussion of the texts, you can progress to how students can be respectful to one another in class.

Even when we teach respect, discuss it, and all agree on its meaning, problems will still arise on occasion. When this happens, the expected behaviour must be discussed again and taught. The difference is that the discourse to solve the problem is much more enlightened and more likely to be successful.

In addition, we have to remember that younger students need to have these concepts explicitly taught. The following example makes the point.

> An experienced colleague was asked by a novice kindergarten teacher to observe her classroom as she was struggling to get the children to take turns and to share, even though **she had told them** what taking turns was and why it was important. After watching, the educator asked if the students could come over to the reading corner. They talked for a moment, and then the educator asked, "Sometimes when you are playing, your teacher asks you to take turns. What does taking turns mean to you?" After a few seconds, a little girl got up off the floor, looked at the teacher, and turned around in a circle. Definitely not the idea her teacher had in mind. Telling is not the same as teaching—teaching engages students in meaningful experiences.

The next step in the process of establishing rules is to ask the class if these rules seem reasonable and if they can live with them. If a few students say, "Yeah, but..." ask them how they would like the rules to be improved. If they cannot make suggestions, ask them to abide by these rules until they can offer improvements. In this way, you do not deny the legitimacy of their concerns but still obtain consensus on a set of rules.

Remain alert to the "Larry Lawyers" in your class who love legal discussions. Our experience is that those students are great at opposing ideas, but not as good at creating positive alternatives. Asking for the alternative is an effective way of defusing their opposition. Finally, explain that the class responsibility is to live according to these rules. Again, you will have to adapt this process, and your words, to the age and skills of the students in your class.

The final step of explaining roles and responsibilities is to request that the class abide by the rules. Be sure to acknowledge that everyone will not always behave perfectly and that you expect students may forget a rule, or make mistakes, on occasion. When this happens, it is your role as the teacher to let the student know the mistake (using low-key responses described in this chapter). The student's role is to stop the misbehaviour. This means both the teacher and student must cooperate and share responsibility for making the classroom a positive place.

3. Dealing with Allies

The ultimate paradox—this is the one time you will have to stop two or more enemies from unintentionally helping each other.

What: The skills to sort out situations where two students cooperate to disrupt the class. The students may be friends, but most often they are not. Below are two scenarios, one simple, one complex.

A Simple Classroom Example

The teacher has asked a question and asked the students to think to themselves. One student calls out an answer, and almost immediately, another student shouts out, "Why don't you give others a chance?" The first student responds, "Mind your own business." Inevitably, in this situation, you will hear a put-down of some sort.

Analysis: In this exchange, the student who responds "Why don't you give others a chance?" is the ally. The first student is obligated to respond and the game of one-upmanship is on. Always deal with the ally first. The other student who called out must be rescued, in a sense, in order to save face. Use whatever response is appropriate. If a low-key response will work, use it. If it does not seem appropriate (as in this example), then select a response from one of the higher bumps. (See Chapters 4 and 5 on how to decide which skill to select.)

Why: These situations can be explosive and can quickly escalate in severity. Efficient skill is essential, or the teacher will become mired in a complex battle of blame versus innocence. "He started it!" "No, I didn't—he did!"

When: Whenever one or more students become involved after an initial inappropriate behaviour.

Artful Nuance: The key is to deal with the problem, not the student (one of the low-key responses discussed in the following section). The goal is to restore order as quickly as possible. Should the low-key responses be insufficient, stop both students and define the problem accurately: "Hold it, please. The problem here is the interruption, not who caused it. At this moment, I do not know who is responsible." Pause for three to five seconds, look at both students, and say, "I'm going to assume it's over. Thank you." At all costs, do not get trapped into sorting out who is right or wrong. You did not see who started it. And even if you did, that student would bring up a mountain of past grievances that would swallow up the most talented criminal lawyer.

A Complex Classroom Example

One student has a foot sticking into the aisle. Typical well-behaving students will either step over the foot, or if they see it early enough, choose another aisle. However, another type of student will see this as an opportunity to trip over the foot. The student whose foot is in the aisle also sees the opportunity and simultaneously raises the foot a minuscule amount, just in case the other student forgets to trip. The "trippee" then takes a dive worth 10/10 on the Olympic scale, turns, and loudly says something like "Watch what you're doing, idiot!" When you look up, the student morphs into Larry Lawyer and exclaims, "He tripped me!" and the tripper says, "No, I didn't!" The case now lands in your court. How do you sort it out?

You now have two Larry Lawyers arguing their innocence before you, the Supreme Court judge. Although the urge to pass life sentences on both is foremost in your mind, you must seek alternatives. The student to whom you need to respond first is the "tripper." He is the ally, because he is responding to the trippee's call-out. Since you didn't see what happened and you don't know who started it, deal only with what you saw and heard. In the classroom, this situation might be played out like this—careful, it gets confusing.

Tripper:	Trips the other student.
Trippee:	"Watch what you're doing, idiot!"
Teacher:	Uses "the look" (one of the low-key responses described in following section) on the student who tripped.
Trippee:	In response to the teacher's look, states, "He tripped me."
Tripper:	"I did not!"
Teacher (To Tripper):	"Hold it, please." (Pause, look at both students.)
Tripper:	Becomes silent.
Teacher:	"Thank you." Teacher continues with the lesson.

Avoid launching into a sermon that typically starts with "Every time there is a problem..." or "I'm sick and tired of..." or "Why can't you...?" These two students probably thrive on teacher overreaction.

4. Winning Over

What: Winning over is a concept identified by Jacob Kounin in the 1970s when he did one of the first studies on effective teachers. The term refers to what teachers do to increase the chances that students will bond to work cohesively with, as opposed to against, the teacher. A teacher's mean score out of 100 is one way to illustrate the extent to which students have bonded with the teacher. The higher a teacher's mean score, the more likely it is that the students will bond with the teacher.

Why: When students bond cohesively with the teacher, it increases the chances that they will behave appropriately. It also means that when students do choose to misbehave, they are more likely to perceive the teacher's response as effective.

When: Winning over never stops. We see it when teachers use students' names, when they frame questions effectively, when they structure groups effectively, when they learn to interact more wisely with students with autism, with gifted students, with students who struggle at home, and so on.

Artful Nuance: Don't forget that winning over is also what teachers do outside the classroom—by saying hi when you walk down the hall; by playing chess with students or starting a bridge club; by going to students' basketball or volleyball games; by asking how students did at a dance competition or how their summer was or their birthday or their visit with their grandma. Research has consistently shown that effective teachers care about students outside the walls of the classroom.

Responding—Pre-Power Approaches

The first four of the bumps are responses to situations that have not moved to power. Even though the bumps are logically described, in sequence, from Bump 1 through Bump 6, classroom situations often defy logic. The decision as to how, when, and where to respond to inappropriate student behaviour must match the level of escalation, and take into account the student's previous behaviour. If the student's first behaviour is a clear push toward a power play, your first response would be to apply a skill from Bump 5. In Chapters 4 (Bump 5) and 5 (Bump 6), we explore responses to power plays in greater depth.

Bump 1: Low-Key Responses

Reflect on what teachers do when students first start to misbehave. For now, consider student behaviour that is deemed simply annoying or irritating, such as talking at the same time as the teacher, tapping a pencil during a test, or calling out an answer when asked not to. If possible, share your ideas with colleagues. Our guess is that you are familiar with all the likely responses, as teachers have been responding to irritating or annoying behaviour for decades (and, as we will see at the end of this book, centuries).

The Most Common Responses (simple, but effective!)

1. Proximity
2. Touch
3. The Look
4. Using the Student's Name
5. The Gesture
6. The Pause
7. Ignoring
8. Deal with the Problem, Not the Student
9. The Signal to Begin
10. Politeness

When we work with teachers who are at risk of losing their teaching position and ask them to identify low-key responses, their answers are the same as those of effective teachers. Clearly, something else must be going on; something akin to the idea that simply buying paint does not make an artist, one has to learn to paint.

Bump 1

The following are in-depth descriptions of the 10 Low-Key Responses. To view Barrie Bennett talking about the subtlety of Bump 1 techniques, go to the *Power Plays* companion website: www.pearsoncanada.ca/powerplays

1. Proximity

To quickly recall the effects of proximity, think of how you react when you are driving and you see a police car in the rear-view mirror—most of us check to make sure we are driving appropriately.

What: This low-key skill refers to the teacher's ability to move toward a misbehaving student.

When: Proximity is used when one or two students first start to misbehave in an attention-seeking fashion.

Why: Moving toward a potential problem area decreases the chances misbehaviour will occur. In the same breath, proximity communicates that you know that a student is misbehaving and needs to stop.

Where: Wherever a student is misbehaving and you can get close to the student without disturbing others.

Artful Nuance: Be aware of how you move toward the student. Moving quickly and directly and standing close to the student with a stern look on your face communicates a different message than moving in a more indirect manner, not standing as close, and not looking at the student.

Caution: Be aware of how close you get to a student. Every student's personal space has different dimensions. The closer you get to the student, the more assertive the stance becomes. If the student's lifestyle is one of power or revenge, the closer you get, the greater the chances you will invite the student to escalate the behaviour.

2. Touch (Usually the Desk)

A gentle reminder that someone is aware and cares.

What: A low-key response that involves the teacher usually placing a hand on the desk between two students talking. It can also be a very light and quick touch on the student's shoulder. The touch of the desk or shoulder is done in such a way that few (if any) other students see it occur.

When: Touch is used when a student first starts to misbehave in an attention-seeking fashion.

Why: To stop the misbehaviour and maintain or re-establish an environment that encourages learning to continue.

Where: If you decide to use touch, we suggest you place your hand on the desk between the students who are talking. If you decide to touch the shoulder, do so with a light, quick touch. Some teachers get away with very quickly tapping the shoulder. It's important to be careful when touching students. Touching the head or leaving your hand on the shoulder invades a student's personal space. In some cultures, touching the head is not acceptable.

Artful Nuance: Avoid eye contact at this time, unless you intend to say something. Eye contact tends to increase the length of the touch and increases the chances you will get involved in a verbal exchange.

Caution: In today's classrooms the use of touch can be an issue—especially for male teachers. Check the school policy so that you have a clear understanding on the permissible use of touch in your classroom and school. Also, be aware of the restrictions on touching in some religions—particularly between sexes.

3. The Look

In the hands of an artful teacher, the look is a quiet way of communicating whether a student's behaviour is acceptable.

What: "The look" has two dimensions. First, the teacher uses the look to quickly and quietly communicate to students that their behaviour is inappropriate. The second dimension is the preventive scan. The frequent use of the scan communicates to students that they are not anonymous and that the teacher is with it. In addition, the teacher can pick up potential problems starting to percolate and stop them before they go too far.

In working with teachers experiencing difficulty, we have found that they frequently fail to scan the room. Consequently, what could have been a minor, single event between one or two students is allowed to develop into a more serious group activity.

Effective teachers seldom have to respond to five or six students who are simultaneously disturbing the class. Yet we often get comments from teachers like, "Yes, but what do you do when there are four or five students misbehaving, or the whole class is misbehaving?" Again, no simple answer exists; however, as you move through the book, you will find suggestions for when groups of students are making it difficult for others to learn. Remember, the reason teachers have to deal with five or six students fooling around is because the issue was not resolved *appropriately* when only one or two were misbehaving. It also usually means that the students are bonding against the teacher.

Why: To communicate that you are "with it" and able to stop things before they go too far, as well as to maintain or re-establish a safe environment that encourages learning to continue.

When: The look is used when a student first starts to misbehave in an attention-seeking fashion.

Where: Give the look from wherever the student can see the whites of your eyes.

Artful Nuance: Know when to look and how to appropriately use body and subtle facial language. The glance, the look, the stare, and the glare each send a different message.

Caution: Be sensitive to the difference between the glance, the look, the stare, and the glare. If you use the glare when all that was required was the look and a smile, you will find the look (as a low-key response) works against you.

4. Using the Student's Name

A minimal verbal skill the teacher uses to remind students that they are not anonymous.

What: From a preventive perspective, using students' names to greet or select them is an effective way of winning students over—especially when the name is said in a kind rather than a nagging fashion.

Why: To stop inappropriate behaviour. As well, as schools get bigger and drop-out rates increase, it becomes more important that we make students feel included. This is particularly important inhigh schools.

When: The student's name is used when a student first starts to misbehave in an attention-seeking fashion. It can also be used as a greeting to acknowledge that a particular student is important enough to have her name remembered.

Where: Anywhere, any time.

Artful Nuance: Appreciate the power of intonation, syllable emphasis, and inflection as you say a name. You can communicate a number of different messages. Try saying your own name in as many different ways as possible and feel the difference. Remember how others have used your name to achieve specific responses from you.

Caution: Using a student's name as the only low-key response will begin to sound like nagging, especially when you hear yourself saying, "David, how many times do I have to tell you?" or "Shilonda, if I've told you once I've told you a million times..." or "Sanda, I am getting tired of telling you to put..." or "Michael, I won't tell you again."

5. The Gesture

A visual response to inappropriate behaviour.

What: This is usually a hand or facial gesture that communicates the expected behaviour. For example, a finger on the mouth communicates "Stop talking" or "Talk quietly." A shake of the head communicates "No" or "Stop." If "Wally Wanderer" is up moving around the room, then quietly saying "Wally" and pointing to his desk gives him all the information he needs. The bonus is that your voice does not upset the flow of the lesson.

Why: The gesture is employed to communicate that you are "with it" and able to stop things before they go too far and to maintain or re-establish a safe environment that encourages learning to continue.

When: It is used when a student first starts to misbehave in an attention-seeking fashion.

Where: Use it from any point from which students can see you.

Artful Nuance: Appreciate the variety of forms that gestures can take, and also how they can be integrated with other low-key responses. For example, moving toward a student who is off task, shaking your head to communicate "not acceptable," and finishing with the "invisible thank you" (also known as a smile).

If you are having a guest speaker in your room, sit to the side near the front so that your students can see you and you can see them. This will also allow you to apply a gesture without interrupting the speaker.

Caution: Be aware that what is considered an acceptable gesture in one culture may not be acceptable in another. Remember that younger students often have no idea what gestures mean—you will have to teach them.

6. The Pause

This is more powerful than you might think. In addition to sending a message to the students, it gives you time as a teacher to take a couple of breaths and a moment to think before responding.

What: The silence teachers intentionally invoke when they notice students or groups of students misbehaving.

Why: To communicate that you are "with it" and able to stop things before they go too far and to maintain or re-establish a safe environment that encourages learning to continue.

When: The pause is used when a student first starts to misbehave in an attention-seeking fashion. The pause is also an important step in other responding skills, such as when squaring off, using choices, and dealing with power—these skills are discussed below and in Chapters 4 and 5.

Where: Often it occurs after a signal to begin a class or a signal to get students' attention. It also occurs when you are giving directions to the class and you notice one or two students or a group of students not paying attention.

Artful Nuance: The pause is usually employed in conjunction with other low-key responses, as well as with other skills for dealing with power.

Caution: Be aware of how long you are prepared to wait and what you will do if you realize the pause is not working. After four or five seconds, you could be getting into a game that could easily escalate to a power situation.

7. Ignoring

A chance to pause and think while simultaneously communicating a message to behave appropriately.

What: The ability of the teacher to communicate that a student's misbehaviour will not achieve the desired effect; in most cases, that desired effect is the teacher's attention.

Why: To *not attend* to a behaviour for which the student is seeking attention or attempting to initiate a move to power.

When: Use ignoring when you perceive a student is misbehaving at an inappropriate time in order to get your attention or the class's attention.

For example, when you use a student's name to get the student to focus and she says, "Why are you always picking on me?" the response of a quick look and then an ignoring would be appropriate. However, if the student has an ally, you cannot ignore the behaviour; you are obliged to act.

Artful Nuance: Make sure your facial gestures don't betray your agitation. If you look annoyed, students get the attention they desire even though you have said nothing. You can also use other low-key responses, such as the look or proximity, while enacting ignoring.

Caution: We suggest you ignore a student when the behaviour does not stop you from continuing what you were doing (e.g., giving direction or explaining something) or stop other students from learning.

8. Deal with the Problem, Not the Student

This skill communicates to students that they are accepted in the classroom, but that the behaviour is not.

What: The teacher focuses on student behaviour rather than on student intentions or personality traits.

Why: This skill deals with what the student is doing and nothing else. The teacher indicates by action or words that the behaviour, not the student, is unacceptable. You communicate that you trust the student to solve the problem. If you focus on students' intentions, you are being judgmental and risk inviting a move to power. Likewise, if you focus on students' personalities, it creates a negative feeling in the classroom and usually unites the class cohesively against the teacher.

Examples of two responses:

A student has engaged in a series of low-key attention-getting behaviours over a span of 30 minutes. The teacher's exasperation is heightened. The student now begins to tap his pencil. Annoyed, the teacher responds, "John, you may not care about your school work, but others do. Show some consideration for the rest of us." John looks embarrassed, then glares at the teacher as he puts his pencil down.

As an alternative, the teacher could say, "John, pencil please," and John puts his pencil down. Or the teacher might use proximity and politely request the pencil—"May I have the pencil, please?"—and follow the request with, "I will return it when you need it, thank you."

In the first example, the teacher is trying to extract a pound of flesh. John has previously irritated the teacher to the point where she now wants a bit of revenge. Even though the teacher achieved the result she wanted—the pencil is down—she has now alienated John and shown the class that anyone might be next on the hit list. Kounin (1977) calls this the Ripple Effect: the teacher's response to one student communicates to the other students how they too might be treated. In the positive example, the teacher achieved the same result without causing resentment in John or lowering the other students' trust in her—the teacher maintained a safe environment.

When: This technique can be used whenever the behaviour is relatively obvious. It is most effective when the student is doing something physical. A particularly effective use is when two students are fighting over a single article, such as a book or a ball. Simply say "Book, please" with your hand extended and "receive" the article. If they are chewing gum, and the rule is no gum, ask them to place it in the garbage—and say "Thank you." Of course, the big issue nowadays is with technology, such as cell phones. The same rule applies. Some teachers simply ask for the battery, which the student can pick up after class or after school or at the end of the week. Keeping the battery preserves students' privacy.

Artful Nuance: For a student racing down the hallway, "Enrico, no running please" is all the information he requires. How we say something is as important as what we say. Voice tone and decibel level have to be controlled. As well, the temptation for the teacher to sermonize often makes the situation worse. The fewer words used, the better. Remember that with some students with fetal alcohol syndrome if the message is too long, as in "David, you know the school rule, no running in the halls," all they hear is the word "run."

As we continue to move through the book, you will no doubt be thinking, "What if this skill doesn't work?" Congratulations! Every time you have a "what if it doesn't work" situation, you are aware that the student's behaviour can escalate. If we take the example of asking for John's pen, and John doesn't relinquish it, the student has chosen to escalate the situation and you must bump up with the student and apply an appropriate skill. In Chapters 4 and 5, we deal with effective ways to respond to this type of escalation.

9. The Signal to Begin

Signals are one of the most extensively used forms of prevention. From a stop sign to the sound of a rattlesnake's tail, signals are all around us.

What: The signal to begin is a sequence of teacher behaviours that results in the whole class or a group becoming quiet and focusing on the teacher. The sequence is (1) the signal; (2) the active pause, which consists of scanning the room to see who has responded (*this goes back to the belief that all students will misbehave at least once at some point*); (3) if necessary, the application of a low-key response to students whose behaviour remains inappropriate; and (4) a teacher response that reinforces the appropriate behaviour, for example, saying "Thank you."

Why: To get the class to focus or refocus.

When: Whenever the class is off task and needs to be regrouped, or when you need the class to come to order at the beginning of the period. Note that a signal is usually necessary at the beginning of most transitions, such as when the students are moving from large-group to small-group activities.

Artful Nuance: With signals, the least important part is the signal itself. The most important part is to "say what you mean and mean what you say." That means you must communicate that you will not continue until the students are attentive. A helpful hint is not to stand apart from the students but to move toward them (using proximity) as you ask for their attention.

In most situations, you should have only one or two signals to get the students' attention. For example, we have observed teachers who will initiate the need for attention by stating three signals within 20 seconds: "Hold it, please." Then they will say, "I need your attention." And then with an agitated voice they say, "Quiet, please!" In these cases, the students have learned to ignore the signals until the teacher's voice hits a certain decibel level.

We also recommend thinking carefully about whether or not to use bells, lights, rainsticks, and so on as signals to begin class or to get the students' attention. If students respond to the prop in class, it

behooves you to carry a bell or rainstick or to be able to access a light switch when outside of the class. Although it is certainly possible to carry a bell outside of class, it is not always practical or socially acceptable. Make the signals practical and transferable to as many situations as possible.

One of the most efficient signals is to raise your hand and say, "Could I have your attention, please?" The five fingers of the open hand can mean five things: turn toward me, eyes on me, hands free, mouth closed, ears listening. This idea of "Give me five" was used in Carol Cummings's (1987) work.

Great Idea: One elementary teacher shared that each week he uses a different signal, a stimulus response idea. He calls out a word and the students provide the response. Usually, he then has their attention. For example, if the teacher calls out "baseball," the students might respond "Blue Jays." When the teacher calls out "pain," students respond "homework."

Each Friday one cooperative group determines the signal for the following week. The signal has to be appropriate—it could relate to a topic being discussed that week. This ties into two concepts related to motivation: *novelty* and *variety*.

Caution: Sometimes teachers have a signal to begin, but unwittingly misuse the signal by pausing too long or using the wrong tone of voice. Overuse of a signal usually occurs because the teacher was unclear with the directions, did not give directions, or realizes that the students are not following the directions. In overuse, you hear the teacher repeating the signal without a receptive audience.

Once, when observing a B.Ed. student in a gym class, an author found it not uncommon to hear 5 to 10 requests for attention. The problem was not with the students, but with the student teacher, who was not really ready to begin the class. He would request their attention, then deal with a student who asked a question, then ask for attention again, then remind students not to pick up their hockey sticks yet, then ask for attention, then... He was a good teacher and well liked, but he had a wee bit to learn about signals for attention.

Don't give a signal for attention if you are not actually ready to start. False starts will defeat you.

10. Politeness

A minimal verbal skill used to let students understand that the teacher is watching and is also respectful.

What: A respectful comment from the teacher that involves words such as "please" and "thank you." The politeness is often attached to the start or end of other low-key responses, for example, "David, please. *(Pause—the look.)* Thank you."

Why: To let the students know that what they are doing is inappropriate in a way that is respectful, and to increase the chances the inappropriate behaviour will not escalate.

When: Politeness is used in a way that communicates that the teacher is with it. This implies that the teacher has eyes in the back of his or her head. As soon as a student is beginning to be off task, the teacher may simply look over and say "Please" and then pause and say "Thank you."

Where: Anywhere, any time.

Artful Nuance: Appreciate the power of intonation, syllable emphasis, and inflection as you use words like "thank you" and "please"—they can also be said in a more sarcastic tone.

Caution: If you use it too often, politeness can come across as nagging. Less effective teachers will use this skill too often and not recognize that the situation has escalated.

Common Characteristics of Low-Key Teacher Responses

1. They are fast; they do not interrupt the flow of the class.
2. They are mostly non-verbal, employing few, if any, words.
3. They are done in a neutral or positive tone; they do not invite an escalation.

If we consider the PMI (pluses, minuses, and most important ideas) of low-key responses, we recognize there is indeed a great deal of depth to these actions. PMI is a decision-making tool developed by Edward de Bono, although we have adapted his *I* to mean "most important" rather than "interesting." Remember that although low-key responses

work, they have an innate flaw. If you are reviewing this chapter in a group, do a Place Mat, with each section having its own PMI. (See Appendix I for descriptions of Place Mat and PMI.)

Look at the diagram that follows to see the potential flaw of low-key responses. It shows two continuums and four quadrants. On the horizontal axis are responses that range from the teacher showing little respect to a lot of respect; on the vertical axis is a continuum that moves from student responsibility to teacher responsibility. Low-key responses fit into quadrant C.

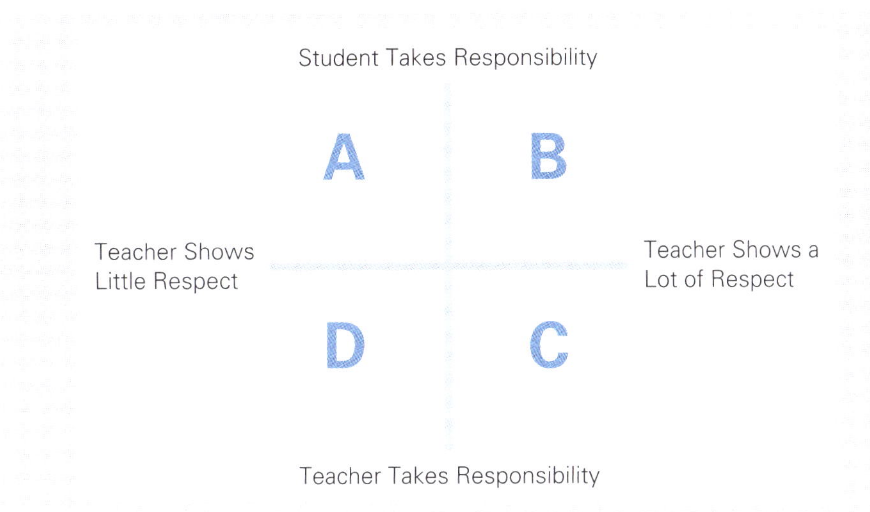

Having the teacher take all responsibility for solving the situation is not effective. Students must learn to take responsibility. Quadrant B is ideal. Programs or approaches such as those found in Jeanne Gibbs's Tribes program work at getting students to shift to quadrant B. Tribes is described in Chapter 8.

Bump 2: Squaring Off

With Bump 2 skills, you communicate the message, "You know that I know that you know...so please stop."

In your classroom, you have tried several Bump 1 skills, and the student continues to behave inappropriately. What do you do next to let students know they need to behave appropriately? If you can, discuss with a group of three or four colleagues what you think a Bump 2 sounds like and looks like.

Compare your thinking with the examples later in this section. This cartoon captures the essence of "you know that I know, so stop."

Rationale for Bump 2

When enacting Bump 2 responses, you are giving students the message: "I have asked you several times, and you know that I have asked, so please stop." You don't have to vocalize this message, although you may. However, you can communicate your point by applying most of the Bump 1 skills a bit more intensely.

Some teachers see Bump 2 as a more intense Bump 1. The key attribute of Bump 2 is that you actually turn to the students when you look at them or say their name so they know you mean business. Again, you do not have to say anything, although saying something is often helpful. *How* you apply the skills will affect your relationship with the students. Bumps 1 and 2, in an effective teacher's classroom, can likely put a stop to 80 to 90 percent of inappropriate behaviours.

Key Ideas to Consider: You do not have to give every student in the class a Bump 1 response prior to shifting to Bump 2. You may enact several Bump 1 responses with one or two students, and when a different student chooses to behave inappropriately soon after, you may enact a Bump 2 response for that student. This is particularly effective when you know that other students in the class are aware of the Bump 1 response.

That said, keep in mind the factors that affect how to choose a response. For example, if the time lapse between misbehaviours is two to three minutes, you may continue to employ Bump 1 with the third misbehaving student.

Artful Nuance: As with Bump 1, the intensity with which you carry out your action has an impact on the effectiveness of your response.

Later in this chapter, we discuss a continuum of intensity from light pink to dark red. With Bump 2 you can increase intensity significantly, but be aware that when you move into the red zone, you may provoke some students into a more defiant stance and escalate to a power situation (e.g., "Why are you always picking on me?" or "Everyone else was talking.") Those types of student responses are dealt with in Chapter 4: Responding to Students Who Move to Power.

Unavoidable Flaw: Like in Bump 1, the teacher takes responsibility for the students' behaviour (quadrant C). However, when Bump 1 and 2 responses are applied thoughtfully, they do not interrupt the flow of the lesson.

Bump 2: Squaring Off—Classroom Examples

When enacting Bump 2 skills, the same conditions as for Bump 1 apply. If the students do not yet respect you as a teacher, and do not enjoy being in your class, then Bump 2 responses will not be as effective. (This connects to the concept of winning over.)

Key Steps in Bump 2

1. The teacher stops teaching, pauses, and turns toward the student (squaring off).
2. The teacher looks at the student, and *may* say something (see the examples below).
3. When the student stops, the teacher says, "Thank you."

The "thank you" de-escalates the situation. Most students find "thank you" more genuine than "thanks." (Ask your students which they prefer.)

Examples of what a teacher may say or do while looking at the misbehaving student:

a. "Excuse me. The talking is making it difficult for me to continue." Pause. When the student stops, say "Thank you."

b. "Mark, what you are doing is stopping others from working." Pause. When the student stops, say "Thank you."

c. "Sari, please put the cell phone away." When the student puts it away, say "Thank you."

d. "Matthew, no." When the student stops, say "Thank you."

(continued)

e. A more intense, assertive look…you move beyond "the glance."

f. Combine the name with the look and a bit of proximity into the squaring off. When the students stop, say "Thank you."

g. "Excuse me, are you finished?" When the students stop, say "Thank you.")

h. "May I continue?" When the students stop, say "Thank you."

Be careful with both (g) and (h). These examples of action work only if your students respect you. If they don't, these two approaches could lead to an escalation where a student moves to power easily.

A student may respond to your "Are you finished?" with a sassy "Not quite." Or a student may answer your "May I continue?" with "Be my guest." If students respond with some sarcasm, do not take it personally. Instead, just add a pause and say "Thank you." These students are simply trying to save face in front of their classmates. At the end of class, when the students start to leave, simply say, "Angela, could I see you for a minute, please?" Now the other students know that she did not get away with it.

Bumps 3 and 4: The Choice and the Follow-Through

Both the humanist and the behaviourist approaches advocate offering choices in the classroom. The works of Dreikurs, Canter, Ginott, and Glasser all champion choice. One reason is because when given a choice, students begin to take responsibility for their own behaviour.

Most parents employ choices. Unfortunately, what parents believe to be choices are often ultimatums. Below are two ultimatums and two choices we might see in classrooms. Which are which? Why would ultimatums be a problem?

a. "Michelle, you can put that cell phone away or I'll take it away."

b. "I've asked politely twice; do your own work or you'll be coming in to do it after school."

c. "David, put the book in your desk or on mine…your decision."

d. "Well, choose to do your homework or choose to have me call your mom. Up to you."

The first two are ultimatums; the next two are choices. Ultimatums send a "do it or else" message that can provoke a student to move to power. They can, in fact, be viewed as an invitation to a power struggle. Because you have more power, you may win the battle but, over time, you will lose the "war" (or, more precisely, your health).

In the following section, we use the example-based Concept Attainment classification strategy to show what makes a choice effective. This Concept Attainment contrasts sets of examples that have the attributes of effective questions against sets of examples lacking those attributes. (See Appendix I for an explanation of Concept Attainment.)

Effective and Less Effective Choices

Focus Statement and Data Set (Phase One of Concept Attainment)

Read the following list of choices. Numbers 1, 3, 5, 7, and 9 are examples of more effective choices. Numbers 2, 4, 6, 8, and 10 are not as effective. Compare the effective choices and contrast them with the less effective choices.

Determine the attributes that make a choice effective. Jot down the characteristics of the more effective choices. When you come up with a hypothesis for the critical attributes of effective choices, determine whether the testers that follow are positive or negative examples of choices.

Data Set: Examples of Choices

1. Louis, take part in the discussion with your group appropriately, or choose to work by yourself at a desk.
2. Jason, stop calling out answers or I'll never ask you a question again.
3. Please put the book in your desk or on mine. What is your decision?
4. You can choose to work quietly together and not disturb the others or complete the assignment at 3:30. What is your preference?
5. Sujata, play the instrument properly or sit quietly and observe.
6. Do your work quietly or I'll send you to the office.
7. You can work quietly together, or you can both choose to have your seating arrangement changed until this assignment is complete.
8. Write your answers neatly, Ahmed, or you can write out 10 dictionary pages after school.

9. Sandra, if you choose to continue using your cell phone, you will be choosing to leave your battery with me and you can pick it up at the end of the day.
10. Amanda, take part in the assembly without disrupting others, or you will not be going on the field trip next month.

Testers

How would you classify the following choices?

- **a.** Please make a decision, gentlemen.
- **b.** My way or else you will not like the alternative.
- **c.** Come prepared for gym class or run five laps.
- **d.** Choose to do your homework or you are choosing to have me call your parents.
- **e.** The classroom rule is no cell phones. You've made a decision to place it on my desk and pick it up after class.
- **f.** Choose to fool around after school and miss the bus, or to get ready properly and not miss the bus.
- **g.** Okay, don't wear your rubber boots outside for recess, but be prepared to have wet feet during class and to call home and explain why.
- **h.** Either put what you have in your purse away or share it with the rest of the class.
- **i.** Great throw, Marlene; fine catch, Stephen. Unfortunately, the classroom rule is no throwing in class. Please put the keys on my desk.
- **j.** Have the assignment done or write lines that double every day they are not done.
- **k.** What you are doing is stopping me from teaching. You can choose to take part appropriately, or you can choose to wait in the office (or hall).

Checking Your Hypothesis (Phase Two of Concept Attainment)

Having considered the choices, compare your list of attributes with the list that follows. Next, review our discussion on the choices. Please understand that our choices might not be right for you—just as sometimes yours might not be right for your students.

We believe A, D, E, F, G, I, and K will work. With F and G you will have to get parental permission. E and I are examples of following

through on a choice that is known to the student, which is a Bump 4 response, described later in this chapter.

Essential Attributes of Effective Choices

1. The choice is related to the misbehaviour.

Effective choices are a function of three variables:

1. the student's misbehaviour
2. choosing a consequence related to that behaviour
3. individual student preferences

Examples 8 and 10 from the data set above and testers C and H have little or no relationship to the misbehaviour. In an effective choice, the options must link to the behaviour.

When constructing a choice, remember that an undesirable consequence for one student could be acceptable to another. For example, giving a student the choice of coming to school on time or staying late addresses the three variables, except in the case of the student who enjoys staying after school. Every teacher has had at least one student who, if given the choice, would rather stay in class and work than go home to an unpleasant situation.

2. The choice is not seen as a punishment.

Examples 6, 8, and 10 from the data set and tester C are not effective because they are likely experienced as punishment. Some punishments, like some ultimatums, are perceived as threats, not as choices. Similarly, the student might consider tester H as punishment, if the exchange is conducted in an embarrassing way.

3. The consequence is given as immediately as possible.

Examples 4 and 10 illustrate cases where students are given the option to continue their misbehaviour and suffer consequences later.

In regard to example 4, if the student chooses to complete the assignment at the end of the school day, you have not resolved your immediate problem. Classroom lawyer students will be quick to point out that they have been given licence to be disruptive until 3:30 and complete their work then. Moreover, in this example, the problem has not been clearly defined. Is the problem refusal to do work or disruptive behaviour?

With regard to example 10, if Amanda continued to misbehave in the assembly and was not allowed to go on the field trip the next month, despite changing her ways after the assembly and behaving well for 30 days before the trip, you have set up a situation that will be viewed as unfair and punitive.

4. The choice is not an ultimatum.

No real choice is offered in examples 2 and 6 and tester B. Instead, the message is "Do it or I'll…" Notice how tester D is worded so that it is *not* an ultimatum. Teachers often mistake ultimatums for choices. It is useful to remember that even if you give an effective choice, it can be reduced to an ultimatum by how you say it and your body language.

5. The choice is offered in a positive or neutral tone.

Any choice stated in a sarcastic or aggressive manner decreases its effectiveness. Example 1 (which is actually Bump 4; the follow-through on the choice) is acceptable if done in good humour.

6. You can follow through on the choice.

It would be extremely difficult to follow through on example 2 and tester J. In regard to the choice offered in J, the teacher had worked herself into a corner. The student was given 100 lines that were to double every day until done. After 13 days, the student was due to write 409,600 lines, and the next day the lines would increase to more than 819,000. Needless to say, the student's parents were not impressed. The principal had to get involved to negotiate a compromise.

By contrast, the choices E and I effectively communicate "I say what I mean and I mean what I say."

Other Types of Effective Choices

The Natural Consequence

Testers F and G are effective choices because the student's decision has a natural, immediate consequence that does not involve another person. Nonetheless, be careful about offering options that entail natural consequences without consulting the school administration and parents. Allowing a student who doesn't want to put on his winter boots to go outside in socks might not look like a good idea when it hits the front page of the local paper.

Also, be prepared to deal with the manipulations that result from the student's likely frustration with the natural consequence. For example (in a case where you are absolutely certain it is the student's fault he

has no lunch with him): "Sorry, Michael, but when you forget your lunch, you get hungry. Tomorrow, you will probably remember it."

Typical manipulations usually involve some combination of the following:

- getting mad, throwing temper tantrums
- tears—adopting a "woe is me" attitude, with the expectation that you could not possibly be so mean to someone who looks this sad
- sweeping generalizations—this is the adolescent's favourite form of argument: "Everyone else lets me phone home."
- lashing out—"I hate you...you're mean...you're stupid."

Once the student makes the choice, the teacher's role is to turn that choice into a reality. Generally, students will attempt to re-involve the teacher as a means to extricate themselves from the consequence. The teacher must be consistent and respond with something like, "This is the choice you made; next time you can decide differently." The worst thing you can do is give in to the manipulation. Once you give in, all you have taught is that you have low tolerance for nagging and you will capitulate.

The Useful Choice

Choice A, please make a decision, is a useful choice. You will probably prefer to use it once your students realize what the choice implies, without a need to state the consequence.

We've seen this used effectively with Grade 1 to university students. The rest of the class do not see it as a distraction, and it can be done non-verbally once your students understand your body language. (Hands come up to about waist level with palms up; this is merged with the look.)

Considerations When Sending Students Outside the Classroom

Tester K allows students to choose to wait in the hall or the office. A choice to wait in the hall is appropriate if the school policy allows a student to sit quietly in the hall.

Where, how, and *for how long* become key factors when you consider this choice. We have seen students sprawled across the hallway or talking to other students who were walking down the hall. Often, other teachers have stopped to have a friendly chat. Certainly, for some students the hallway is great—they love it. If a student prefers the hallway to your class, don't use the hallway as a way to change behaviour. (Remember the individual student preference variable—what you may think is punishing may, in fact, be fun for the student.) Instead, give the student the option of going to the office or to an isolated place in the room. If you find that you are sending too many students to the hallway or office, you should look carefully at changing how you engage students in learning or your behaviour to help solve the problem.

For example, one middle school teacher often had more students in the hall than in the classroom. When he gave a choice, it wasn't unusual for other students to ask if they could leave as well. Although this individual was a nice person, he struggled in the classroom. Getting a degree in education and standing at the front of the class does not make a teacher; at best, it means a nice person has an invitation to become a teacher.

Further, if the choice offered to the classroom lawyer involves "...and come back when you can behave appropriately," expect to be told "I'm not ready yet" when you ask the student to return. At best, you can reply, "My mistake. If I ever need a good lawyer, I'll call you. I'm now asking you to return to your seat, please." The line "If I ever need a good lawyer, I'll call you" is useful because it uses humour to admit that the student is correct and that you are not perfect. "I'm now asking" and "please" are important to decrease the chance of inviting a power play. If students refuse your request, they are moving toward power. We'll be looking at responses to this situation in Chapter 4, where we look at Bump 5, Defusing a Power Play.

Choosing to go to the office can be effective or ineffective, depending on the number of times it is applied and the administration's procedures for dealing with students sent to the office. For it to be effective, the principal and teacher must have a common understanding of the teacher's classroom practices to prevent and respond to student misbehaviour. The principal must assume the teacher attempted to prevent misbehaviour, and most likely applied invisible discipline, squaring off, and choices (Bumps 1 to 3) appropriately. The principal must also recognize that students made the choice to come to the office because they were, in some way, disrupting the learning environment.

At this point, depending on the school's discipline policy, a number of possibilities exist. Ultimately, all possibilities must respect the fact that the problem is between the teacher and the student, and those two individuals must eventually resolve the issue. Expecting the principal or vice-principal to come up with a solution, given that they were not in the room (a "long-distance" solution), does little to assist the teacher and student to resolve the problem. That said, when the behaviour becomes severe or intolerable, the school administration must become involved. Whenever possible, administration involvement should be part of a plan, not something whipped together, ad hoc, in the moment.

Holding Tank Strategies for Teachers

Holding tank strategies allow teachers to maintain a positive learning environment for other students, while simultaneously taking time to think before tackling a student's inappropriate behaviour.

In the following cases, school staff should agree on actions to prevent and respond to inappropriate behaviour before giving the student the choice to leave the room.

A. Sit and Wait for the Teacher in the Office

In this option, the student quietly sits in the office, knowing that during the next break (class change, recess, lunch, spare) the teacher will come and have a brief chat. This gives the student (and the teacher) time to let adrenalin levels return to normal so that a meaningful and reasonable exchange can occur. The teacher should attempt to have a three-to-five minute chat with the student within 15 to 20 minutes. (See Bump 6, The Informal Chat, described in Chapter 5.)

The benefit of this approach is that office staff are not interrupted. As well, the teacher does not usurp the power of the principal or other administrators who deal with discipline issues. If administrators get involved in all problems, they are not as effective when more severe issues arise.

B. Complete the Personal Plan

In this option, the staff designs a one- or two-page planning form (which could be different for primary, junior, intermediate, and senior students). At the top, the form might read, "Why I made the decision to leave the room" and partway down, "What needs to happen in order to solve the problem?" The student carefully and neatly completes the plan. (See the two samples in Appendix B. The second plan is intended for the student to take home.)

When the form is completed, the student hands the form to whoever is responsible in the office to have it checked and signed, and then returns to the classroom. In the room, the teacher accepts the form, reads it, asks if the student agrees with the solutions that he wrote in the plan, and invites the student back into the room on the understanding that he will behave.

Younger students, or those who struggle with reading or writing, can verbalize the plan to a person in the office who will write it for them. The student's teacher reads the plan, asks the student to explain what she will do now, and then invites her back into the room.

A spin-off benefit of the plan is that it documents the student's trips to the office. The documentation allows for more precise discussions with parents and decreases the likelihood that the student will misrepresent the situation. If you're interested in research, you might consider tracking whether or not the use of cooperative learning methods (such as Tribes) reduces the number of referrals to the office.

Finally, there is always the possibility that, on occasion, the plan will not work and the student's misbehaviour will escalate. In this case, the teacher has to interpret the escalation as a bump and choose an appropriate response. This often shifts to Bump 7, The Formal Contract. See Appendix A.

C. Take a One-Hour Time Out

Time out is a form of in-school suspension—a more severe response to student misbehaviour. If you are using a time out, we recommend that parents be alerted. If not, the student may go home and complain, "My teacher stuck me in a room and wouldn't let me do my math." If this happens, you can expect a phone call seeking clarification of the value of the time out. However, when parents understand the logic of how and why you employ this strategy, they are more likely to accept and support it.

This option is useful if a location exists where a student can sit quietly and be observed, and yet not see other students or staff. Some teachers believe the students should bring their work, others that they should sit and do nothing. Both options have strengths and weaknesses. We prefer the do-nothing option because if students are sent with work and refuse to do it, the power play continues. Doing nothing is the unexpected; it catches them off guard and increases the chance that they will reflect on why they received an in-school suspension.

The do-nothing option also ensures the time out is not an enjoyable time of rest and relaxation. After 15 or 30 minutes, bored students are usually asking for relief, such as "Can I get a book to read?" However, before the humanist in you takes over, please consider the rationale of the time out. You don't want this time to be viewed as a welcome, peaceful respite from the rigours of the classroom. From our perspective, the most effective answer is, "No, I'm sorry. This is an opportunity for you to consider how you want to be involved in your class." The language you use to respond to the student is important. Consider a staff member who responds, "Be quiet. If you worked in class you wouldn't be down here!" That teacher has unwittingly issued an invitation for an escalation of the situation.

Ideally, a time-out room is reasonably bare, with perhaps only a chair or a desk. The room itself should not offer an incentive to continue misbehaving. Create a room for reflection and calming down that communicates acceptance and caring, but be careful it does not unintentionally encourage misbehaviour.

Also, we would suggest that the time out be used only after other strategies have been attempted, such as the Informal Chat and Personal Plan. In certain situations, students should be sent to a guidance counsellor rather than be put by themselves in a room—they need to talk. Be judicious in your application of all techniques to prevent and respond to student misbehaviour—especially time outs!

D. Work in Another Classroom

Through the use of choices and follow-through on the choices (Bumps 3 and 4), students can also make the decision to work alone and quietly in another teacher's class. For example, "Alison, you can choose to work appropriately with your group, or you can choose to work quietly in Ms. Manzin's class."

This option requires that teachers agree beforehand to help each other out when one is having a particularly hard time with a class or student. Such support among colleagues contributes to collegiality in a school.

The class to which the misbehaving child is sent cannot be one that encourages misbehaviour. That means that all teachers involved in such exchanges must take the time to explain and discuss this procedure with their students.

In most cases, placing the student in a class of older students is more appropriate. The older students will know they are to ignore the visitor. As well, sending students to a younger class can be humiliating. That said, for some students, going to a lower grade classroom can be better. For example, if you are using it to build responsibility by having the students help younger ones read—great! Just be sensitive to the effects on the students.

E. Read Quietly in the Library Until You Are Prepared to Rejoin the Class

Again, this is an example of how staff members can work together. It is important not to use the library as a punishment zone, but rather as a place for students who need time to be alone, to reflect, and to gather their thoughts while being quietly supervised and supported at a distance. If students are sent to the library, they should be expected to read or work quietly.

Bump 3—The Choice...A Quick Review

1. **Stop teaching, pause, and turn to the student,** or approach the student privately if you anticipate a power struggle.
2. **Provide the student with an appropriate choice** or allow the student to make a choice by simply saying, "A decision, please." This can be a quiet, kind request or a more assertive one. The art of using the choice is deciding on its appropriate intensity.
3. **Wait for an answer.** The answer could be verbal and appropriate, non-verbal and appropriate, verbal and accompanied by a comment to save face, or non-verbal in a way that saves face.
4. **Finish with "thank you."** If the student persists, follow through with Bump 4. The following are examples of choices designed by teachers for common misbehaviours. Remember that an effective choice to some teachers might not be appropriate for you. Modify and adapt them to meet your needs. Creating the right choice is a skill. It is your decision about *how, where,* and *when* that determines the effectiveness of the choice.

Sample Choices for Common Misbehaviours

It is not always easy or possible to create effective choices on the spot. Consider taking the time to prepare a few effective choices for your situation.

a. **Talking at an inappropriate time**
"Linus, please choose to listen quietly, or choose to have your seating arrangement changed. Your decision."

"Terri, take part when it is your turn, or you are making the decision not to participate in this discussion. What's your preference?"

"Excuse me, although you are working hard, the noise level is too high. I've asked twice. Work quietly within your group or choose to work on your own. I'll give your group a minute to decide. Thank you."

b. **Tinkering with an inappropriate object in class (toy, hat, cell phone)**
"Interesting trinket, Janice; however, this is not the time or the place. Please put it in your desk—or on mine."

"Mack, the school rule is no hats in class. You've made the decision to leave it on my desk. You can pick it up after class. Next time, you know you have donated it to charity."

"Becky, I'm also addicted to cell phones, but the issue is time and place. Please put it away or bring the battery up to me."

c. **Calling out answers**
"We've discussed why I don't accept call-outs. Choose to respond appropriately or choose not to take part in this activity." (Or "Choose to sit at the back of the room and come back when you can take part appropriately.")

"Michael, we all have the right to 'turn on our own light.' Choose to wait your turn or write your answer on a piece of paper and I'll read it when you finish."

d. **Fooling around in small groups so others can't work**
"You are stopping others in the group from working effectively. Choose to work appropriately, or choose to work by yourself. The decision is up to you."

Wait a few seconds for a response. If there is no response, continue, "Thank you, I'll assume by your silence you will work with your group." If the misbehaviour continues, follow through on the choice by having the student work alone (Bump 4).

Bump 4—The Follow-Through...A Quick Review

Bump 4 is simply the other half of the choice—the part where you act on the choice given. This is the critical time when students learn that you "say what you mean and mean what you say." There's no way to isolate Bump 3 from 4; they work in tandem.

In classrooms, we hear Bump 4 responses such as these:

- "I'm sorry, Akim, you've made the decision to work on your own over here. Thank you."
- "Thank you, Andrea, you've made the decision to put the cell phone on my desk."
- "You've decided, through your language and aggressiveness, to be suspended. We did not suspend you; you suspended yourself."

In life, rules and laws are akin to Bump 3, The Choice; if you break them, then Bump 4, The Follow-Through kicks in. If you rob a bank, you are choosing, if you get caught, to go to jail. If you drink and drive, you are choosing, if caught, to lose your licence. If you speed in a school zone, you are choosing to pay a hefty fine. If you forget to pick your spouse up at the airport, well, you know there will be consequences!

Of course, if no enforcement is enacted, then rules and laws are of little value. In life, if rules and laws are inconsistently applied, you will take your case to court. Only a fool would forget to pick his wife up at the airport a second time, especially when his wife is a principal… who'll phone his mother.

Classrooms are no different. As students and teachers make choices, life plays out. If, as a teacher, I choose to structure groups effectively, then I am choosing to maximize student learning and decrease my management problems. If, as a student, I choose not to study and do homework, then I am quite likely choosing not to be successful in school. If, as a teacher, I am sarcastic, boring, disorganized, and humourless, I am choosing to have students bond against me—and I deserve what I get.

Note that some consequences (Bump 4) happen by default: if I choose to touch the hot frying pan, I will get burned; if I choose to text while crossing the street, I may be run over.

Implied Choice in Bump 4

Follow-through can make use of "implied choice" on two levels. First, you follow through on the choice that was provided to the student earlier. Second, you convey the message that a choice given to one student applies to all (assuming that the other students heard the choice).

For example, two students who are not staying on task are given the choice of working appropriately or changing seats. For a short time, the students behave, but after five minutes, they act inappropriately once again. The implication is that they will now have their seating arrangement changed—the follow-through on the choice they had been given earlier.

If other students heard the choice, and two different students are also off task, they too can expect to have their seating arrangement changed, without having been given the option directly. In this situation, the teacher does not need to give the choice before taking action.

The next day, as the class starts, if the same students start the period by behaving inappropriately, you could simply invoke Bump 4. Or you could choose to use a low-key response instead to remind the students of appropriate behaviour, then square off, and renegotiate with a choice (Bumps 1 to 3).

The decision on how to respond and in what order the responses will occur differs for different students on different days—such are the vagaries of classroom life. As stated previously, for Bump 4 to work, you must offer a choice on which you can follow through. The option should not be perceived as unfairly punishing or hurtful to the dignity of the child. No matter how logical and fair the choice seems to you, some students will initially see the choice as unjust and illogical. However, when things calm down, an effective choice, enacted with respect, will certainly increase the chance that the student will in time bond with you and not turn against you.

Earlier we talked about Kounin's (1977) concept known as the Ripple Effect. If students know they are being treated fairly, the likelihood is that they will also treat you fairly. Over time, this helps the teacher become respected as a caring person and an effective teacher. If students respect us, they are less likely to defy us and move to power, where we feel the locus of control shifting to the student.

Nuances in Responses

The nuances that occur within each of the teacher responses are critical to how successful the response will be. Those nuances are the art of applying a particular response. For example, if the skill is proximity, the nuance, or art, is how fast you move toward the student, how long you stay, how much you say, and the loudness and tone of your voice.

The nuance sets the intensity of the response. Imagine an intensity continuum running from light pink to dark red. Light pink is polite; the response is carried out with a smile. At medium pink, the teacher remains polite, with a calm face but no smile. At dark pink, there is still politeness but now we sense intensity. Moving into light red, the teacher's expression is intense and her voice becomes more assertive. You have to be careful when you shift to medium and darker red, as these shades can invite an escalation.

Nuances also refer to the subtle messages that the student is communicating. In most cases, the teacher needs to have experience with students who move to power to pick up on the clues students provide as they invite and push the escalation. A teacher who does not apply nuances in responding to student misbehaviour risks being out of sync with the student. You may underrespond or overrespond to the student. As a result, students may see the teacher as "not with it" or "muggable." When teachers are muggable, they send out the message that they are weak, and so they are at risk being taken advantage of.

A Mini-Bump Example

The student taps a pencil.

The teacher asks the student to stop (the nuance is in how the teacher asks, what the facial message is).

The student maintains eye contact, taps one more time, and puts the pencil down.

(The extra tap serves as a warning shot to let the teacher know the student will stop when he wants to stop.)

A Maxi-Bump Example

Now the student gets out of his desk without permission.

The teacher asks the student to sit down (the nuance is in how the teacher asks, what the facial message is).

The student ignores the teacher and continues to the back of the room.

The teacher threatens with a trip to the office if he does not comply (this is usually a darker red, and often invites an increase in the escalation).

The student responds, "This class sucks; no one likes this class."

When he is kicked out, he slams the door as he leaves.

Chapter 3 Conclusion

The more skilled we are at dealing with less complex student misbehaviour, the less likely it is for the misbehaviour to escalate into a power situation. Bumps 1 through 4 are designed to de-escalate behaviour, so that the power struggle does not emerge.

This chapter described four sets of skills that effective teachers have likely been using in the classroom for hundreds of years, and parents even before that. Bumps 1 through 4 as responses to escalation are not complex to understand. They are common sense, and no one "owns" them. As the authors, we simply collected, described, and organized them for you. The complexity is in *how, when, where,* and *with whom* you apply them. Our guess is that if you are an effective teacher, when you read this chapter, you will say to yourself, "Now, I know why I am effective," or "Now I understand why my choices work." That said, applying responses effectively is one thing; realizing what you are doing is another. Remember that mentoring others in classroom management is difficult if you don't recognize and understand what you are doing. This is especially important to keep in mind when student teachers are in their practicum. If university instructors and classroom teachers are not well versed in classroom management, the dialogue with student teachers will be simplistic.

As you enact those four bumps, keep in mind the spectrum of light pink, medium pink, dark pink, light red, medium red, and dark red. The same skill can be enacted with any of these intensities. Keep in mind, if you use a light pink when you should have used a dark pink, or vice versa, you can be perceived as too soft or too assertive. Each of the bumps is the science; how you enact them is the art.

Responding to Students Who Move to Power

4 Key Areas of Bump 5: Defusing a Power Play

Recognizing the Move to a Power Play Situation

- sense defiance
- heart races/adrenalin
- sweaty
- voice changes
- student smirks

etc.

Determining Where It Started

- hallway
- another teacher's classroom
- at home
- in your class

etc.

Knowing Who Started It

- another student
- another teacher
- a parent/guardian
- you

etc.

Having a Set of Responses to De-escalate the Situation

- ignore
- humour
- a choice
- language of attribution

etc.

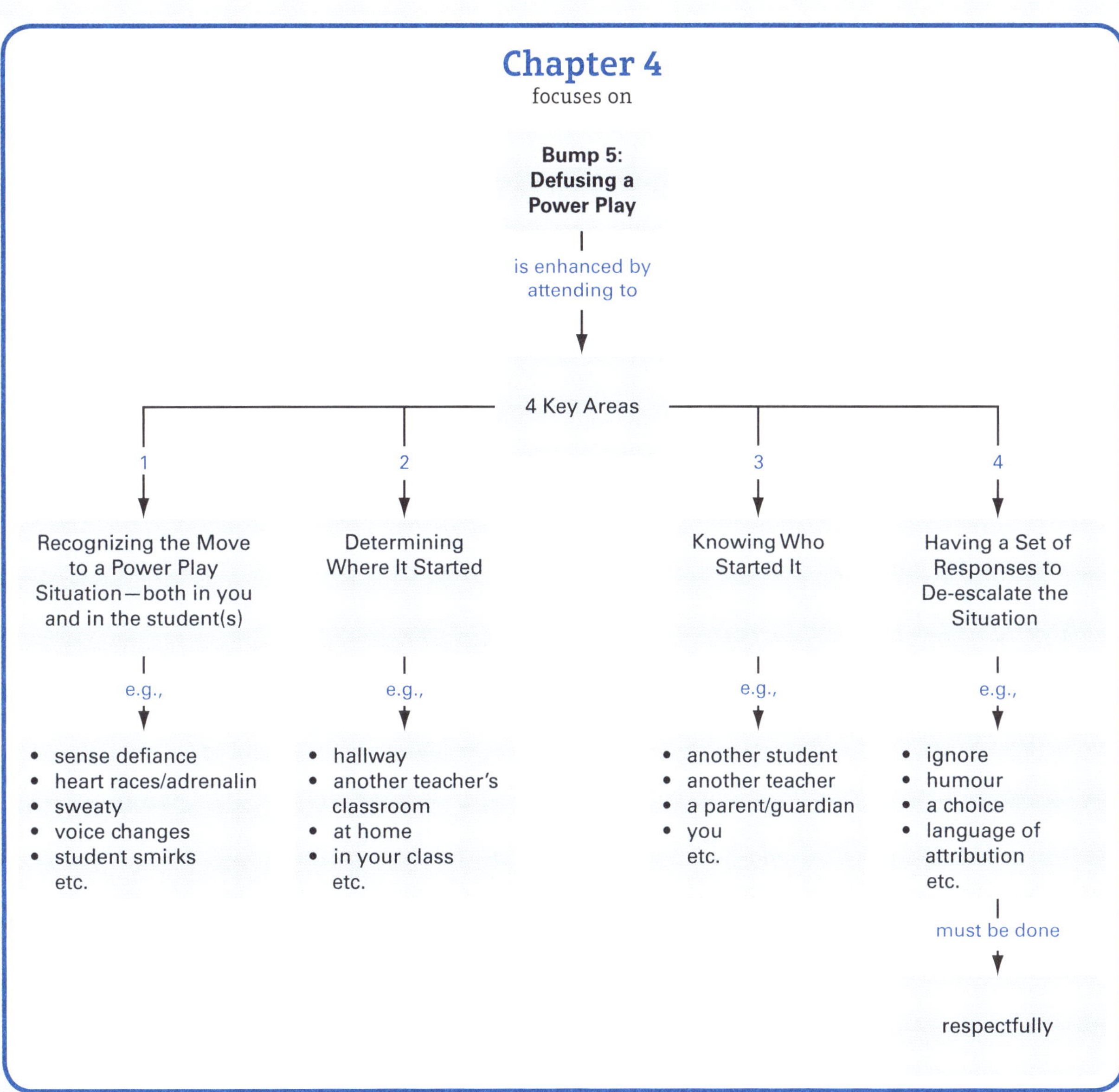

Chapter 4
focuses on
Bump 5:
Defusing a
Power Play
is enhanced by
attending to
4 Key Areas
1
Recognizing the Move to a Power Play Situation—both in you and in the student(s)
e.g.,
• sense defiance
• heart races/adrenalin
• sweaty
• voice changes
• student smirks
etc.
2
Determining Where It Started
e.g.,
• hallway
• another teacher's classroom
• at home
• in your class
etc.
3
Knowing Who Started It
e.g.,
• another student
• another teacher
• a parent/guardian
• you
etc.
4
Having a Set of Responses to De-escalate the Situation
e.g.,
• ignore
• humour
• a choice
• language of attribution
etc.
must be done
respectfully

In this chapter, we discuss how effective teachers respond to students who initiate power plays in the classroom. This represents Bump 5 in our theory of bumps. Although the responses we examine in these pages are not the only actions that can restore order efficiently, we offer them to provide insight into why some actions are particularly successful in de-escalating situations. As you move through this section, you will also see how the Bump 1, 2, 3, and 4 skills are still in play. These less complex skills are still needed to effectively enact the responses to power.

Teachers experience degrees of aggravation. When a student tells you to "f—k off" or that your lesson is "boring," or ignores your request to put away her cell phone, you experience a different feeling than when a student calls out an answer, chews gum, passes a note, or sits without working.

Power struggles are not just limited to tensions between teachers and students. For example, consider what happens between adults in the staff room when one person neglects to tidy up after making a mess at lunchtime. And what about the dynamics of a staff meeting—does everyone suspend judgment, listen attentively, disagree agreeably, and encourage equal voice?

Power Plays in the Workplace

A study conducted in Canadian hospitals illustrates that bad behaviour and bullying do not disappear as we shift into adulthood. As one example, the *Globe* article "Defusing the Uncivil Workplace" (Immen, 2011) revealed that conflict and power plays take place in hospitals between employees at all levels. The article describes a program entitled Civility, Respect and Engagement at Work (CREW) that was launched in five Canadian hospitals (three in Nova Scotia, two in Ontario) to collect data on workplace tensions and initiate a process to resolve the incivility.

As a result of the CREW program, incivility dropped by 30 percent and absences fell by 15 percent. No change was observed in the level of incivility among employees who did not participate. A key component of CREW was to provide employees with release time

for skill training on how to appropriately discuss conflict issues and resolve them.

The five CREW steps to reduce incivility are the following:

1. Bring the issue out into the open.
2. Formalize a code of conduct in writing.
3. Set enforcement standards.
4. Commit to consistent enforcement.
5. Provide resources for counselling and stress reduction.

The measured results of the training confirm the value of the process. The five steps are not unlike what we teachers do, and should be doing more of, in our schools.

The Cost of Bad Behaviour

For their book *The Cost of Bad Behavior*, authors Christine Pearson and Christine Porath (2009) surveyed a large sample of U.S. professionals and determined that bad behaviour negatively affects productivity, health, and economics in the workplace. The findings below illustrate the prevalence of incivility; the parallels between workplace and school are striking.

Results of Pearson and Porath's Study of Professionals

Percent	Workers Who
96	have been insulted or bullied in a workplace
78	reported that their commitment to an organization declined as a result of being bullied or insulted
63	lost time at work to avoid the offender
48	said they intentionally decreased work effort after uncivil treatment
47	said they intentionally reduced time at work after uncivil treatment
38	said they intentionally allowed their work quality to slip

Case Studies

Below are examples of conflicts in school situations where either no structure was in place to resolve the conflict or no support system existed within the school for the teachers.

Situation 1: One of the authors of this book was working with a teacher at risk of losing her job in a public school. The school administration sought help from the Teacher Effectiveness Program, in which trained consultants provide support to struggling educators.

This at-risk Grade 9 teacher planned excellent lessons and was kind and respectful to students. Unfortunately she came across as vulnerable, a "muggable" target for students. During a unit test, the president of the student union sat on the back of his seat, with the globe of the world, and told the students the answers to the questions. The teacher tried to get him to stop, but he refused. At this point, the consultant informed the offending group of students that they had made the decision to go to the office. They left, smiling.

Within two minutes, they returned. The office had sent them back. The consultant took the students to the office and asked for the principal. He was not in, and the assistant principal was teaching. When asked, the secretary said the administration did not have a plan to deal with students sent to the office. The consultant then sought out the assistant principal and asked him to step out of his classroom and into the hall.

The power struggle that ensued between the two could have made a most entertaining YouTube video. The consultant emphatically made the point that the two administrators were unethical; they were showing no initiative to assist the at-risk teacher. From the perspective of the consultant, the administration was incompetent when it came to dealing with at-risk teachers and creating a school-wide discipline action plan.

The upshot: The at-risk teacher was moved to a Grade 3/4 class and became a very effective teacher.

What can we learn from this situation?

Power struggles play out between students and teachers and between consultants and administrations—we all get caught. We also see that schools that don't have a plan of action for students who choose to go to the office leave the classroom teacher at risk. We also learned that a consultant, who is an expert on how to deal with power struggles, can nonetheless initiate a power struggle with another adult rather than resolve one. In other words, power struggles can happen to anyone. The key is to learn from them.

Situation 2: A consultant was assigned to work with an at-risk secondary teacher. After observing the situation, the consultant noted that the at-risk teacher had the potential to change, but was totally unaware of how poorly he was dealing with situations.

The teacher willingly agreed to release time to devote three days to following a group of his students into other classrooms. That experience opened his eyes to what he was doing wrong and ways he could improve his own practice. The end result is that he is now thriving as a teacher.

What can we learn from this situation?

Often the issue of classroom management and instruction, especially with newer teachers, is one of simply not knowing. Few teachers receive high-quality programs related to instruction, especially related to classroom management. Newer teachers often need to see what is possible, observe what others are doing, and then, with support, make necessary shifts.

Situation 3: Below is an email from a frustrated teacher.

> Barrie, you may not remember me but I attended your classroom management classes at OISE [Ontario Institute for Studies in Education] and your workshops when you worked with our district. I am only four years from retiring and I am struggling to keep going. I am on leave for a few months (doctor's orders) and I am now okay to go back. I have a class that is really doing me in. I am fine with other classes, but this one class just gets me. Parents complained after I yelled at a student and it was suggested I take a break. After all these years, I thought I was over issues around classroom management...

What can we learn from this situation?
Classroom management issues never go away. Things may go well until we are put into a subject area that is not our specialty or we get a group of students who are difficult to handle in a school that has no support system for teachers. When it comes to classroom management, we can never stop learning. We have seen a large number of teachers who require stress leave because of acute tensions related to classroom management issues.

Four Key Factors in De-escalating Power Plays

There are four factors that must be understood for de-escalating power struggles by students.

1. Recognize When You Are About to Get into a Power Play

This ability to recognize the onset of a power play starts with identifying what you are feeling when you are about to get into a power situation, as well as noticing the actions and behaviours of the student who is moving to power.

a. **You:** We have all experienced situations involving some sort of struggle for power. What do you notice about yourself when you sense you are sliding toward a power struggle? Record what happens to you. Compare your answers with those of other teachers.

b. **Students:** What do you notice about students when they are inviting a power struggle or starting to move to power? Record your observations. Compare your answers with those of other teachers.

Rationale: If you are not skilled in anticipating the event, you will get caught and end up too far into the power play to effectively de-escalate the situation and restore social order so that learning can continue.

Recognizing the Onset of a Power Play

What Teachers Notice About Themselves

- I feel I am flushing...my face gets red.
- My adrenalin starts to pump.
- My hands get clammy.
- I clench my hands…my stomach hardens.
- I puff up (males).
- I make myself look bigger (males).
- My voice cracks…gets louder.
- My heart starts to race.
- I start to sweat…
- I move toward the student.
- I move away from the student.
- I feel and think like I would like to throttle the students.

What Teachers Notice About Their Students

- They talk back...sort of arrogant.
- They glare at me.
- They sit and do nothing…maybe cry.
- They swear.
- They smile at me.
- They do something that sucks me in like saying, "Why do we have to do fractions?"
- They pretend I don't exist and keep talking.
- They start to get other students going.
- They bring up something from the past as a precedent.

2. and 3. Note Where the Power Play Started and Who Started It

Where It Started

As a teacher, having a sense of where the power play started helps you decide how to effectively respond. Below are five of the most common places for power plays to start.

a. **In Your Classroom:** A power play that begins in the classroom allows you greater understanding of what prompted it and puts you in a better position to deal with it effectively. However, if you started it (intentionally or not), the solution is more complicated.

b. **In Another Classroom:** When a power play starts in another classroom, the upside is that you know that you are not the reason for the conflict. The downside is that you have little understanding of why it started, which makes it harder to work out a reasonable approach to restoring social order. If you can pick up that something is amiss as the student walks into your classroom, you may be able to nip a potentially difficult situation in the bud with a quick private chat (see Chapter 5).

c. **In the Hallway:** If you see a conflict between two students, you are well placed to resolve it. The challenge is that you most likely have no idea who started it, so do not take sides. If the conflict is not serious, you can usually step in and ask the students to stop and move on to their classes. If the conflict is more intense, offer students the choice to stop or to solve their dispute at the office. Of course, if it is serious, you need to get help. Your relationship with the students is critical in this case. If they know and respect you, your intervention will be more effective.

d. **At Home:** Like conflicts that start in another class or in the hallway, the upside is that you are not part of the reason for the conflict, so you are in a better position to resolve it. The downside is that you have little influence over what happens in the home. Keep in mind that boys who witness violence in the home often become bullies; girls who witness violence at home tend to withdraw. Being a bully (more aggressive) and withdrawing (more passive) can result in power struggles. The difference is that passive power does not stop you from teaching; the struggle is in motivating those students to come to school and learn.

e. **On the Way to School (for example, on the bus) or into the School:** Given that you have no idea who started the conflict, the key is to not take the power play personally—you were not the cause.

Who Started It

Knowing who started a power play helps teachers decide how to respond, especially if you're the one who somehow started it. In any event, the possibilities are not endless. The most common "who" scenarios follow.

a. **Another Student or Students:** How you respond depends on whether or not the struggle started in your classroom or outside of it. If it started outside, you may have to enact the Informal Chat described in Chapter 5. A power struggle started by another student means that at least one other student in your classroom may be involved. In this case, you will also have to deal with that other student and possibly with more allies.

b. **Parent or Parents:** You can't control what goes on in the student's home. However, you can be fairly sure that, since one in six students in Canada lives in an at-risk environment, what happens within the family is likely not teaching the student the skills to effectively deal with conflict. You must make sure you do not model what goes on in the home. For example, if family members raise their voice to resolve conflict, then when you raise your voice in the classroom you are modelling that "might is right." The key is to model, and balance, reason and kindness with assertiveness. Over time, you will begin to have an impact.

c. **The Teacher (You):** When the struggle starts with you, and you have an internal locus of control (that is, you understand that this is your responsibility to resolve), you can work to solve the problem. The downside is that if you have an external locus of control (that is, you believe that others are responsible—your job is to teach) you are more likely to blame the students because you hold the belief that all students should behave (this is a problem expectation, discussed earlier). Note that you can shift your locus of control. For example, if you fail to check for understanding effectively, to frame questions effectively, to structure groups effectively, and so on, you increase the chances that students feel unsafe and will be unsuccessful academically. Students who do not feel safe and who are unsuccessful are more likely to misbehave. Start to change how you teach, how you engage students in learning, and how they engage with one another.

d. **The Student Moving to Power:** Responding to a student who is moving or has moved to power is not easy. Remember that the more the students respect you as a teacher and as a person, the greater the chances are that your response works. If your class is boring, you are not organized, you do not make learning meaningful, and the classroom environment is unsafe, you are far less likely to de-escalate the move to power.

Rationale: If you do not know who started it, and where, you may select an inappropriate or less effective approach to de-escalate the situation.

4. Respond to De-escalate the Move to a Power Play

What thoughts do you have when a power play is about to start in your class? When working with Grade 6 teachers from the Medicine Hat School District, we asked them to capture what comes to mind when a power play is about to start. Below are some of their comments.

- Choose your battles—is it worth the effort?
- Define the issue.
- Identify the reason behind the behaviour—the background to what is happening.
- Be respectful—it's not about me.
- Empathize.
- Did I start it?
- Should I ignore it?

- Change the focus from the issue to the solution.
- Understand the student thinks she is correct, and it is worth the fight.
- Find out why it started.
- Don't get sucked in—come back later when you're ready to deal with the situation.
- Be calm—understand the issue before dealing with it.
- Make sure each person has the chance to state their feelings/opinions.
- Understand the points of view of those involved—look at both sides.
- Allow students to maintain their dignity.
- In some situations, remove the peer influence from the situation.
- Consider that the student wants the power…so give it to him in appropriate ways.

When we ask teachers to think back on how they resolved power struggles in the classroom or at home, we find they already know most of the tactics people employ to de-escalate these situations.

Interestingly, even though many teachers "know" the tactics, they may not always enact the responses at the right time, in the right way, or in the right place, often because emotions get in the way. Moreover, they consistently miss one key skill related to the "language of attribution" that they use, often without realizing it (see pages 102 to 103).

Rationale: Without a large repertoire of responses, you will not be able to wisely and effectively respond to different power situations.

If someone asked you to identify how you respond when it looks like a power play is about to start, what would you say?

What Other Effective Teachers Have Told Us

As you read through these ideas, you may find it obvious that they are simply common sense. And if you are a more effective teacher who has built a relationship with students, you know these responses work. After each idea, we provide a PMI (pluses, minuses, most important ideas) commentary as a critical analysis of each approach. The PMI model was developed by Edward de Bono. Note that the "I" usually stands for "interesting," but for these situations, the notion of "Important" is more useful.

1. Ignore What the Student Said or Did and Deal with It Later

You look at the student to let her know that you are aware of what is going on, but you choose not to deal with the situation at this point in the lesson. Teachers often tell us that when students are about to leave class at the end of period, they will ask that student (whom they had earlier ignored) to stay for a moment. This ensures the student does not have to save face in front of the other students and that other students know that she did not get away with the inappropriate action. The key is that the behaviour stopped when ignored, and it was not a major offence such as a racial or gender slur.

Plus: Ignoring is fast, allows you to continue teaching, and doesn't disrupt the flow of the lesson. It can also be integrated with some of the other responses. As stated earlier, the other bumps are also part of the teacher's repertoire of power responses. So the use of ignoring is virtually the same as the Bump 1 move, except that it will often be connected to "the look" with a bit more intensity.

Minus: Ignoring the behaviour may imply to other students that you're doing nothing. It may appear that the student "got away with it." If you hear a student mumble something, do not inquire, "What did you say?" You will most likely regret asking.

Most Important: When ignoring, you are less likely to get sucked into the power play, and the student will find it more difficult to continue the escalation. If the student does something to save face, let it go if it is not too inappropriate. As an example, the student may complain, "This sucks." In response, simply say, "You're right, sometimes it does," or "Whatever," or just ignore it.

2. Use Humour to De-escalate the Situation

This approach implies that you are able to keep your sense of humour when a student begins to initiate a power move.

Plus: The teacher's use of humour informs students that you are not going to buy into their invitation. It also makes it difficult for the student making a power move to get support from allies. Of course, humour implies a range of actions, from a smile to acknowledgement to making a joke.

Minus: Humour may come across as sarcasm. If it does, the student may lose face and therefore turn further against you.

Most Important: Remember not to take the student's behaviour personally. If you take what the student did personally, then you are more likely to use sarcasm in a negative way. Keep the humour light and related to the misbehaviour.

Below are some examples.

a. A student says, "This is boring."

Teacher response: "Boring for you? I had to plan this lesson last night, plus I have to teach it today. You should be feeling sorry for me right now."

Teacher response: "Boring, well, enjoy today because I get worse every day of the year."

b. A student says, "This sucks."

Teacher response: "Well, there are moments in life that suck; it would be a boring world if every minute was always perfect."

Teacher response: "At least now tomorrow's lesson will look so much better because I sucked in today's lesson...Thanks for letting me know."

c. A student says, "F—k off" (directly at the teacher).

Teacher response: "Whoa, another F-bomb—not good; hope that's the last one."

Teacher response: "What you asked is not possible. But thanks for the idea."

Continue teaching. At the end of the lesson let the student know that you need to see him so the other students know that this student did not get away with it.

If the student continues to push in this situation, you'll have to shift away from humour. You might say, "Clearly, this is not stopping. We've talked about this before. What you said is a major issue; you've now chosen to go to the office—this is your decision, not mine."

The student may reply, "I'm not leaving" or "You can't make me leave." In this case, you may respond, "I can't make you, so you can choose to leave on your own or you can choose to have me invite the principal." You could also say, "Class, please pick up your books and go to the library. I will be down in a couple of minutes." If the student has cooperative parents you can say, "You can decide to go to the office to solve this problem, or you can choose to have us call your parents in to help resolve it—your decision."

This situation is about as difficult as it gets. Obviously, if you do not have a clearly articulated discipline policy—with an administrative support process in place—your options are severely limited. In a secondary school, you can treat this kind of verbal aggression as disturbing the peace, and if you have a police liaison, you can bring that person in to resolve it by escorting the student out of the room.

d. A student says, "Oh, f—k" or "This is f—ing ridiculous" (indirectly to the teacher).

Be careful on this one; this kind of comment is often just the result of frustration. Don't overreact and turn it into a power situation. Some students live in homes where "f—k" is just a word—they know it is inappropriate to use it in class, but it will just slip out.

Teacher response: "Sammy...you're lucky I'm deaf and have a bad memory." (Give him a quick glance and move on.)

Teacher response: "You're right, it may be ridiculous; I probably confused everyone. Tell me what I did for you to talk to me that way." (Note that you ignore the f—k component.)

Student: "I have no idea what I am supposed to do!"

Teacher: "My fault. I did not check to see if everyone understood; sorry about that. Next time, maybe just put up your hand and tell me I'm not being an effective teacher and I'll make the shift."

e. A student says, "You're a bitch."

Teacher response: "That's the third time someone has told me; I'm beginning to believe it's true."

Teacher response: "Thanks, I know...glad my practice is paying off."

Teacher response: "Only when there's no chocolate in the house."

In order for these responses to work, the majority of students must respect the teacher and want to be in the class. If that is not the case, nothing will work. Notice that agreeing with students takes all the wind out of their sails; it leaves them with no place to go and nothing to push against.

f. Two students start to get into a friendly disagreement and you see one student (Mark) lightly hit another student (Rod) on the shoulder.

Teacher response: "Rod, the next time I see your shoulder hit Mark's fist, you're in trouble. Your fist okay, Mark?" (Pause, walk away.)

Teacher response: "Gentlemen, I'm going to pretend I did not see this."

g. To try to irritate the teacher, a student says, "Learning about history is torture."

Teacher response: "Sarah, you're right. And you should know that I spend my evenings planning ways to torture you with history...and now I see it's working."

h. A Grade 1 student comes into the classroom with muddy outside shoes that are supposed to be left outside the room. When asked to leave the boots outside, she replies, "No, I want to wear these."

Teacher response: "That's okay, Shannon. Just take your legs off and hang them outside." (One of the authors witnessed this exchange, and saw the student laugh and reply "I can't do that" before walking to the hall to change her shoes.)

Summary: With these teacher responses, once you've responded, pause, perhaps offer a small smile, and continue teaching.

When appropriate, deal with the incident later to ensure the student (and others) know their behaviour was not acceptable. Try saying, "Maria, can I see you for a minute, please?" If the student walks out, let it ride until she calms down and conduct an Informal Chat at a later time (see Chapter 5).

3. Describe the Situation and Move On

This approach is designed to let students know in advance that you are not going to buy into the power situation by telling them how the situation will play out.

Plus: The time to describe the situation provides students with a few more seconds to rethink what is happening; it also lets students see the future unfold and gives them a way out without having to argue or say anything to save face.

Minus: This tactic takes more time, so is more likely to stop the flow of learning.

Most Important: This approach allows students time to think about what is happening and provides a way out, while still allowing them to save face.

a. Two students argue, evidence of a mini-power play between the two.

Teacher response: "Excuse me, this happened last week and you both ended up in the office with detentions. I am going to assume that you don't think going back to the office is good idea so you'll stop and we can get on with the class... [*pause*] Thank you."

b. One student in a group refuses to work.

Teacher response: "Michael, it looks like this is not working; you're upset and so is your group. I am going to walk away and assume you will all try to make this work. Thank you." (This response is unlikely to work unless you have a high mean score and your students really respect you.)

Teacher response: "Janice, yesterday you did the same thing and ended up working on your own. I was upset, you got upset, and that clearly did not solve the problem. I am assuming you will now prefer to work with the group... [*pause*] Thank you."

c. A student continues to text after being asked to stop.

Teacher response: "David, I've asked twice; last week you made a decision to lose your cell phone for a week. I am going to assume that you will put it away... [*pause*] Thank you."

d. A student tells the teacher to "F—k off."

Teacher response: "If you are trying to make me upset, it's working. I must have done something wrong to cause you to talk to me like that. Can you tell me what it was so I don't do it again?"

e. A student says, "Why are you always picking on me—others were talking too."

Teacher response: "Sorry I missed them; all I saw was you. Next time I will pay more attention. Thanks for letting me know. I'll assume this is over. Thank you."

4. Provide a Choice

This response is similar to Bump 3, The Choice. The choice has to relate to the misbehaviour. The choice is offered in a positive or neutral tone; it does not come across as an ultimatum (see pages 66 to 67). It is not seen as a punishment, and the choice is one you can follow through on. Note that Bumps 3 and 4 also work in power plays.

Plus: Choices allow students an opportunity to make a decision—to take some responsibility for their behaviour. Choices have a logic to them.

Minus: Given that the choice is designed by the teacher, sometimes students see it as forced and don't like it.

Most Important: Students have the opportunity to decide their future. Students have a voice, albeit a limited one. They may say, "I don't like those choices." You can respond, "That's fine, do you have a better one?" If their choice makes sense, allow it. If not, say, "Sorry, not acceptable. Now decide or you are deciding to have me decide; it's up to you."

a. One or two students are not working effectively in their group; you've asked them to refocus a couple of times, but they are still not complying.

Teacher response: "I've asked twice, so you now have a choice. You can work in your group effectively and do your part, or you can both work on your own to complete the group task."

b. A student is continuing to use a cell phone after being asked to put it away; this has happened in previous classes.

Teacher response: "Marsha, I asked in previous classes and once today. You can put your phone away and leave it there or you can choose to put it on my desk and pick it up after class. Your decision." (The student does not say anything.) You continue, "I'll assume by your silence you are going to put it away. Thank you."

c. Two students are arguing in the hall.

Teacher response: "Excuse me, this is not appropriate. [*Wait a couple of seconds.*] We can agree this is over and you move off to your classroom, or we take this to the office...up to you. [*Wait a few seconds again.*] I'll assume this is over. Thank you." Walk away, taking three to five steps before turning to see what the students have done.

You must follow through on the choice. If the students have moved, it's over. If not, you say, "You've chosen the office; violence and threats are a major off a protocol for students being sent to the office. If you don't have a clearly articulated discipline policy that spells out what happens when students end up at the office, then the office is *not* an option.

d. A student calls the teacher an "a—hole."

Teacher response: "We've talked about this before. I talk to you respectfully, and I expect you to talk respectfully to me. You know this is a major offence in the school and you knew that if it was to happen again, you were deciding to go to the office. And it just happened again. Your behaviour just made the decision for you to leave; not me."

5. Provide a Time Out

A time out, which is also a possible outcome of Bump 4, The Follow-Through, works if you have a good relationship with all your students, including the student involved in the power situation. It usually works best if you've already worked this possibility out with the students, so that they know that when they get into a situation that may escalate, a time out is an option, and they know where to go and what to do.

Plus: The student has the chance to move away from the situation and spend time alone to calm down and think it out. You have time to figure out what to do while the student is away.

Minus: Not all students will make wise use of the time out, and those students should not be allowed to leave the classroom for a time out. Also, students are not involved in learning while calming down.

Most Important: Try to establish the procedures, location, and options for the time out with students in advance so that they know that when they feel they are about to lose control, they can self-invoke the time out. For younger students, try to have a place in your room where students can go to calm down. It's also not a bad idea to tell them that sometimes you will also use it when you need a time out.

a. A student is getting agitated and struggling to work with other students.

Teacher response: Walk over to the student and quietly say, "Sujata, it's okay to get upset. Do you want to take some time on your own? You can walk down and read in the library for a while."

b. A student is sitting at her desk doing nothing, clearly upset.

Teacher response: Have an envelope ready in advance for a student to take to the office (this is especially useful for younger students). The office should know that when this envelope comes to the office, the student should be told to wait a minute and be asked how things are going. The office will then give the student something to take back to the teacher. "Amanda, could you take this back to your teacher for me? Thanks."

6. Use "Tai Chi"

This approach is designed to align the student with the teacher so that you are saying the same thing; it deflects the student's comment so you are both heading in the same direction.

Plus: This approach has the student agreeing with you when the situation is starting to escalate and is not too severe.

Minus: This is not an appropriate choice if the behaviour is more severe or challenging.

Most Important: Use this approach when the situation is just starting to evolve: when the student is, intentionally or not, doing something to get the situation going.

a. A student says, "This is boring."

Teacher response: Pause for a few seconds and respectfully say, "So what you're saying is that I am not doing a very good job of teaching today." Pause. The student may shrug or say, "Yeah." Continue, "You're right, I could do a better job; I'm sorry, tomorrow I will make it more interesting."

b. A student says, "I'm not doing it."

Teacher response: Kindly say, "So what you're saying is that no matter what, you are not going to do it." The student might say, "Yeah." Respond, "Okay, thanks for letting me know. I can't make you, so it's okay if you sit there for a while." If appropriate, you could also add, "Would you like to go to the library to read for a while?"

c. A student asks aggressively, "Why do we have to learn fractions?"

Teacher response: "Good question; there's no point learning something that has no value. I forgot to take the time to explain the value of this. I'll do it now. Thanks."

7. Use the Language of Attribution

This approach is based on attribution theory, which informs us that whether a situation gets better or worse depends on our response to it. Attribution theory says we can use language to pass responsibility to the person who needs to accept the responsibility. In the classroom, the student needs to take responsibility.

The language of attribution can come across somewhat like a ping-pong match, as the teacher keeps deflecting responsibility for the student's problem back to the student.

Student: "I'm not doing it."

Teacher: "And I can't make you. So where do we go from here?"

Student: "I don't know. Do whatever you like."

Teacher: "Thanks, I will keep on with this boring lesson."

Student: Mumbles. The teacher lets it go, knowing the mumble is just a face-saving tactic.

Plus: The teacher makes the decision not to buy in and passes the responsibility to decide whether the situation escalates or de-escalates back to the student.

Minus: The student has the freedom to say what he wants.

Most Important: Whether the situation is resolved or not is up to the student.

a. A student says, "This is boring" or "Why do we have to study algebra?"

Teacher response: "The issue is not about studying algebra; the issue is that you are stopping me from teaching and others from learning. So what's next?"

Student: "Do whatever you want."

Teacher: "Thanks." (Now keep on teaching.)

b. A student says, "You can't make me do it."

Teacher response: "You're right, I can't make you. So where do we go from here?"

Student: "I'm still not doing it."

Teacher: "Thanks for letting me know. Can I assume you won't stop others from working and me from teaching?"

Student: "Whatever."

Teacher: Ignore it and move on. The "whatever" is a face-saving move on the student's part.

If the student continues, then you have no choice but to say, "You can choose to stop or choose the office—you do not have the right to stop me from teaching and others from learning. Your decision." If the student still continues, buzz the office and have someone come down and get the student—keep calm, and be respectful and polite. This makes it easier for the student to come back to your room. Although the student has burned his bridge, yours is still intact and he can come back across it. The other students will also see you as a fair and reasonable teacher.

c. A student says, "F—k off!"

Teacher response: "I'll take it that you are upset. So what do you want me to do?"

Student: "F—k off."

Teacher: "I tried to be polite; clearly it did not work. That kind of talk is a major offence; you've made the decision to leave. You do not come back until you explain to me why you said it and your plan for coming back into my class. I like you, but I can't accept that behaviour. Thank you."

This situation may escalate—you may have to phone to get help or get another teacher next door to assist you. You may have to take your class to the library so this student does not play off allies or worry about saving face. This situation demands the teacher have a high mean score; it is difficult to resolve if the class has bonded against you.

Chapter 4 Conclusion

To effectively respond to students who are moving to power, teachers need to identify when the shift to power starts. This is critical, because if you don't first recognize the actions leading to a power conflict, you will quickly become too involved in it to extricate yourself from the situation. You also need the skills to de-escalate the situation once you have recognized the shift to power.

Another scenario: You can recognize the shift and have the skills, but if students do not respect you as a teacher and as a person, your effectiveness will be compromised. This goes back to the idea of the teacher's mean score (akin to the value of a stock on the Toronto Stock Exchange, which moves up and down based on what happens during the day). If our "stock value" at that moment in the classroom is high, our chances of being successful are high. Conversely, if we have a low stock value at that moment with students, then our chances for success are low.

Finally, as well as being able to recognize the start of a power play, and having both the skills to de-escalate it and the respect of students, we need to know how to apply responses in an artful way. We can define artful as being sensitive to the student and the situation. We always run the risk of being too wishy-washy or too assertive. Responding is an art, guided by the science of understanding our students and their moves to power.

Clearly the school staff (teachers, aides, secretaries, custodians, administration) must work together to create a safe school environment and build a collaborative, supportive school culture. When the student makes a decision to leave the room and go to the office, those in the office must have a policy in place for dealing with the student.

Power Responses: The Informal Chat

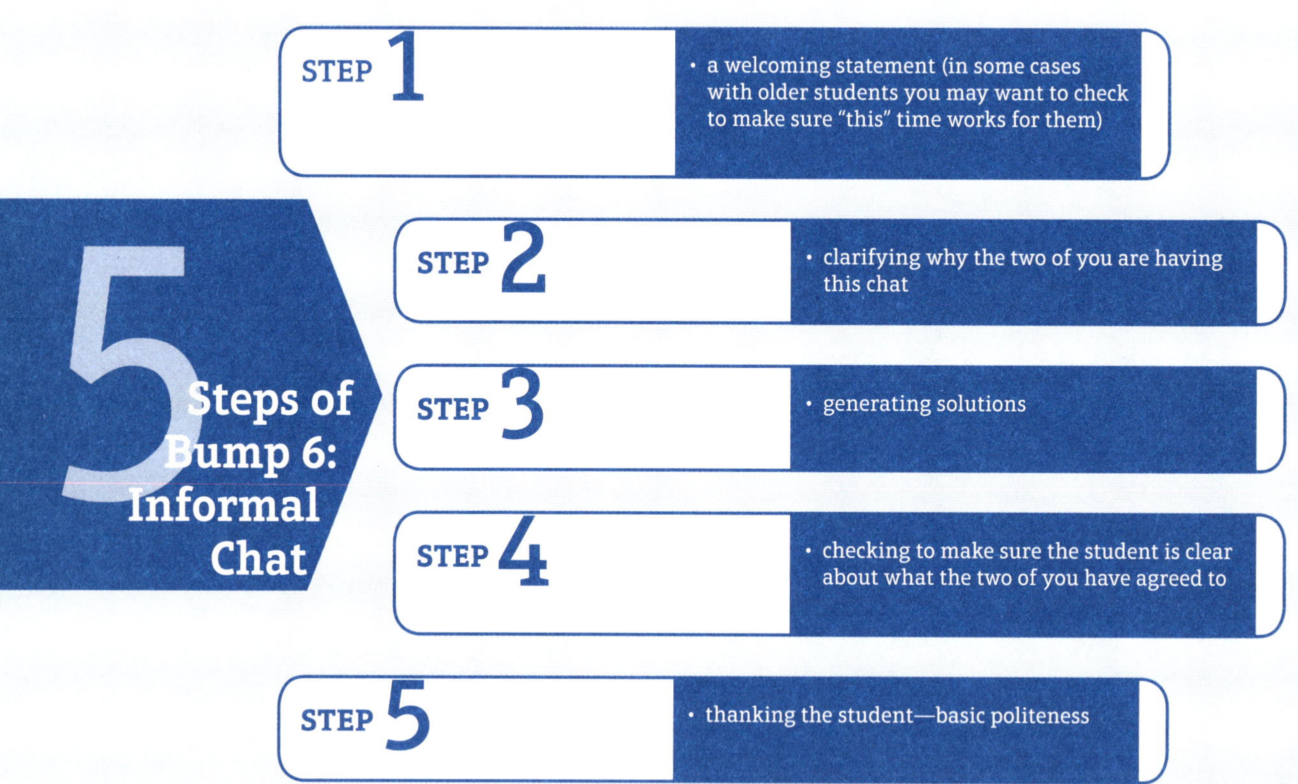
5 Steps of Bump 6: Informal Chat
STEP 1
• a welcoming statement (in some cases with older students you may want to check to make sure "this" time works for them)
STEP 2
• clarifying why the two of you are having this chat
STEP 3
• generating solutions
STEP 4
• checking to make sure the student is clear about what the two of you have agreed to
STEP 5
• thanking the student—basic politeness

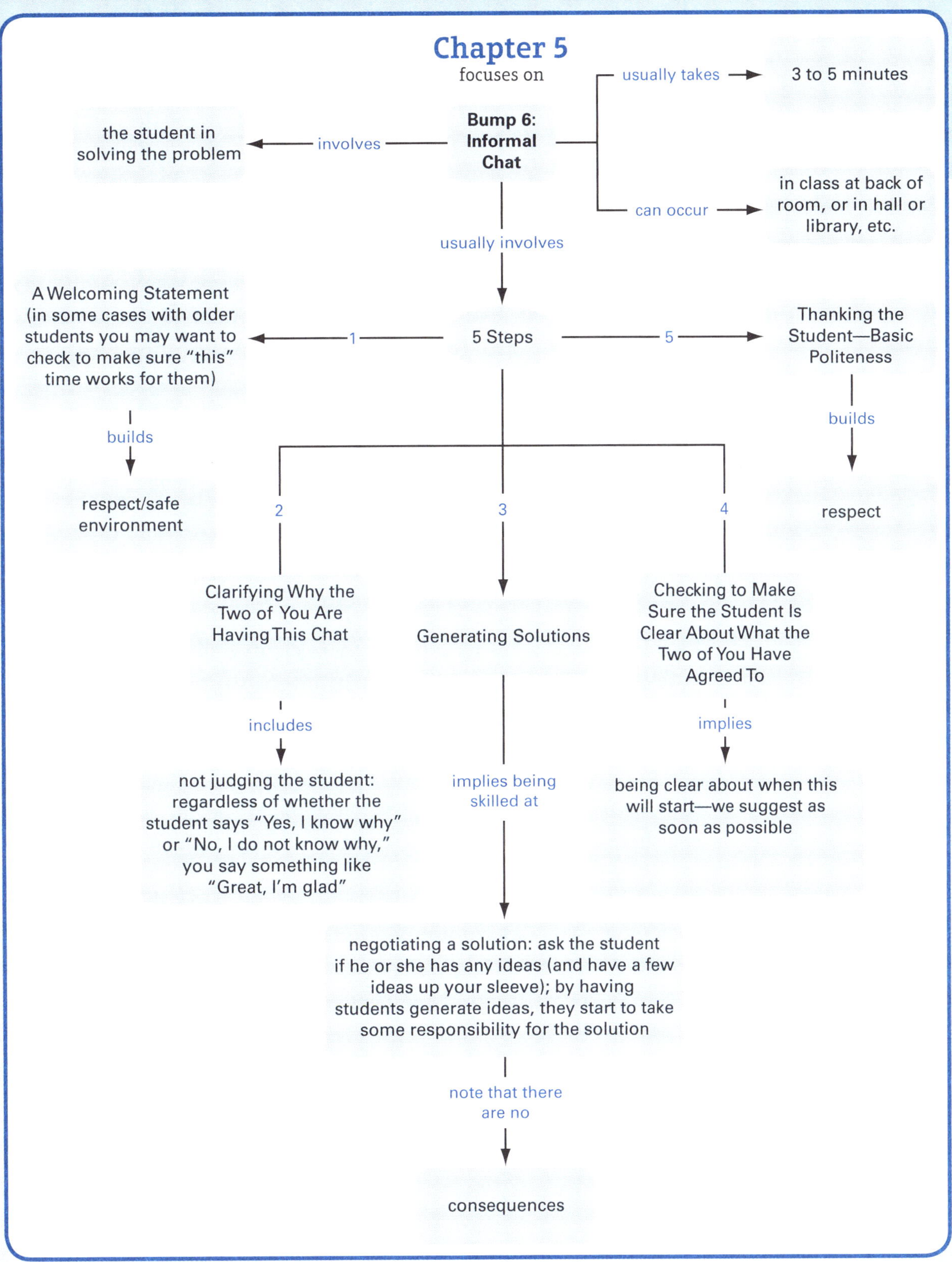
Chapter 5
focuses on
Bump 6: Informal Chat
usually takes
3 to 5 minutes
involves
the student in solving the problem
can occur
in class at back of room, or in hall or library, etc.
usually involves
5 Steps
1
A Welcoming Statement (in some cases with older students you may want to check to make sure "this" time works for them)
builds
respect/safe environment
5
Thanking the Student—Basic Politeness
builds
respect
2
Clarifying Why the Two of You Are Having This Chat
includes
not judging the student: regardless of whether the student says "Yes, I know why" or "No, I do not know why," you say something like "Great, I'm glad"
3
Generating Solutions
implies being skilled at
negotiating a solution: ask the student if he or she has any ideas (and have a few ideas up your sleeve); by having students generate ideas, they start to take some responsibility for the solution
note that there are no
consequences
4
Checking to Make Sure the Student Is Clear About What the Two of You Have Agreed To
implies
being clear about when this will start—we suggest as soon as possible

The focus of this chapter is Bump 6, The Informal Chat. We illustrate the ways in which a teacher can sit down with a student and resolve a classroom conflict. The conflict usually involves a misbehaviour that happens too frequently, is moving to power, or has erupted into a power struggle.

The chat may take place before, during, or after classroom time. The key condition is that the student has to agree to meet; if not, you do not have an informal chat. Instead, you have moved to Bump 7, The Formal Contract, which arises out of a formal chat in which other people will become involved. This book does not explore the formal chat, but focuses only on initiatives teachers can implement in the classroom. We briefly explain the formal chat in Appendix A.

Key Attributes of an Informal Chat

In analyzing the informal chat from the perspective of pluses, minuses, and most important factor (PMI), we conclude the following:

Plus: The teacher has an opportunity to clarify and solve a classroom problem without other students being involved. Perhaps more importantly, the student is part of the problem-solving process. The informal chat is applicable with students from Grade 1 to university.

Minus: The chat takes time. When done during class time, it takes time away from other students. You will often need more than one or two chats.

Most Important: The key plus is the opportunity to talk to the student and to build a relationship—and to do so without other students around. Note that during the first chat, consequences are not discussed or even implied. The goal is simply to agree to try to solve an issue. In subsequent chats, simple co-constructed consequences, such as tidying the classroom, can be discussed.

The Informal Chat: A Personal Perspective

We've all had chats with someone to try to resolve an issue, with a friend or family member, perhaps with a student in our class or in a previous class. What five steps would you follow for a successful three- or four-minute chat? Write down your thoughts. When finished, compare your ideas with those of other teachers.

The Informal Chat: Five Steps

Paulo Friere

Paulo Freire, in his book *Pedagogy of the Oppressed* (1970), states that dialogue is the only way to solve a problem. He argues that in the absence of hope, faith, trust, critical thinking, and love, true dialogue cannot exist. The informal chat is a place to have a dialogue—an open, free discussion. It is not a talk where the teacher adopts the position of power and speaks of imposing consequences if the student continues to misbehave.

Below are the steps effective teachers typically take when having a chat to solve a problem. We will explain each in greater detail. Of course, teachers will modify, adapt, or re-sequence the steps to meet different situations.

1. **Set a positive climate.** Thank the student for agreeing to chat. When appropriate, check to make sure the time is right for the student to meet. If you sense resentment, let the student know she can choose to meet now or tomorrow. This gives the student a wee bit of control over the situation. For power students, this is important.
2. **Clarify the issue.** Ask the student if he knows why he was asked to chat.
3. **Generate possible ways to solve the problem.** Try to get the student to contribute ideas for resolving the issue, but have a few ideas up your sleeve, at the ready.
4. **Check for understanding.** Make sure the student understands what you both agreed upon, and when the agreed-upon actions will start.
5. **Thank the student.** Let the student know you appreciate her taking the time to work through the issue.

The Five Steps Explained

1. Set a Positive Climate

This chat has to take place in a safe and inclusive environment. Both the student and the teacher have to want something positive to happen; they have to trust that each will do their part.

When the chat takes place during lunch or after school, it's a good idea to check with students, especially older ones, to make sure they are okay about taking three to five minutes out of their free time. The two chairs you use for this chat should be the same, for equal status. As well, it is less imposing to sit at an angle, rather than directly in front of the student.

Caution: Keep your classroom door open, but situate the student so that a passerby can't see the student but can see you. Being seen could cause the student embarrassment. However, if you suspect the student might use the situation of the chat against you, we recommend that you have a colleague pop by several times and unobtrusively listen or stick her head in the room to say hello. Another option is to hold the chat in the library where other people are around, but at a distance.

Example 1: Setting the climate for an after-school meeting with an older student:

"Thanks for agreeing to meet with me. Do you have the time to meet now, or is tomorrow better?"

Example 2: Setting the climate for an in-class meeting with a younger student:

"David, thanks for sitting back here to talk with me. This will only take a few minutes. Is that okay with you?"

2. Clarify the Issue: Inquire If the Student Knows Why She Was Asked to Have a Talk

Regardless of whether the student says "yes" or "no," respond with, "Great..." This sets a positive, upbeat tone for the conversation, and helps the chat stay informal. A friendly dialogue that is conversational in nature is power-neutral.

For example:

a. The student says "no": "Great, then this gives me a chance to clarify something that has been bothering me."

b. The student says "yes": "Great, now you don't have to listen to me talk at you. Can you tell me why we are meeting?"

Sometimes the student will mumble something. When this happens, one option is to say, "It does not seem like this is the right time to solve this. Would you like to do this now or tomorrow?" Or you may respond, "My guess is that you really don't want to do this now. We can do this later. Thanks, Michele, have a good afternoon. Sorry to have kept you." (Smile kindly and leave.)

3. Generate Possible Ways to Solve the Problem

Encourage the student to contribute ideas, but have some of your own at the ready.

This is the pivotal step in the process. The student has to feel and believe that her voice is heard. It helps for you to approach this step with a little humility. Consider what you could do differently, not just what the student can do. Begin by asking the student how she thinks the issue can be resolved. She may or may not have an idea, or she may have one that is not acceptable. In every case, your response should be encouraging. "Great, that's fine," or "It's okay not to know—this is tricky."

A chat intended to generate solutions may proceed like this:

> Teacher: "I'm glad you know why we are meeting. You also know that I got a bit upset. Do you know why I got upset when you kept calling out answers?" Pause.
>
> Student: "Not really."
>
> Teacher: "Okay, that's fine. When you call out, no one else has to think—you don't let them turn their own lights on. Each student has the right to think for themselves and also to participate in class. How do you think we could solve the issue of you calling out answers?"

> Student: "I'll stop calling out answers."
>
> Teacher: "That would be nice, but you've probably been calling out answers since Grade 1, so my guess is that it will be hard to stop. What if we try to get it to no more than three in the morning and two in the afternoon? Would that be okay?" Or in a secondary school class: "What if we try for no more than two in the period? Can you live with that?"

In addition, reflect on what you can do as a teacher to increase the chances that the issue does not happen again. For example, if the student is calling out answers, you could adjust the way you introduce questions to the class. You may want to suggest to the student, "What if I remind the class not to call out, and at times let the class share with a partner before sharing with the class, so that everyone gets a chance to talk? What do you think of that idea? Then I can randomly call on people to share. I know you are bright and like to think. What if once others have had a chance, I ask for hands from anyone who would like to add any information...that would be a good place to let your mind work a bit harder. Would that help a bit, if I did a better job of how I asked my questions?"

As the teacher and student brainstorm on solutions, the student will often suggest consequences for his misbehaviour. For example, the student may offer, "What if whenever I call out, I have to clean up the paper around the school fence?"

We suggest you focus on positive solutions, and refrain from punitive consequences. You may say something like, "I appreciate your idea. What you are suggesting is a lot of work. Let's keep consequences out of this for now and see if we can come up with something that works for both of us, and doesn't have you feel like you're being punished or punishing yourself."

Once you have both agreed on actions, students will often ask about what will happen if they don't have perfect compliance. For example, if you agreed to two call-outs per period they may ask, "What if I do more than two?" Express confidence, not distrust. "Let's not worry about that; let's try what we agreed to do." If, during the class, the student makes two call-outs early in the period, go over and say quietly, "Thanks for trying. Do you need two more?" The key is to not get upset, but keep your word and let the student know you are not going to impose a consequence.

4. Check for Understanding: Make Sure the Student Understands What Was Agreed On and When the Agreement Will Start

This is a brief step. After ideas are shared, make sure you and the student are clear about what you agreed upon. We suggest you say something such as, "Okay, we've talked a bit and you know that teachers can sometimes confuse students, so could you please tell me what you think we agreed to?" This is an opportunity for you both to clarify the next actions.

The student has to know when the agreement kicks in. It should be as soon as possible. If the informal chat happens during recess, let the student know the agreement begins after recess. If the chat happens after school, clarify that it will start the next day or next class.

5. Thank the Student for Being There

Simply let the student know that you appreciate she took the time to chat. Possibly, apologize for taking up her time outside of class.

For example: "I appreciate you taking the time to work this out; sorry this took away from your time. I simply want to maximize learning in our class. Thank you."

Rationale for the Informal Chat

1. It shifts the responsibility for the misbehaviour to the student.
2. The chat is a proactive response for dealing with a persistent problem.
3. It minimizes the time spent dealing with misbehaviour during instructional time.
4. The chat allows the student and the teacher to work together to develop a positive plan of action in which they both take responsibility for implementation.
5. It allows the student and teacher to re-establish a more positive relationship.

Artful Nuance: If your mean score is low, the chat is unlikely to work. The student must have some respect for the teacher for this response to be effective.

Examples of Informal Chats

1. Bachelor of Education Students and One of This Book's Authors

The chat below occurred between one of the authors of this book and two students in the B.Ed. program at the Ontario Institute for Studies in Education (OISE) at the University of Toronto. Ironically, the chat played out at the end of the author's class on classroom management practices. During the first class, two students, sitting in a group of four, would be off-task while their group was working and would talk while the author was speaking. The author could see other students were not impressed. In the second class together, the author went over to the two students when they started to talk again and asked if they could please see him at the end of class. They came as requested, and they did have a few minutes to chat.

Author (*smiling*): "My guess is that you probably know why I asked you to see me."

Students: "Because we were talking while you were talking, but we were just talking about what you were saying."

Author: "That may be the case, and that is fine. The issue is that others around you are somewhat annoyed because you are talking during group work, and when I am talking. You are adults and you pay a lot of money to be here, but so do the others. So how will we resolve this?"

Students: "We won't talk anymore—it's okay."

Author: "That would be fine, but I think stopping talking may not be in your best interests either. What if when you feel you can't wait to talk about something that is important to both of you, you let your group know and step outside the room to talk. Would that be okay?"

Students: "Yes, that is good, but we can stop."

Author: "Okay, so what did we really agree to here?"

Students: "If we want to talk when others are working or you are talking, we can just step outside and talk."

Author: "That would be great. This is your course, you are paying for it, so you also need to do what works for you. Sorry to keep you; thanks for helping me not get too grouchy."

Two classes later, the author held a class on the Informal Chat. The two students started to laugh and shared with their classmates that the author had used this approach with them, and it really worked. The entire class had a laugh.

2. A Grade 6 Student and His Teacher

Teacher: "Grant, I need you to think about when a good time would be for us to talk, either today or tomorrow. I will ask you at lunchtime what works best for you."

(At lunchtime, when asked, the student said he could talk now.)

Teacher: "Thanks for talking right away. I appreciate that. I promise I will do this as fast as possible—no one is in trouble here—I just want to try to see if we can solve a small problem. Do you know why I asked you to see me?"

Student: "Not really."

Teacher: "Great, then maybe it is my fault that this is happening. When we are learning something new and I ask students to work in groups, you aren't happy when I choose the groups or partners for you. Would I be right?"

Student: "Yeah."

Teacher: "Do you know why I put students in groups when learning new ideas?"

Student: "Not really."

Teacher: "I guess I did not explain this effectively to the class. My fault. I try to do things that maximize how all of you learn. Research shows that when they are learning something new, students often explain things to each other in ways that the teacher does not. Some students are a lot less stressed when they discuss ideas with each other rather than when the teacher comes by and talks at them. Remember when we did the job ads, what did the employers expect from people being hired?"

Student: "Had to work with others, and not always just your friends."

Teacher: "So I am not trying to punish the students; I am trying to make our learning connect to life outside of school. So, how can we solve the issue of you getting upset when you have to work in groups?"

Student: *Shrugs indifferently.*

Teacher: "Is it okay if I share a few ideas?"

Student: "Okay."

Teacher: "One option is that I simply make it so you don't have to work in groups; you can work on your own. But if I agree to this, I know that I am not being an effective teacher...even though you would prefer it. And sometimes, you can tell me when you're ready to work with a partner.

"Another option is that you let me know who you would like to work with and whenever possible, I will try to make that happen—on the condition that when you work with that person or, say, two other people, you do your work. That would also mean that I am not really structuring the group work as effectively as I should, but I can live with it for a while.

"A third option is that we take turns: sometimes you work alone, sometimes with someone you've agreed to work with, and once in a while you will work with someone I've picked.

"Do any of those ideas sound fair?"

Student: *Shrugs.* "The first one."

Teacher: "What was the first one?"

Student: "I work alone and maybe sometimes I will work with someone, but I can sort of pick who I work with."

Teacher: "Okay, so for tomorrow, write down on a piece of paper the names of students you could work with eventually, or who you would be okay doing a Think-Pair-Share with. Is that okay?"

Student: "Okay."

Teacher: "Thanks, Grant. I know you are not a fan of group work; some students prefer to work alone. In life, there are lots of times where you have to work alone. I just want you to have the skills to work with others, as well. Tomorrow, I will be more thoughtful about letting you work alone and try to have you work with a student or two that you might be able to work with. Please understand that when you work alone, you don't have the right to stop others from working.

"Sorry this took a bit longer. Thanks for helping me understand you a bit better. Enjoy the rest of your lunch."

Chapter 5 Conclusion

The key to remember about the informal chat is that the student has to agree to be part of the chat. If a student indicates that he does not want to be there (by intonation, body language, or words), you need to politely let him know this approach is over, at least for now. For example, if the chat is an after-school or lunchtime meeting, respectfully say something such as, "I can tell that right now is not a good time for you. We will talk at another time. Enjoy your evening (or the rest of your lunch)."

If you are talking during class time, at the back of the room or out in the hall, offer a choice: "This may not be the best time. We can decide to chat for a few minutes now, or we can chat at the start of lunch or right after school. What works best for you?"

Another option is to say, "Clearly, you do not want to talk about this now. That is fine. I will assume then that when you're ready, you will go back to your seat, and you will work by yourself and not stop others from working." (Wait for a few seconds.) If you feel that won't happen, say something like, "If that is not possible, then tell me what you think you should do to solve the issue of you stopping others from working." Once again, you can expect that if the student is not bonded positively with you (that is, you have a low mean score), the situation will be difficult to resolve—even if you enact your responses perfectly.

SECTION 2

TEACHER PRACTICE

The Teacher Continuum: Moving Toward Effective Teaching Practices

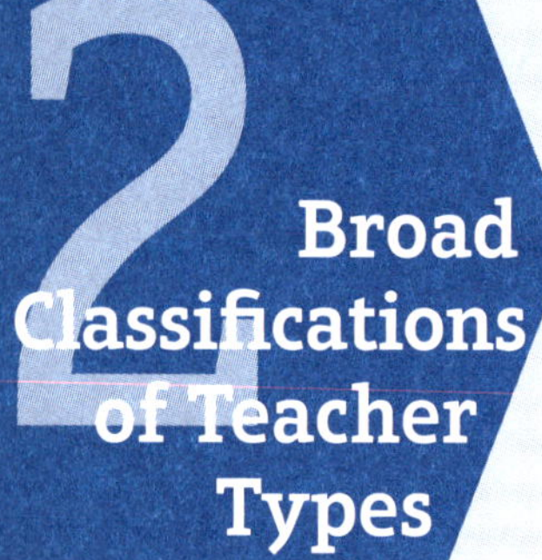

Effective Teachers

- are skilled interpersonally
- have a more extensive enacted repertoire of responses
- believe that all students at some time will misbehave
- will continually develop their repertoire of skills, resulting in a more differentiated and effective set of skills
- are seen as being highly effective and respected
- have a high mean score

Less Effective Teachers

- are less skilled interpersonally
- have a more restricted enacted repertoire of responses
- believe that all students should behave
- are less likely to continually develop their repertoire of skills, resulting in a less differentiated and less effective set of skills
- are seen as being ineffective and not respected
- have a low mean score

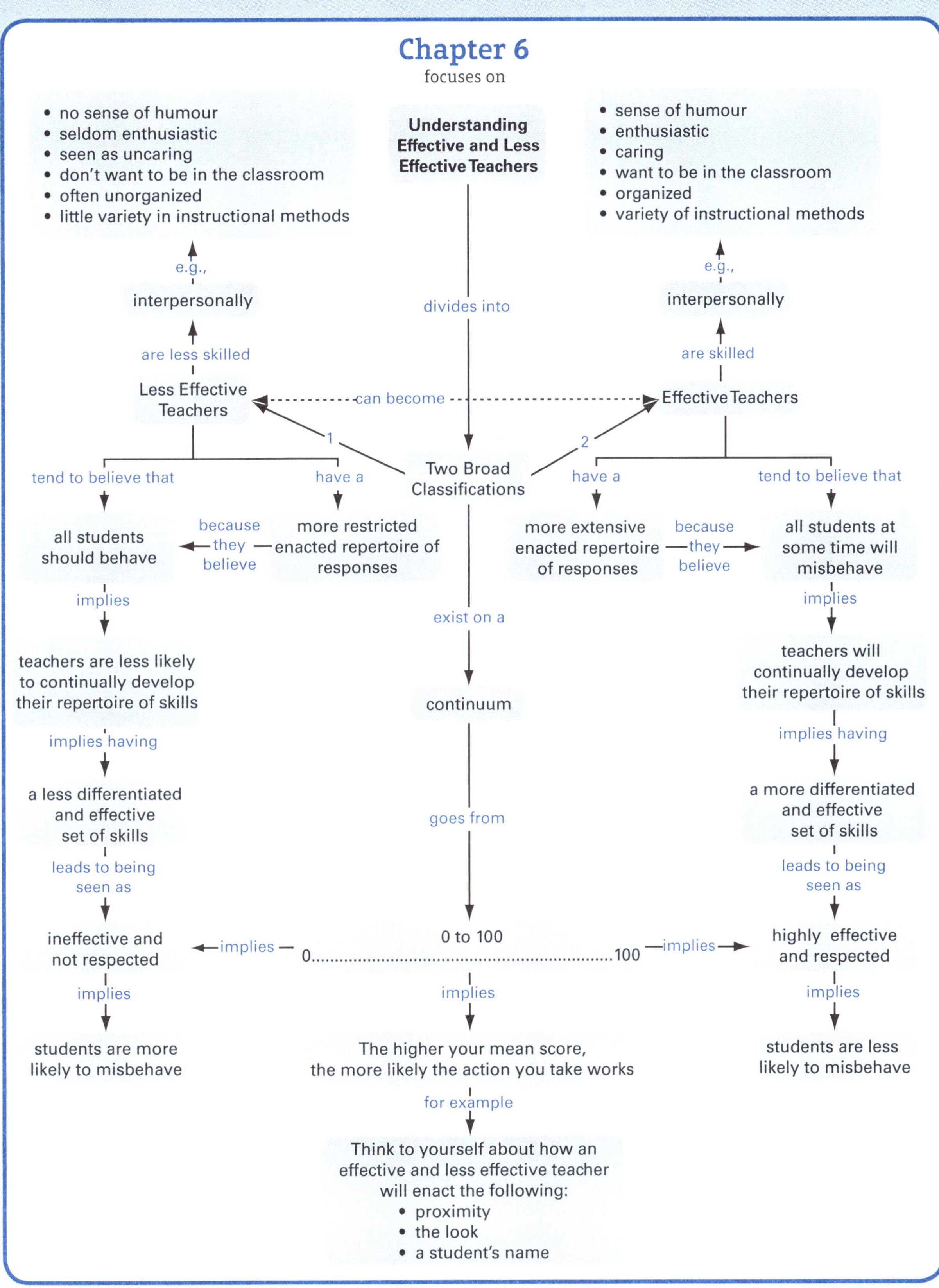
Chapter 6
focuses on
Understanding Effective and Less Effective Teachers
divides into
Two Broad Classifications
1
Less Effective Teachers
can become
2
Effective Teachers
are less skilled
interpersonally
e.g.,
• no sense of humour
• seldom enthusiastic
• seen as uncaring
• don't want to be in the classroom
• often unorganized
• little variety in instructional methods
are skilled
interpersonally
e.g.,
• sense of humour
• enthusiastic
• caring
• want to be in the classroom
• organized
• variety of instructional methods
tend to believe that
all students should behave
have a
more restricted enacted repertoire of responses
because they believe
implies
teachers are less likely to continually develop their repertoire of skills
implies having
a less differentiated and effective set of skills
leads to being seen as
ineffective and not respected
implies
students are more likely to misbehave
have a
more extensive enacted repertoire of responses
because they believe
tend to believe that
all students at some time will misbehave
implies
teachers will continually develop their repertoire of skills
implies having
a more differentiated and effective set of skills
leads to being seen as
highly effective and respected
implies
students are less likely to misbehave
exist on a
continuum
goes from
0 to 100
implies
0......100
implies
implies
The higher your mean score, the more likely the action you take works
for example
Think to yourself about how an effective and less effective teacher will enact the following:
• proximity
• the look
• a student's name

This chapter explores how effective teachers create a classroom environment where students experience success, feel safe and respected, and actively participate in their learning. In effective teachers' classrooms, students rarely misbehave, and when they do, the behaviour is minor and not sustained. The situation is resolved with minimal loss of academic time and the students' sense of self is left intact, even in the most complex classrooms.

Comparing Effective and Less Effective Teachers

What differentiates teachers who have few classroom management problems from those who continually have problems? Principals tell of teachers who always send students to the office and others who never do, even though they teach the same students. The question is why.

The authors of this text were involved in a teacher effectiveness program, working with the most effective teachers in a large district (200 schools, 154 of which were involved in the project) and with teachers who were at risk of losing their teaching positions. The experience provided insights into the belief systems of effective and less effective teachers, and confirms that it is possible to shift from one to the other.

Developing a Perspective

Read the following descriptions of four teachers. In which classroom are students more likely to learn and behave? Which teacher would you as a parent want to teach your children? Would your students see you as teacher A, B, C, or D?

Teacher A is not enthusiastic, has no sense of humour, and shows little interest in students' lives in or outside the classroom. He has a high IQ but has learned little about how to teach. Students always sit in rows. He does not frame questions effectively, and students are seldom actively involved in meaningful learning. The teaching process is repetitive and lacks novelty or variety. This

teacher does not act on what is known about how students learn (e.g., multiple intelligences, learning styles, students at risk, gender issues).

Teacher B is polite, can at times be enthusiastic, and will periodically see the humour in classroom life or show an interest in students' lives. She allows students to work in groups, but the students choose whom they work with and the groups tend to be too large. She enjoys asking questions, but usually the same three to five students answer most of them. At times, she will do something interesting to make learning meaningful. This teacher's instructional repertoire is somewhat limited to the simpler instructional methods, such as Think-Pair-Share, Place Mat, Word Webs, and Venn diagrams. Her instructional methods are never integrated. She tries to attend to multiple intelligences and learning styles, but has not done so effectively. She would like to learn about differentiated instruction.

Teacher C is frequently enthusiastic, has a sense of humour, and is always polite. He shows an interest in his students' lives. He is more thoughtful about putting students in groups; he will allow friendship groups but often randomly assigns students to groups, with group size usually between two to four students per group. He frames questions and gives students time to think before being randomly selected to share answers for greater accountability, safety, and active participation. He will sometimes integrate a wider instructional repertoire, using Think-Pair-Share, Place Mat, 4 Corners, Mind Maps, Venn diagrams, Fish Bone diagrams, and so on. He is quite skilful and intentional about attending to multiple intelligences, learning styles, and children at risk, and is working on differentiating his instructional methods to meet the diverse needs of students.

Teacher D is consistently enthusiastic, has a great sense of humour, and is always respectful of students' lives both within and outside the classroom. She is an expert at structuring groups and balances group work with individual and competitive opportunities to learn. For example, she will use Teams Games Tournaments to review before an exam. For the most part, she uses teacher-selected groups. This teacher frames questions so that all students are held accountable to think; her questions are intentionally designed to attend to the appropriate level of thinking (such as those found in Bloom's Taxonomy—see Appendix C) and reflect the types of questions found on exams. She often has students share with a partner before being randomly selected to share with the class. She has an extensive instructional repertoire that has students integrate multiple instructional methods, for example, integrating a Mind Map, Concept Map, Venn diagrams, Fish Bone diagrams, and a Concept Attainment data set to summarize a unit of study. She is an expert at attending to multiple lenses related to how students learn, such as multiple intelligences, learning styles, students at risk, gender, brain research, and so on. She offers workshops on differentiated instruction for other teachers.

The Belief System of Effective Teachers

Effective teachers believe that no matter how skilled they are as teachers, how much they know about their content, and how enthusiastic they are, most if not all students will, intentionally or unintentionally, behave inappropriately at some time. These teachers also realize their responsibility is to deal with that inappropriate behaviour.

Result: Effective teachers are not disappointed when students misbehave. They do not generate negative emotions. They understand students will misbehave, and continually work at extending their repertoire of responses. They rarely have students choose to go to the office.

Research: Effective teachers spend far less time dealing with misbehaviour. Research by Soar and Soar (1979, 1987) shows that negative classroom environments have a negative effect on achievement. More interestingly, their research also shows that positive affect environments are unrelated to student achievement. A positive environment will not hurt learning, but more is needed to *improve* learning. Soar and Soar further show that when student behaviour is closely monitored, student learning is affected positively; however, controlling learning activities does not show a relationship to student

achievement. Given the complexity of classroom management, their research informs us that teachers require feedback on how they manage their classrooms.

The Belief System of Less Effective Teachers

Less effective teachers usually believe that all students should behave, and that as teachers, they are there to teach, not to respond to students who misbehave.

Result: Less effective teachers are almost always disappointed when students misbehave. These teachers often have a chip on their shoulder. They move to anger quickly, and although they may "know" what effective teachers should do, they choose not to use such approaches. They apply a much more restricted range of skills to encourage appropriate behaviour and to respond to students who are behaving inappropriately. They frequently send students to the office rather than take the time in class to deal with the problem, often because they do not have the skills to respond.

Research: The research informs us that teachers who know their subject matter deeply and are extremely enthusiastic about their subject are more likely to have an "expert blind spot" (Ing, 2006; Nathan & Petrosino, 2003). Those with a blind spot believe their knowledge and passion for their subject overrides their responding to the needs of their students. They are more likely to believe they do not need extensive knowledge of how students learn, nor a more extensive repertoire to design effective learning environments.

Teacher Attributes

Think back on teachers you've had or have known as colleagues who were effective and less effective. What criteria put them into one of those two categories? Chances are that you found the teachers demonstrated the attributes listed on the following page.

Attributes of Effective Teachers

- Had a sense of humour
- Was alive, enthusiastic, wanted to be in the room
- Challenged us
- Was caring and polite
- Really knew his stuff
- Apologized to us when she was wrong
- Was creative
- Made learning meaningful; had lots of hands on things
- Used drama to get us to understand math
- Would spend time with us outside of school; came to our games
- Let us into their lives—showed they are human

Attributes of Less Effective Teachers

- Boring...monotone
- Did not enjoy teaching
- Had favourites
- Never learned our names
- Did not mark our work—no feedback
- No thinking, we just took notes
- Embarrassed us publicly if we made a mistake
- Could not teach—always taught the same way
- Always seemed to be angry, often inconsistent, unpredictable
- Was sarcastic

A Personal Perspective on Effective Teaching

With the critical determinants for effective teaching in mind, take a look at the rubric on the next page and ask yourself how your students would score you on the key attributes. If you are consistently at Level 3 or 4, you will find student misbehaviour in your classroom easier to resolve.

Attributes of Effective Teaching Rubric				
Area	**Level 1**	**Level 2**	**Level 3**	**Level 4**
Displays enthusiasm and humour	Little to no enthusiasm; no sense of humour; does not seem to care about student learning	Some enthusiasm; at times shows a sense of humour; at times seems to care about student leaning	Often enthusiastic; usually has a sense of humour; usually cares about student learning	Consistently enthusiastic; great sense of humour; always cares about student learning
Motivates learners	Lesson rarely if ever interesting or meaningful; no variety	Lesson at times interesting and meaningful; minimal variety	Lesson usually interesting and meaningful; often has variety	Lesson always interesting and meaningful; a lot of variety
Is organized	Little to no sense the lesson and teacher are organized	Some evidence the lesson and teacher are organized	Lesson and teacher are usually organized	Lesson and teacher are always organized
Invokes safety and accountability when asking questions	Little to no accountability or safety invoked	Some attempt to invoke safety and accountability	Safety and accountability usually invoked when appropriate	Safety and accountability always invoked when appropriate
Structures groups effectively	Does not demonstrate how to structure groups effectively	At times, attends to a few attributes of effective group work, but more by default	Often structures groups effectively; understands the research	Always structures groups effectively; deeply understands the research
Shares/discusses the objective and purpose of the lesson	Rarely if ever discusses the objective and purpose of the lesson	At times may discuss the objective or purpose of the lesson	Usually discusses the objective and purpose of the lesson, when appropriate	Whenever appropriate, always discusses the objective and purpose of the lesson
Checks for understanding	Rarely if ever checks to see if students understand	May at times check to see if some students understand	Usually checks to see if most students understand	Always checks to see if most students understand
Differentiates instruction	Has a limited instructional repertoire; rarely if ever integrates instructional methods	Has an evolving instructional repertoire but does not intentionally integrate instructional methods	Has a substantial instructional repertoire and often integrates a variety of methods	Has an extensive instructional repertoire and integrates a variety of instructional methods

If you assume that all students will behave appropriately at all times, you will likely be undone by frustration and discontent when they fail to meet your expectations. However, if you recognize that all students may, at times, misbehave, you will be prepared to anticipate their actions, and therefore be in a more controlled, less emotionally charged, position to respond.

Consider that boxers are rarely knocked out by a punch they see coming, because they are prepared for it and take actions to avert it. Typically the punch that they don't anticipate is the punch that puts them down. Here is a classroom example.

> A principal noticed a Grade 7 student sitting in a chair in the office and politely asked the student why he was there. The student replied his teacher had sent him, "Because I turned around in class." The principal, who is not naive, asked, "How did you turn around?" The student replied, "I was talking to the student behind me and the teacher told me to turn around, so I got up, turned around and kept talking to the student behind me. **[The student was smiling as he told this last part.]** Then the teacher yelled at me to get down to the office."

If you were the teacher, what would you have done to solve this problem? The student's action was, after all, what a young Robin Williams or Jim Carrey might have done.

The wisest response: laugh and say, "Very good; perfect response. My fault, let's try a 180—someday you will make a great lawyer!" The teacher who sent the student to the office held the belief that all children should behave. By living on the edge of anger in the classroom, the teacher fuels power plays. By understanding why and how a student engages in a power play, the teacher can maintain an effective classroom.

Responding to Misbehaving Students

Think back again to teachers you've had or known as colleagues. How did the effective teachers respond to inappropriate actions? How did the environment they created help to curb misbehaviours?

Thinking of an *effective teacher*, can you remember how that teacher responded to students who misbehaved? What specific actions did she take? List your recollections. When finished, compare your answers with those we've received from other teachers, below. Did you find it difficult to recall what the teacher actually did?

Thinking of a *less effective teacher*, can you remember how that teacher responded to students who misbehaved? What specific actions did he take? List your recollections. When finished, compare your answers with those we've received from other teachers, below. Did you find it easier to recall what the teacher did?

Responses of Effective Teachers

1. respectful
2. did not embarrass you publicly
3. talked to us in the hall
4. used humour
5. got us to focus on something else
6. they did not have to respond—we behaved
7. I don't remember what they did
8. just had to look at me
9. would ask you politely to stop

Responses of Less Effective Teachers

1. yelled—embarrassed us publicly
2. didn't solve the problem
3. sent us out of the room or to office
4. slammed a book or metre stick
5. sent us to the front of the room by the teacher's desk
6. detention—punished us all for one or two students
7. threw a piece of chalk or brush
8. made us write lines
9. threatened to call our parents

Which two of the nine responses of effective teachers listed above do you think are most common? The answer is at the bottom of the next page.

How Effective Teachers Decide When, Where, and How to Respond to Students Who Choose to Behave Inappropriately

Effective, experienced teachers typically consider the following factors when deciding how to respond to a student who misbehaves and moves to power.

1. Past behaviour of the student
2. Severity of the misbehaviour
3. Frequency of the misbehaviour
4. Time between misbehaviours
5. Time and place
6. Reaction by others in the class
7. The school discipline policy
8. The student's life at home
9. The student's respect for the teacher

The first six of these variables assist the teacher to interpret levels of student defiance. The remaining three variables affect the teacher's response.

1. Past Behaviour of the Student

Teachers are more likely to respond differently to a student who has had more infractions in their class than to a student who has had fewer infractions.

For example, two students have been sent to the office for fighting. For one student, this is the sixth occurrence in two days. For the other student, it is the first. When dealt with in the office, either by the teacher who sent them or by the office administration, the response to the two students should be different. The teacher/administrator will be perceived as unfair if the response is the same. The apparent difference in the response to the two students is understood (and more likely to be seen as fair and consistent by the students) when it reflects sensitivity to past student behaviour.

2. Severity of the Misbehaviour

A teacher will respond differently to a student who calls out a racial slur than to a student who is observed whispering to another

Answer: the sixth and seventh examples.

student. To be recognized as fair and earn class respect, it is critical for a teacher's response to fit the severity of the misbehaviour.

3. Frequency of the Misbehaviour

The more often the behaviour occurs, the more likely the teacher will perceive it as a disturbance or defiance. Often, the student will use a variety of behaviours. If the student wants to carry on the game, he will show remarkable creativity. On the other hand, if the student wants to upset the teacher right away, the same behaviour will be repeated. In most cases, the nature of the student's actions depends on how long the student wants to engage (the teacher/other students) to meet his need for attention, power, or revenge.

4. Time Between Misbehaviours

Although a student may misbehave five times a day, teachers are more likely to interpret the misbehaviour as a disturbance or defiance if the five misbehaviours occur within a five-minute period.

5. Time and Place

What is acceptable in one situation, or at one point in a lesson, could be interpreted as defiance in another. For example, a student who whispers to another or explains answers to another during a test period is engaging in unacceptable behaviour. Students are usually aware of, and sensitized to, the expectations of time and place.

6. Reaction by Others in the Class

If the student's misbehaviour is ignored by the other students (e.g., a funny comment provokes no reaction), the teacher can choose to overlook the action or use a low-key response that does not disrupt the class. However, when other students pay attention, the teacher must engage. For example, in a Grade 10 class, one student put his head up and pretended to whistle while the student behind him actually whistled. The teacher smiled and politely asked him to stop whistling. The teacher's response to the "pretend" whistler evoked a few chuckles from the class. In this case, the student's agenda was to entertain. The teacher's response would likely be influenced by the other variables.

The next three variables assist teachers in deciding *how* to respond.

7. The School Discipline Policy

The school discipline policy, or lack of a policy, provides boundaries that guide teachers. For example, where the administration does not want teachers to send students to the office, the teacher's repertoire cannot include giving a misbehaving student the choice between behaving or going to the office. Moreover, where students may be sent to the office but the administration does not have a policy for dealing with those students, the choice is available but provides only the illusion of effect.

8. The Student's Life at Home

The more we know about the students, the more sensitive and appropriate we can be in responding to their misbehaviour. Some students carry such complex baggage into the classroom that it is a miracle that they attend class, never mind attempt to respond appropriately. For example, there may be physical, mental, or sexual abuse in the home, or they may have to cope with parental addictions or other family problems.

9. The Student's Respect for the Teacher

Obviously, if students do not like us, our responses to their misbehaviour will not be as effective. At the beginning of the year, the teacher is not yet likely to have "won over" the students. As a result, teachers will respond in less assertive ways, and be more tolerant and watchful as they begin to implement the management system. Where a student who moves to power does not respect the teacher, the teacher can predict that giving the student a choice in front of the class will result in a negative outcome. Students will escalate their behaviour with just the slightest indication of support from even one other student. Teachers should watch *The Breakfast Club* to see an illustration of this point.

Consideration: The Organisation for Economic Co-operation and Development's 2010 Programme for International Student Assessment (PISA) results show that respect for the teacher is a critical success factor in student academic performance. (Four hundred and seventy thousand 15-year-old students representing 65 nations and territories participated in PISA 2009. An additional 50,000 students representing nine nations were tested in 2010.)

PISA

How Less Effective Teachers Respond to Students Who Choose to Behave Inappropriately

Virtually every response of a less effective teacher falls into one of these nine categories.

1. Uses sarcasm or ridicule (usually referring to lack of intelligence or maturity on the part of the student)

Examples: "Act your age." "Stop acting like a kindergarten kid." "Grow up." "Keep it up and you'll be working at McDonald's for the rest of your life."

2. Appeals to higher authority: administration or parents

Examples: "Keep it up and you'll be going down to the office." "Do you want me to call your parents?"

3. Uses anger, screaming, or long sermons (often referring to number)

Examples: "How many times do I have to tell you?" "If I've told you once, I've told you a million times…" "I've had just about enough." "That's it, you're out of here."

4. Activates whole-class punishment (eliminating something that students enjoy)

Examples: "You don't go out for lunch until everyone is ready." "If you don't want to do your homework, we will do it during Phys-Ed class."

5. Sends students to the hall or to the office

Often two or three students are already in the hall, so the next one has to go to the office.

6. Gives up; "discipline by prayer"

Knowing that intervening will only escalate the situation, the teacher appears to do nothing, seeming to be praying to a higher authority.

7. Uses or threatens to use punishment

Example: Slamming an object (e.g., a book or metre stick) on a student's desk in a threatening manner.

8. Hands out weird punishments—that often make the newspaper

Examples: Students who chew gum are required to put it in a box of previously chewed gum and then take out another piece of previously chewed gum from the box and chew it. Students are given 100 lines a night, and they double each night until the lines are done. If students dye their hair, they are not allowed to attend graduation.

9. Tears up, uses guilt

Example: "How can you do this to me? I've tried really hard to make this interesting."

Personal Positioning

Consider your reflections on effective and less effective teachers and ask yourself where your students would place you on a continuum of 1 to 100, with "1" representing the least effective teacher and "100" the most effective teacher. The students' mean score is the critical score. We discussed this idea earlier; to review, the metaphor of the Toronto Stock Exchange is useful. The higher the teacher's mean score, the more the students have bonded with the teacher rather than against the teacher. The higher the mean score, the more likely it is that the intervention the teacher invokes to restore social order will be effective. A teacher's mean score will move up and down during the day; when the school bell goes at the end of the day (akin to the bell ringing at the end of trading), that value is what the teacher brings into the classroom at the start of the next day. We don't know the exact point at which things get worse or better; however, if classroom management is working poorly in your class, you may want to stop and think about how students are perceiving you and your class and what you might do to increase your score so students work with you rather than against you.

1 ____ 100

Two teachers can take the same classroom management workshop and learn the same classroom management repertoire, and yet the skills one applies will work and the skills the other applies won't. In our long history of working with effective and less effective teachers, we have observed that the higher the teacher's mean score, the more likely the intervention the teacher uses will work.

Conversely, the lower the score, the less likely that same intervention will work.

A Grade 10 student from Charlottetown, Prince Edward Island, with an 87 percent average in all her classes spoke with one of the authors of this text. The student said all of her teachers were good, except for her history teacher. "Everyone gets kicked out of his class," she explained. She herself had been kicked out several times. She added, "Just before the Christmas break, the teacher told the students not to move; one boy bent over to pick up his pen and was kicked out of class...because he moved." She continued, "Now we don't even care, we just sit there; [the teacher] sits there and sometimes he makes us write notes; he teaches us nothing. When we get kicked out we just wander the halls. Parents have complained, students have gone to see the principal, written letters to the principal; the principal simply says there is nothing she can do."

Interestingly, many effective teachers have little idea about why they are effective; they also have very few classroom management problems. Effective teachers avert or subdue misbehaviour so effortlessly and quickly that it can be difficult to catch their precise actions. In seconds, an effective teacher may move toward a student, maintain the ideal proximity, give the student a purposeful glance, and politely say the student's name ("David, please") in the right tone.

When our B.Ed. students go into their practicum and work with a less effective teacher, they gain an appreciation of the classroom management techniques they are learning and a confidence in their abilities to apply these techniques effectively. Interestingly, when they work with an effective teacher, our students often feel worse about themselves. They recognize the teacher is effective, but do not necessarily know why. When they ask the teacher what they should do to be effective, the associate teacher often does not know. The teacher may say, as one inner-city teacher did, "Well, just watch me and do what I do." Or as another said, "You just have to love kids." Those comments are of little value to those who want to learn. Imagine if you were to simply watch someone juggle three flaming torches before you tried it. Or if you just developed a love for juggling flaming torches before you gave it a go. Ouch.

Chapter 6 Conclusion

In the 1970s, Jacob Kounin (1977) completed one of the first studies of effective teachers. He identified a number of actions they took to design more powerful learning environments. Below we briefly describe his findings. Do any of these *not* apply today?

1. Withitness

These teachers are proactive; they seem to have eyes in the back of their head. They stop situations before they get out of hand, and they can sense when things are working or not.

2. Overlappingness

This refers to teachers' ability to metaphorically chew gum and walk at the same time. While continuing to teach, they walk toward a student who is misbehaving (proximity), give the student a glance, quietly say the student's name (in the middle of a sentence), and continue talking.

3. Winning Over

This concept refers to the teachers' ability to build a more cooperative relationship with students—students bond cohesively with the teacher.

4. No Slow Downs or Jerkiness

Effective teachers are able to keep the flow of the lesson going; they set routines, are clear with directions, and have smooth efficient transitions. When students move from seat work to group work or into centres, the time lost is minimal.

5. The Ripple Effect

When a teacher interacts with a student, the effect of that interaction ripples to all other students in the class, like a rock dropped into a body of water. The students come to understand that this is how they will be treated in this class.

It is important not to confuse a fun classroom with an effective one. Research, known as the Dr. Fox effect (see Naftulin, Ware, & Donnelly, 1973; Williams & Ware, 1976), shows that a university lecturer who made students laugh and was interesting but provided virtually no useful content scored much higher in terms of being effective than a lecturer who was less enthusiastic and humorous but did

provide key information. Students, however, need a merger of interest, enthusiasm, and relevant content.

There is an art to classroom management. In the same way that we know we cannot become a Monet through paint-by-numbers, we must recognize that excelling as a teacher is more complex than learning techniques to add to our instructional repertoire.

Instructional techniques alone can only take us so far. Keep in mind that no matter how extensive your repertoire, few of your choices will work unless you get to know your students, show them that you are enthusiastic and that you care, see the humour in what they do, be polite, and learn their names and something about their lives. With these caveats, the more diverse the instructional methods in our repertoire, the more likely we are to effectively differentiate our instruction to meet the diverse needs of students.

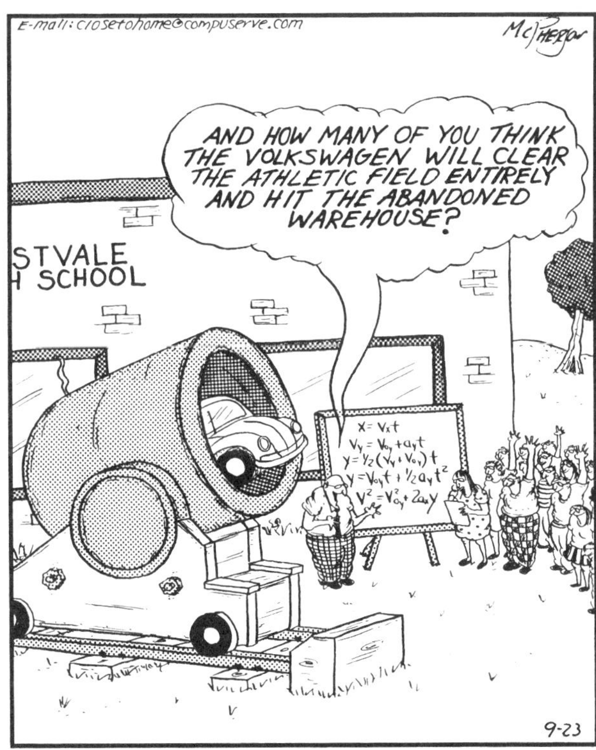

Thanks to the innovative labs of teacher Herb Krenley, physics quickly became Westvale High's most popular course.

How We Talk to Students: Questioning, Responding, and Checking for Understanding

5 Key Areas of Questioning

Safety

INCREASES WITH
- wait time
- sharing with a partner before sharing publicly

Types of Thinking

EXAMPLES
- open ended
- convergent
- inductive
- deductive
- sequencing
- prioritizing

Levels of Thinking Involving Taxonomies of Thinking

INCLUDE
- recall
- comprehension
- application
- analysis
- evaluation
- synthesis

Framing Questions and Providing Parameters

INCLUDE
- how much wait time
- how students will be selected to respond
- who students should talk to before they are selected to respond publicly

Responding to Student Responses

INCLUDE
- correct response
- incorrect response
- partially correct response
- no response
- a guess
- a silly response
- a convoluted response

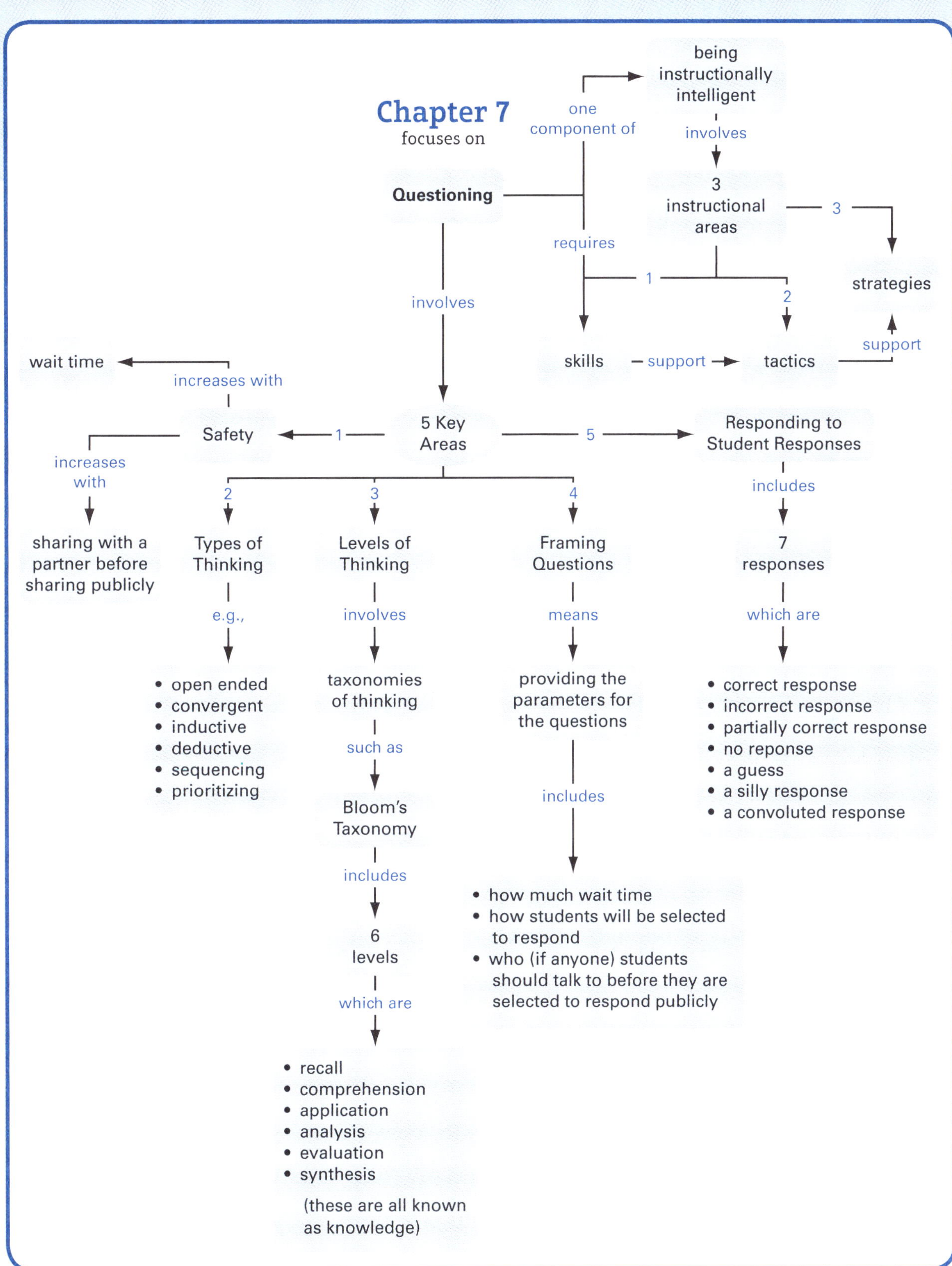
Chapter 7
focuses on
Questioning
one component of
being instructionally intelligent
involves
3 instructional areas
3
strategies
requires
1
2
skills
support
tactics
support
involves
wait time
increases with
Safety
1
5 Key Areas
5
Responding to Student Responses
increases with
sharing with a partner before sharing publicly
2
Types of Thinking
e.g.,
• open ended
• convergent
• inductive
• deductive
• sequencing
• prioritizing
3
Levels of Thinking
involves
taxonomies of thinking
such as
Bloom's Taxonomy
includes
6 levels
which are
• recall
• comprehension
• application
• analysis
• evaluation
• synthesis
(these are all known as knowledge)
4
Framing Questions
means
providing the parameters for the questions
includes
• how much wait time
• how students will be selected to respond
• who (if anyone) students should talk to before they are selected to respond publicly
includes
7 responses
which are
• correct response
• incorrect response
• partially correct response
• no reponse
• a guess
• a silly response
• a convoluted response

Framing questions is an instructional skill that teachers employ to have students experience the instructional concepts of safety, accountability, and active participation. We estimate that about 95 percent of teachers do not frame questions *effectively*, even though the literature and research in this area have been around for over 100 years. Framing questions effectively will increase the chances that students behave appropriately.

Mrs. Mortleman made sure that everyone participated in class.

Below is an excerpt from a book by John Millar titled *School Management and the Principles and Practice of Teaching* (1897):

> Generally the best way of asking a question is to address the whole class. Each pupil should understand that he may be expected to reply. In stating the question no sign should be shown that would indicate who is to answer. The main thing is to secure that every student is held on the alert. Each question should be given to that student, who, with due regards to the interests of the class stands in most need of receiving it. (p. 232)

Framing Questions and Requests

How you frame questions and requests makes a difference in managing classrooms. That does not mean you should not ask for hands or call-outs or zing particular students; some students love to put up their hand, to call out, or to be zinged. The key idea is to realize the strengths and weaknesses of each approach to framing questions and requests.

Effective and Less Effective Questions

On the next page is a Concept Attainment data set that illustrates two ways to question students. Even-numbered examples represent one way; odd-numbered examples represent the other. Reflect on what the

even examples have in common that differentiates them from the odd ones. As you read the examples, ask yourself, "Is the way I frame questions and requests more aligned with the odd- or even-numbered examples?" Also consider the effect framing questions in these two ways would have on student behaviour. For now, don't focus on Bloom's Taxonomy.

1. Take 10 seconds to consider whether or not the way I factored this equation was done correctly, and why or why not. In 10 seconds, I will randomly call on you to share what you think. Please just think quietly. If I select you and you are not sure, just say pass, but keep thinking because I may come back to you.
2. David, how would you explain the idea of "push" and "pull" as it relates to people leaving one country and moving to another?
3. No hands please. First think, then when you're ready, share with a partner. Then I will select three people to share with the class. If you were Tuck, would you drink the water? Why or why not?
4. Hands, please: what are three examples of 3-D shapes?
5. Think-Pair-Share first and then be prepared to come to the board to show how you would edit this paragraph. On your own, please think for 30 seconds. Okay, you have 45 seconds to discuss with a partner before I select some of you to edit.
6. Who can explain the difference between sarcasm and ridicule?
7. In your group, label yourselves A, B, and C. Now, discuss how you are going to complete your draft of a concept map. In about 90 seconds, I will select a person from your group to share your group's idea. Murphy's Law tells us that you will be picked, so make sure you are ready to share.
8. What were the factors that led to the First World War? Anyone? Lisa?
9. Look at these three pieces of art, and rank them in terms of how they affect you emotionally. Be prepared to share with the class, but before you do that, you can share with a partner or simply think to yourself. I will select a few of you to respond in about one minute.

10. Can anyone come up to the board and show us how to correctly balance this equation?

Testers

In the following set of example questions and requests, choose which you think are similar to the odd-numbered questions and requests in the above set, and which you think are similar to the even-numbered questions and requests.

a. Marcus, the other day you gave a great answer. Could you explain it to the class?

b. Brainstorm in your group, please, then I will ask for volunteers to tell me what your group was thinking.

c. Could I have three people come up to the board and show the class how they solved the problem?

d. Hands up if you know why this happened. Okay, could one of you share with the class?

e. Think-Pair-Share, please. Why are scientists arguing that we should be concerned about global warming? (*Students are given 90 seconds to discuss.*) Okay, thanks. Who would like to share what you and your partner were thinking?

f. When I say "Go," move to the corner that best represents who you think was most responsible. Find a partner, no groups larger than three. Discuss and when I sense you are ready, I will randomly call on different people to share with the class. "Go."

Why the Odd-Numbered Questions and Requests Are More Effectively Framed

Our research supports previous findings (Rowe, 1974; Tobin, 1987) that students are more likely to be successful responding to the odd-numbered examples. Students feel less vulnerable when they have the opportunity to reflect before speaking and to consult with peers on their answers. Students who feel less vulnerable are more likely to participate, to feel accountable to participate, and to offer longer, more complex answers. When students experience this success and safety, they are more likely to behave appropriately.

Attention to a Taxonomy of Thinking

Bloom's Taxonomy (Bloom, Krathwohl, & Massia, 1956) is one of the key factors when it comes to almost every area of the teaching and learning process. See Appendix C for a brief explanation of why Bloom's Taxonomy is so critical. Clearly, if teachers can control the level of complexity of their questions, they will more skilfully engage all students, especially when employing wait time when framing questions. Bloom's Taxonomy is a key component of differentiating one's instruction.

Bloom's Taxonomy

The taxonomy comprises six levels. Note that the top two levels have been flipped from their original order. All six levels are now known as "knowledge."

Synthesis	putting things together in a new way
Evaluation	judging or assessing or ranking with criteria
Analysis	comparing and contrasting or deconstructing
Application	doing something to prove understanding
Understanding	sharing examples or describing in own words
Remembering/Recall	restating ideas; retelling word for word

What do you think are students' thoughts about the types of questions teachers ask? How would you rank questions that students most like to least like to answer in terms of Bloom's Taxonomy?

Framing Questions: A Personal Perspective

Take a look at the rubric below and ask yourself how you would score. If you score Level 3 or 4, you are more likely to create a classroom atmosphere of safety, accountability, and active participation.

Rubric on Framing Questions

Area	Level 1	Level 2	Level 3	Level 4
Wait time	No wait time considered or provided	Wait time provided periodically, but usually not enough or too much	Wait time usually provided, and the time is usually appropriate	Wait time always applied effectively
Accountability	Students feel no accountability to participate; easy to opt out	A few students may feel accountable; most feel they can opt out	Most students feel accountable; few feel they can opt out	All students feel accountable; opting out is almost impossible
Active participation	No students are actively involved	A few students are actively involved	Most students are actively involved	All students are actively involved
Framing of questions or requests	Students have no idea how much time they have to think or how they will be expected to reply	Students, at times, have some idea of how to respond	Students usually have an idea of how much time they have to think and how they will be selected to share	Students always know how much time they have to think and how they will be selected to share
Attention to a taxonomy of thinking (Bloom's Taxonomy)	Teacher has heard of Bloom's but does not understand the levels of thinking; students do not know about different levels of thinking	Teacher has some idea of different levels of thinking but seldom acts on it; students do not know about different levels of thinking	Teacher understands different levels of thinking and often considers them when framing questions; students know very little about levels of thinking	Teacher and students understand the different levels of thinking and the levels are always considered when framing questions

Responding to Students

The Ways Students Respond to Questions

In the 1970s, Madeline Hunter of Saskatchewan, and later at the Graduate School of Education at UCLA, one of the most respected and practical educators of the past century, analyzed the different ways teachers respond to student answers. Hunter identified that students answer questions in one of seven different ways. In looking at each of these seven approaches, we will include the effective teacher's appropriate response. Note that the silly response may be an invitation to a power play, if you are not careful in how you deal with it.

1. Correct response
2. Partially correct response
3. Incorrect response
4. Guess
5. Convoluted response
6. Silly response
7. No response

Note that students may attach an attitude to certain response methods—some students, unfortunately, have a masterful ability to weave in defiant attitudes, including one of disdain and a "who cares" attitude. These occasions prompt us as teachers to want to scream mightily, but we are wise to do so only in the theatre of our mind.

Hunter discussed the importance of creating a safe classroom in her writing on motivation. She stated that "positive feeling tone" is a key factor. This applies to framing questions. If the teacher's mean score is too low, then having the skills of framing questions and responding to student efforts are not going to have as great an impact on classroom management. This reinforces the need to win students over and the importance of cohesive bonding.

If students have bonded against the teacher, and you have not won them over, then your efforts are going to be less effective.

Responding to Students' Responses

1. Correct Response... Why did he respond correctly?

The question was too easy or he just memorized the answer (no understanding).

Perhaps don't pass judgment so that you encourage more thinking.

2. Partially Correct Response... Why was it only partially correct?

Maybe the question was too long, you asked more than one question, or you talked too much after the question, making it difficult for the student to remember the exact question.

Highlight the part of the answer that was correct, then repeat the question more precisely and ask for an extension to that part that was missed.

3. Incorrect Response... Why did she respond incorrectly?

Possibly, the question had multiple components and the student was confused.

Try breaking the question down into simpler parts. That said, the key piece is to understand that when students provide an incorrect response they are telling you three things: (1) they have a piece of information; (2) they do not know where it fits; and (3) they need to find out the right answer. So the teacher must respectfully let them know where their piece of information fits and assist them to get the answer.

4. Guess... Why did he guess?

Perhaps he felt pressured to say something; telling you he is not sure or would like to pass is not an option. Was he afraid to respond?

Have students discuss with a partner or in a group first or let them know it is okay to say "pass," knowing that you can ask them to respond later.

5. Convoluted Response... Why is she beating around the bush?

Possibly the question was vague or unclear, or the student doesn't know the answer but feels obligated to say something, or she is thinking while she is talking.

Listen for a brief time to be respectful, then stop the student at the end of the sentence. This can be tricky, so try saying something like, "I hadn't thought of that, thank you." And then select another student. Alternatively, probe to find out what she meant.

6. Silly Response... Why did he respond with a silly response?

Perhaps the student does not feel he belongs in your class; he needs attention. Perhaps you asked a potential Jim Carrey and this is the comedic opportunity he cannot pass up.

Find the grain of truth in the response—and state, "I hadn't thought of it in quite those terms, but that last point makes a lot of sense." Or laugh and move on.

7. No Response... Why didn't the student respond?

Maybe the question was too complex. Perhaps the classroom is not safe. Perhaps the student did not hear the question. Watch the student's eyes; if she is looking up or to the side, she is thinking and should be left alone; if she looks at you or her eyes move from side to side, jump in.

Have an escape clause so she can save face, for example, "Sorry Jennifer, I worded the question in a confusing way; I even confused myself. Let me rephrase it." Now allow all the students to think and share with a partner before selecting someone to respond.

Checking for Understanding and Student Behaviour

When students do not understand what they have to do or why they have to do it, a greater chance exists that they will misbehave. Checking for understanding affects success; when students are successful, they are more likely to behave appropriately.

Unfortunately, from our experience in classrooms, we find the following three key instructional practices are usually ignored or done superficially:

- Teachers do not share or discuss the objective and purpose of the lesson with students.
- Teachers do not structure group work effectively.
- Teachers do not effectively check for understanding.

Checking for Understanding

Let's begin with the concept of checking for understanding during the lesson. Few teachers we work with, even effective teachers, effectively check for understanding. A key characteristic of effective group work, which we'll discuss in Chapter 8, is having the group reflect on how successful they were both academically and socially.

Below are six examples of teachers checking for understanding. How are the first three examples (A, B, C) similar? How are they different from last three (D, E, F)? As you read them, which triad reflects your classroom?

A. "Okay, does everyone understand?" (*one-second wait*) "Are you sure?" (*two-second wait*) "Okay good, let's move on."

B. "Hands up if you have any questions about what you need to do." (*two-second wait*) "No questions?" (*three-second wait*) "Okay, you can start."

C. "Now, can someone explain how to factor this equation? David?" (*David explains it correctly.*) "Does anyone not understand how David did it?" (*two-second wait*) "No one? Great. Go ahead and start."

D. "Michelle, do you understand how to do this?" Michelle says, "Yes." The teacher says, "Great, can you please explain to me how you will do it?"

E. "Quickly share with a partner what you learned from your experiment. I will call on three pairs to share in about 45 seconds."

F. "Think to yourself how you think you would solve this question. Hands up if you think you can do it." (Several hands go up; the teacher selects two students to share with the class. After they share, the teacher does not judge their answer.) The teacher then asks the other students to share with their teacher-selected partner what they heard the two students say. The teacher tells the students that several of them will be selected to share their thinking.

Consider the example at the top of the next page. Would you include it with group A, B, C or with D, E, F?

"I am going to explain how to do this. When I am finished, I will randomly select three of you to tell me what I said. As you don't know who I will pick, I suggest you listen carefully."

If you said A, B, C you are right. The teacher in this example does not give the children thinking time or foster a sense of safety. That said, he does increase the students' accountability to listen.

Checking for Understanding and Empathy

If someone asked you what the key consideration of empathy is when asking questions and checking for understanding, what would you say? Read the following case studies and see what you find.

Case Study 1: A Grade 9 Class

A Grade 9 student tells this story. "I was in an Algebra class in a school in Calgary, Alberta. The teacher came around and asked me if I understood what to do. It was halfway through the school year, and I was a new student from Cranbrook, B.C. In my old school, we had just started fractions. B.C. was about a year and a half behind Alberta in Math. My response was, 'Yes, I just haven't started yet.' There was no way I was going to admit in front of the class that I did not understand; the other students would have heard me. I ended up having the fourth-lowest mark in the province on the provincial exam. I was put in a vocational program in secondary school and informed that I would not be going to university. The important point that gets pushed aside is that my teacher was very kind and I really liked being in her class. She was just not a very good Math teacher...for me."

Analysis: Students rarely put up their hand and admit in front of their peers that they do not understand. Teachers must be empathetic and check to see if students really do understand. As teachers, we must consider our questions and check for understanding from the students' perspective, taking into account their need to belong, to be safe, not to be exposed, and not to fail publicly. If we fail to do this, students will bond against us and we will get what we deserve. One cooperative learning structure that facilitates students checking with other students is to employ a Ghost Walk (see Appendix I).

Case Study 2: A Graduate Class

In my graduate class at the University of Toronto, I start by asking if there is anyone who does not understand what is meant by a "fact." (I wait seven seconds and no one puts up their hand.) I then ask if there is anyone who does not understand what is meant by a "concept." (I wait seven seconds and no one puts up their hand.)

Next, I look around the room and select a student to share what he thinks is meant by a fact and a concept and how the two are related. I've never had a student who can answer the questions. Once I select the student, I wait five seconds. The selected student is clearly embarrassed. I ask the class, "How many of you are glad I picked Mark?" They all raise their hands and laugh. I ask them, "Why didn't you raise your hands when I asked who doesn't understand 'fact' and 'concept'?" They respond that they did not want other people to know they were not sure, or that they thought they understood but later realized they did not. I ask the student I selected how he felt about being singled out publicly. The typical reply is, "I was starting not to like you." I then ask, "If we feel this way as graduate students, I wonder how our students feel in our classrooms."

"Columbus, will you sit down and stop asking all these dumb questions?"

Analysis: The key concept is "public vs. private" failure. We do not mind working on something, struggling, and failing when we do it privately, or when we can predict we will be treated with respect for our efforts. When we ask students if they would like to be selected to respond publicly without sharing with a partner, or if they would prefer to have time to think and share with a partner before sharing with the class, almost all opt to share with a partner first—even Grade 1 and 2 students, not just university students. We must create a safe, respectful environment as part of our empathetic approach.

Cartoonists often employ our fear of public failure as grist in their cartoons.

On a scale of 1 (not skilled) to 10 (skilled), how would your students score you on empathy and checking for understanding?

Checking for Understanding: A Personal Perspective

In classrooms, we rarely see checking for understanding at an effective level. Below are eight statements. Which ones would students most likely experience in your classroom?

1. Who can explain...?
2. Hands up if you have an idea of...
3. David, how would you explain...?
4. When I say three, thumbs up if you agree, thumbs down if you disagree.
5. Think to yourself for 10 seconds, and I will randomly call on several of you to respond.
6. Explain to your partner what you think...and I will call on three of you to tell me what you and your partner thought.
7. Write how you solved the problem, and I will quickly come around in two minutes to see how you solved it.
8. Work in your group of three for four minutes. Make sure you can all explain how to solve the problem. One of you will be randomly selected to go and explain the solution to another group.

On the next page is a sample rubric that connects to the questions or statements numbered 1 to 8 above. The higher the level, the more effective the check for understanding. How do you think your students would score you?

Rubric on the Teacher's Skill at Checking for Understanding				
Attribute	**Level 1 # 1, 2, 3**	**Level 2 # 4**	**Level 3 # 5, 6**	**Level 4 # 7, 8**
Accountability	Teacher does not consider accountability; no evidence of accountability; students can easily escape	Emerging sense that accountability is important, but still easy for students to escape	Teacher clearly understands the need for accountability, most students accountable; difficult to escape	All students accountable; very difficult to escape
Participation	1 or 2 students involved on a voluntary or teacher-selected basis	3 to 5 students involved, often on a voluntary or teacher-selected basis	Most students involved; most often on a teacher-selected basis—volunteers may respond later if appropriate	All students involved on a teacher-selected basis—volunteers will respond later if appropriate

Chapter 7 Conclusion

The maxim "an ounce of prevention is worth a pound of cure" certainly holds true for the classroom. Students rarely run through the door with bated breath and palpitating hearts, crying, "Teach me, teach me, I love algebra, I live for history. How many languages can I learn today?" As teachers, we all know that if we do not structure aspects of fun, interest, and novelty into a lesson, students will attempt to include these for us—and usually at our expense. It is a complex task to ensure enthusiasm for six hours a day, 200 days of the year, for 30 students, all of whom learn differently and are interested in different things that are often not school related. That said, it is still less difficult than dealing with classroom management issues, every day of the school year.

By practising safe questioning, responding, and checking for understanding, we increase the likelihood that our students feel safe, involved, and motivated to learn. This, in turn, affects success and achievement. In addition, when we understand what our students understand, we can more wisely select and integrate our instructional methods to meet the diverse needs of a group of students. What's important to note is that all of this increases the chances that students do not misbehave.

Cooperative Learning and the Inclusive Classroom

3 Main Areas of Cooperative Learning

Creating a Safe Learning Environment

KEY IDEAS
- mutual respect
- attentive listening
- appreciation statements (no put-downs)
- right to pass

Critical Components of Effective Group Work

BASIC COMPONENTS
- individual accountability
- face-to-face interaction
- teaching collaborative skills
- processing the academic and collaborative objective
- enacting positive interdependence

Group Structures

APPROXIMATELY 300 SMALL GROUP STRUCTURES
- Place Mat
- Inside/Outside Circles
- 4 Corners
- Jigsaw
- Academic Controversy
- Group Investigation

etc.

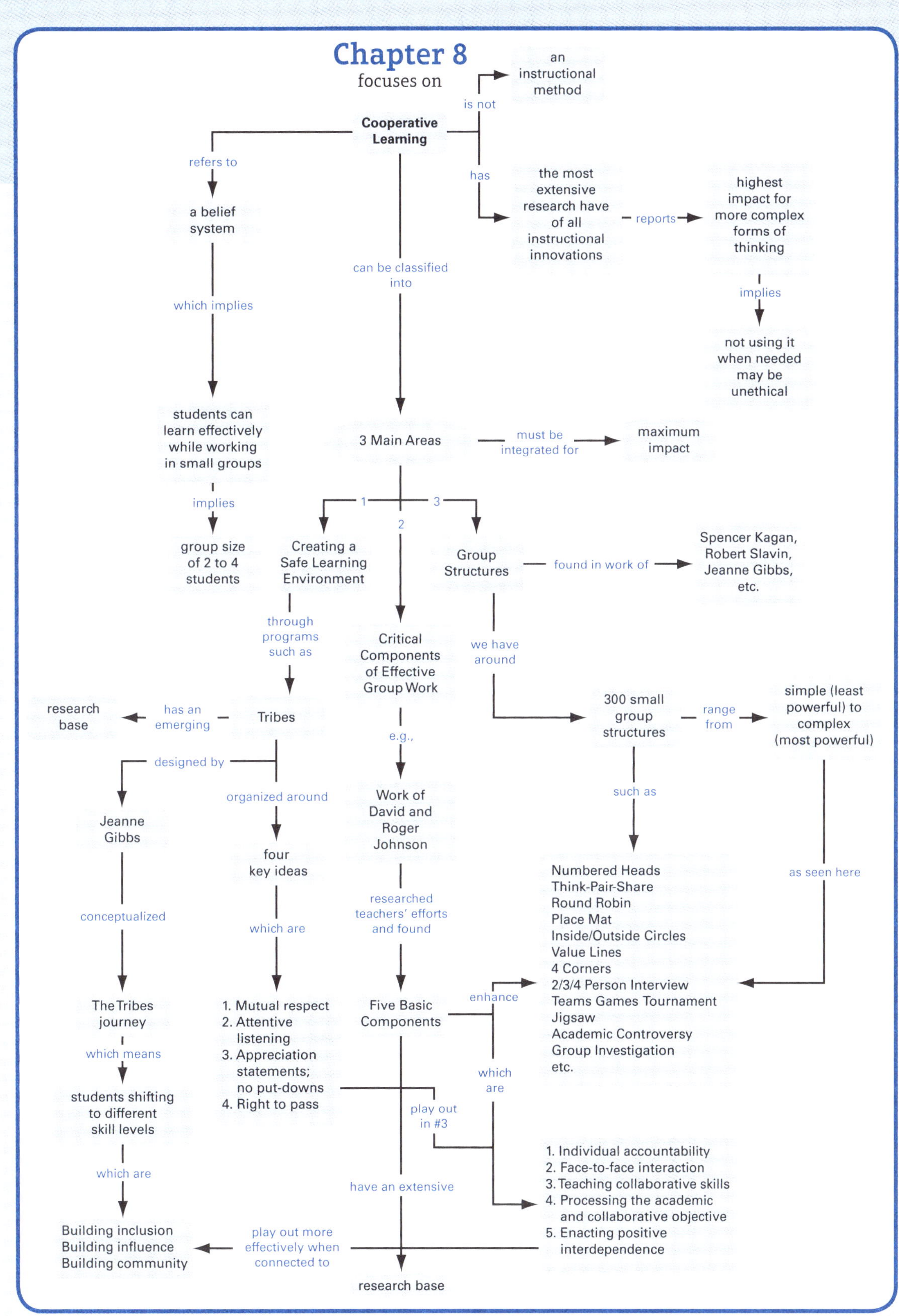
Chapter 8
focuses on
Cooperative Learning
is not
an instructional method
has
the most extensive research have of all instructional innovations
reports
highest impact for more complex forms of thinking
implies
not using it when needed may be unethical
refers to
a belief system
which implies
students can learn effectively while working in small groups
implies
group size of 2 to 4 students
can be classified into
3 Main Areas
must be integrated for
maximum impact
1
2
3
Creating a Safe Learning Environment
through programs such as
Tribes
has an emerging
research base
designed by
Jeanne Gibbs
conceptualized
The Tribes journey
which means
students shifting to different skill levels
which are
Building inclusion
Building influence
Building community
organized around
four key ideas
which are
1. Mutual respect
2. Attentive listening
3. Appreciation statements; no put-downs
4. Right to pass
Critical Components of Effective Group Work
e.g.,
Work of David and Roger Johnson
researched teachers' efforts and found
Five Basic Components
have an extensive
research base
play out in #3
enhance
which are
1. Individual accountability
2. Face-to-face interaction
3. Teaching collaborative skills
4. Processing the academic and collaborative objective
5. Enacting positive interdependence
play out more effectively when connected to
Group Structures
found in work of
Spencer Kagan, Robert Slavin, Jeanne Gibbs, etc.
we have around
300 small group structures
range from
simple (least powerful) to complex (most powerful)
such as
as seen here
Numbered Heads
Think-Pair-Share
Round Robin
Place Mat
Inside/Outside Circles
Value Lines
4 Corners
2/3/4 Person Interview
Teams Games Tournament
Jigsaw
Academic Controversy
Group Investigation
etc.

In this chapter, we illustrate how to create a safer, more inclusive classroom through effective group work, first focusing on instructional techniques and later on collaboration-building programs. The purpose of these techniques and programs is to create situations in which students feel safe and know that their voice is valued. We also discuss the essential attributes of effective group work, and how less effective group work leads to classroom management problems.

Later in this chapter two rubrics are presented. The first relates more broadly to effective group work, and the second to the Johnsons' Five Basic Elements of effective group work. In Appendix E we add a third rubric that applies a modification of the Levels of Use component of the Concerns Based Adoption Model (CBAM). This rubric will assist you to assess your use of the research on effective group work.

Developing a Perspective

Read the following descriptions of four teachers. In which classroom are students more likely to learn and behave? As a parent, determine which teacher would you want to teach your children. As a teacher, assess whether your students would see you as teacher A, B, C, or D.

Teacher A had virtually no training in structuring groups effectively during his B.Ed. degree, and has taken only a couple of workshops where cooperative learning was discussed. His students work in groups of five or six that they select themselves (friendship groups). In most cases, one or two students do all the work and others sit back and do virtually nothing. The teacher does not think about making sure all students are accountable and does not take the time to teach the collaborative skills students need to work more successfully in groups.

Teacher B was trained in Tribes during her B.Ed. program, but in the school she is in no one uses it so she has let it slip a bit. She did Tribes at the start of the year and reminds students of the Tribes agreements. She attended a workshop on Kagan structures and is beginning to apply some of these in her class. She has students in Tribes groups of five, and she had a say in how the groups were structured.

Teacher C was trained in Tribes and Kagan structures during his B.Ed. program, and is teaching in a school where both of these programs are used. He uses teacher-structured groups and random assignment to groups; he rarely allows friendship groups, especially if the learning is going to be complex. He reminds students of the Tribes agreements, and the students reflect on how they are using the agreements and work hard to implement them.

Teacher D was not trained in Tribes or Kagan structures during her B.Ed. program, but has worked in a school and district where co-operative learning is considered critical. She has attended a four-day workshop on the Johnsons' Five Basic Elements of effective group work and is certified in Tribes. A teacher in the school has been running workshops on Kagan structures after school. Teacher D's students have been doing Tribes since kindergarten and they all attend to the Tribes agreements. She also works to encourage additional social, communication, and critical thinking skills. Her students work in groups of two to four, and the groups are almost always teacher structured. Her Tribes groups meet each Friday to discuss how they are doing.

Effective vs. Ineffective Group Work

Today most teachers employ "group work," some minimally, others more extensively. The problem is that many don't employ *effective* group work. And, unfortunately, ineffectively structured group work is one of the worst approaches to teaching and learning. Why? Five key reasons are identified below.

1. **No Individual Accountability:** It's too easy for one or two students to take over and do all the work. In some instances, students are forced to take over because no one else in the group will do the work—others hitchhike off their efforts.
2. **Poor Composition of Groups:** Students too often sit in friendship groups rather than teacher-selected groups (the most effective) or randomly assigned groups (the second most effective and the most like real life). Friendship groups are often based on homogeneous characteristics such as gender, culture, academic ability, and popularity. When you have friends in a group, you also have one or two students who have the power and control because of their popularity.

3. **Unfamiliarity with the Social Processes of Collaboration:** Teachers rarely take the time to teach and have students reflect on key social, communication, and critical thinking skills required to effectively complete the task in the group.
4. **Inappropriate Group Size for the Academic Task:** Often, the groups are too large. Groups larger than four reduce work time, and it is too easy for students to hide and not participate.
5. **Inappropriate Choice of Task:** Some tasks should not be done as group work—they are inherently more suited to individual work.

Vignette on Cooperative Learning: The Grade 10 teacher had assigned a group project and Annie was placed in a group with three boys who did virtually nothing on the project. Annie did almost all the work, yet each student received the same grade. Annie is bright and easily saw that the teacher was not skilled; the student knew what should have happened. When asked by a researcher, Annie said the teacher should have made sure the other three students were held accountable to take responsibility for their part—to check the efforts of each member, to make sure they were all involved in giving the report. Annie understood this better than the teacher.

Most students are more than willing to work in groups when the time to complete the work is appropriate and when group work is balanced with opportunities to work individually and competitively. Below are a few comments from Grade 2 students who work in a classroom with a teacher who is very skilled at structuring group work.

"I like cooperative learning because it is fun, you can learn more, you might pass and go to grad three."

"I like cooperative learning because we worke together and worke very hared. But some times we fite in my grop and then we figr it out."

"I thing I like to work in groups because I feel lonely when nobody sit with me and I feel nobody loves me. I have a group and thair names are Vanessa, Dianne, Terra..."

Why Implement Effective Group Work?

Pioneers in education have always argued that learning is socially constructed. The champions of this theory date back to Charles Dickens and include Jean Piaget, B.F. Skinner, Paulo Freire, John Dewey, Lev Vygotsky, and Howard Gardner.

No other approach to teaching has as much research support as cooperative learning in the classroom. For statements of leading educators and research on the subject, see the work of Johnson and Johnson (1989), Slavin (1995), Ellis (2001, 2005), and Hattie (2012). Despite the hundreds of studies showing the positive impact of effectively structured groups, today most teachers fail to structure group work effectively.

Cooperative Learning

As educators, we must recognize that both poorly and effectively structured group work results in classroom management problems. Consider that groups are, after all, a collection of individuals, each having unique sensitivities, idiosyncrasies, and working styles that can clash in any circumstance. Factor in differing levels of abilities, and the chance that issues will arise increases exponentially.

Effectively structured group work is intended to deal with the inevitable conflict of group work—it won't prevent it from happening. Effective group work is designed to create opportunities for conflict so that students learn to confront and resolve it.

A Personal Perspective on Effective Group Work

The irony of using cooperative learning is that it was intended to create opportunities for students to learn how to deal with conflict. (See Appendix D for an overview of how the Johnsons' Five Basic Elements actually create problems.)

An author of this text was recently working with a new secondary teacher who was struggling with group work. She insisted that she was doing everything right, but it just wasn't working. The teacher had students work with their friends, the groups had five to six students, she had not taught any appropriate social skills, and the class was trying to do Jigsaw. Jigsaw is one of the most complex of the 300 group structures. She had not taken any course work or workshops on cooperative learning. The teacher had never heard of Kagan, Gibbs, or the Johnsons. Given these facts, her struggles are no surprise.

Take a look at the rubric below and ask yourself how you would score on the key attributes of effective group work. Your goal is to work toward consistently scoring Level 3 or 4 in each area, an indication that you are using group work effectively to create a safe learning environment in which students can express ideas and learn new concepts.

Teacher's Use of Effective Group Work Sample Rubric

Attributes	Level 1	Level 2	Level 3	Level 4
Group size	No attention to group size; teacher does not sense that group size is relevant; often more than four students per group	Some attention to group size, but some groups unnecessarily bigger than they need be, especially given the skill level and age of the students; may be two to four per group, but some groups still more than four	Group size is usually considered in most situations, although group size at times may not match the size needed for the academic task or skill level of the group	Group size always considered; group size reflects the skill level of the students and the needs of the academic task; teacher rarely uses group larger than four, unless necessary to successfully complete the task
Group structure	No attention to how groups are chosen—usually friendship or location groups; teacher has no idea that, or fails to act on the idea that, different group structures exist, such as friendship, random assignment, and teacher-selected	Some attention to who works with whom, but again, mostly friendship groups; teacher beginning to periodically act on the different ways to structure groups, such as random assignment and teacher-selected groups	Teacher attends to how groups are structured and will usually carefully use teacher-selected groups or, at times, random assignment to groups; will seldom use friendship groups	Teacher is conscious of the need to structure group work carefully, that teacher-selected groups are usually the most effective, then random assignment to groups; teacher will let students work with friends at times, once they have proven that they can work effectively with all students in class
Task clarity, relevance, and interest	Task is not clear; students do not see the relevance and have little interest in doing this task in groups	Task is somewhat clear; some students see the relevance and a few are interested in working on this task in groups	Task is clear; most students see the relevance and are interested in working on this task in groups	Task is very clear; all students see the relevance and are interested in working on this task in groups

(*continued*)

Teacher's Use of Effective Group Work Sample Rubric (*continued*)				
Attributes	**Level 1**	**Level 2**	**Level 3**	**Level 4**
Readiness for group work	Students are placed in groups with no opportunity to acquire the skills needed to work together effectively; teacher has no idea that collaborative skills can be classified into social, communication, and critical thinking skills	Teacher may explain skills, but students do not understand what those skills look like and sound like; teacher is beginning to act on the idea that collaborative skills can be classified into social, communication, and critical thinking skills; students do not reflect on their use of these skills	Students are taught the appropriate skills needed to complete the task; the teacher is more often acting on how social skills, communication skills, and critical thinking skills play off each other; students are beginning to reflect on how they implement these skills	Students are taught the appropriate collaborative skills needed to complete the task; teacher and students understand how social skills, communication skills, and critical thinking skills play off each other; students consistently reflect on how they implement these skills

How to Start Developing Effective Group Skills

Although a number of excellent programs and books exist on cooperative learning, three solid places to start are with the work of David and Roger Johnson, Spencer Kagan, and Jeanne Gibbs. We briefly discuss their work in this section.

The diagram on the next page illustrates how one might layer or intersect the work of Gibbs, the Johnsons, and Kagan. The bottom layer involves creating the safe classroom. Jeanne Gibbs's work on Tribes is one of the most widely applied processes for structuring a more inclusive, safe learning environment. One of the author's doctoral students recently completed her Ph.D. on the implementation of Tribes in a B.Ed. program (Phillips, 2011).

The middle layer refers to having a deeper understanding of how groups function, akin to understanding how an engine works. When the group breaks down, you need a process to fix it. The Johnsons' work is a key lens into understanding the process of group work. (See Johnson, Johnson, & Johnson Holubec, 2008, for more in-depth information in

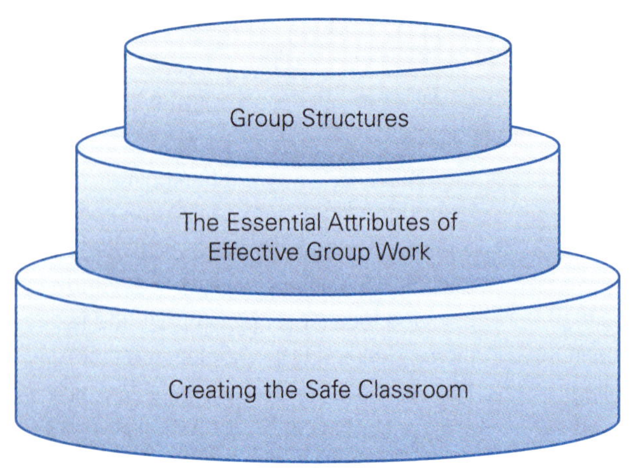

this area.) The top layer involves the multiple ways we can structure group work to facilitate a more differentiated way to meet the diverse needs of students, as well as to weave in novelty and variety in the classroom. Kagan and Kagan's (2009) new work would be a key resource to begin developing a variety of small group structures.

On the next pages, we briefly explain each of the three approaches.

Spencer Kagan: Small Group Structures

Spencer Kagan has been involved in assisting teachers to implement a variety of small group cooperative structures for more than 30 years. He has the most comprehensive collection of structures that range from simple (Numbered Heads) to more complex (Inside/Outside Circles). The value of these structures is that they allow teachers to address a number of important classroom issues. The cooperative learning structure One Stay the Rest Stray, for example, addresses the need for students to get up and move around. Think-Pair-Share and Two/Three Person Interview, for example, develop students' intrapersonal and interpersonal skills. Jeanne Gibbs also has an extensive collection of small group structures that form part of the Tribes program.

One key motivational factor is interest, which can often be divided into novelty and variety. Having a variety of these small group structures allows the teacher to engage students in different ways.

Kagan talks about the importance of simultaneous interaction. In the 1970s and 1980s Madeline Hunter talked about the importance of having all students actively involved. Most of the cooperative learning structures make it difficult for students to sit back and hitchhike off the efforts of others—they all must participate.

Two Examples of Cooperative Learning Structures

The two structures that follow illustrate the importance of reflecting on how your practices support student participation and feelings of safety in group situations.

1. Place Mat

Place Mat is a cooperative learning tactic where a piece of paper is divided so that each person has a place to write, with one additional space allocated for summarizing the group's ideas. Usually, this shared space is in the middle of the paper. Although this is a useful cooperative learning structure, some students may consider it unsafe, since their on-the-spot thinking is clearly visible to other group members.

There are several ways to increase the safety of the Place Mat tactic.

1. Provide students with time to think before they start writing.
2. Start with another small group tactic known as Milling to Music, where students have a chance to talk with others before sitting down and starting to work.
3. Provide at-risk students with a heads-up, allowing them to think through the problem the day or evening before.
4. Cut the Place Mat into pieces so students work individually and privately before they come back and tape the Place Mat together. This allows you to walk around and check how each student is doing, providing extra help where needed—and no one is the wiser because you visited with all students.

2. Think-Pair-Share

This structure, developed by Frank Lyman, involves asking students to think on their own, then share with a partner, and finally share with the entire class. The underlying premise in classrooms is that all students need to feel safe and wish to be successful. When we provide time for students to think before they share, we increase their sense of safety and their chance to be successful. It is more beneficial still if you allow them to share with a partner before sharing with the class. Students from elementary to graduate levels state that they prefer to have time to think and then share with a partner before sharing with the class. When asked why, they report that they feel safer; that they are more likely to be "right" publicly. Our graduate students confide, "We can't afford to be *wrong* publicly in this class."

The key for using Think-Pair-Share effectively is that teachers must be skilled at framing questions and allowing appropriate wait time. This structure is more complex than it appears. Our teaching students report after their first practicum that their efforts to get the students to Think-Pair-Share often cause classroom problems. We asked these students to list all the factors they must consider for Think-Pair-Share to work effectively. Below is their list.

1. An even or odd number of students in the classroom. If there's an odd number, the student left over will be the one no one wants to work with; when you ask him to join another group, he will refuse and/or the other group will complain about having him join. This is a recipe for a power play, to say nothing of how the student left behind feels.
2. What do you do with a student who is an English language learner? Who does she pair up with?
3. When you put boys and girls together, they will often struggle to talk to each other.
4. They have to have the skills of attentive listening and be able to paraphrase what the other person said.
5. You have to give the students enough time to think first before they share, or they may have nothing to talk about.
6. If you don't know the level of thinking involved, say, using Bloom's Taxonomy, then you may not allow the appropriate amount of wait time.
7. You need to understand how to reply to a silly response, or a guess or a no response, or a partially correct response, or you may have classroom management problems.

You would be wise to refrain from pointing at students when selecting for a Think-Pair-Share. Instead, use an open hand that suggests an invitation rather than a "stabbing." How you frame your questions also counts: "Marsha, what were you and Meila thinking?" Our students tell us they prefer to be asked, "What were you *and your partner* thinking..." If they are going to be wrong publicly, they do not want to "go down alone."

The challenge for Faculties of Education is to ensure that B.Ed. students understand how to structure group work effectively. To superficially know a few group structures, such as Think-Pair-Share and Place Mat, without the background knowledge of how to structure groups is akin to putting a piece of paper on a comb, humming through it, and calling yourself a musician.

Popular Programs for Cooperative Learning

In this section, we explore two of the leading programs to promote effective collaborative learning within the complex learning environments of schools: Jeanne Gibbs's Tribes and the Johnsons' Five Basic Elements of Effective Group Work.

We have completed a PMI (pluses, minuses, most important factors) for each program. Note that, as in earlier chapters, although the *I* in Edward de Bono's decision-making tool is meant to denote "interesting," for our purposes we have changed it to mean "most important."

Jeanne Gibbs: Tribes

Tribes was started by Jeanne Gibbs back in the 1970s to create a classroom environment that makes it easier for students to assist one another to feel they belong. Today Tribes is being implemented in countries around the world. Currently, Jeanne Gibbs has a Tribes book for elementary, middle school, and secondary school teachers and students. (See the References. page 254, for those books.)

The Tribes program involves a four-day, 24-hour program designed to move students through three progressive phases. In the first phase, the program provides a variety of tactics to build a safer classroom environment by building inclusion. In the second phase, students shift to developing skills to influence and be influenced, and as part of that to confront and deal with conflict. In the third phase, students learn the skills to work as a community. The program has, as its core value system, four Tribes agreements.

1. Mutual respect
2. Attentive listening
3. Appreciation statements/no put-downs
4. The right to pass

These agreements are non-negotiable and should always be invoked during individual, cooperative, and competitive learning situations. We have found that most teachers who take Tribes training fail to effectively implement its intent. Although they may typically implement the program at the start of the year or just after attending a workshop, usage soon drops to only a periodic mention of the Tribes agreements and to displaying posters of the agreements on a classroom wall. Below is our PMI chart on Tribes.

PMI Chart on Tribes

Pluses	Minuses	Most Important
Provides intensive/practical introductory training—information, modelling, practice is provided (theory, demonstration, practice)	No follow-up for those taking the training—transfer is minimal unless teachers come in teams or do it as a school staff; principal has to support it (no peer coaching)	Initial training in how to create a safer, more inclusive classroom environment
Provides activities to engage students to develop the disposition to acquire basic social competence	Does not make the connection between social, communication, and critical thinking skills	Participants get an introduction to social theory, but must make further connections by integrating Tribes with other approaches on their own
Introduces the Johnsons' Five Basic Elements and connects to multiple intelligences	Connection to the Johnsons' work and to multiple intelligences is minimal	Acknowledges and respects other cooperative learning approaches
Has the potential to assist teachers in implementing more complex instructional methods, including non-group-related methods	Does not connect the three phases of the Tribes Journey to other instructional methods, such as Jigsaw or Academic Controversy	Explains why more complex instructional methods (e.g., Jigsaw) do not work; if a method pushes "influence" and the class has no "inclusion," the method fails
Teachers are the trainers—minimal research, but expanding	Trainers often know very little about other cooperative approaches	Have to connect Tribes to other approaches; Tribes is a patch on a quilt, not the quilt

Tribes has students work through three increasingly complex dimensions. First the teacher works on building inclusion and trust. Once that is accomplished, and it may take months or even all year, the students shift to developing the skills to influence and be influenced. And finally, the students evolve to building community. You can see how framing questions, wait time, and the cooperative structure of Think-Pair-Share or Place Mat can be used to work on inclusion. A Jigsaw or Academic Controversy would be an influencing strategy. Group Investigation and role plays and enactments in the classroom relate to building community. Tribes has an extensive number of tactics teachers can employ with students to build inclusion, influence, and community.

School One: York Region District School Board

These comments are from Denise McLafferty, the principal of Moraine Hills Public School from 2006 to 2011, regarding the use of Tribes in her school.

> I have been the principal of a Tribes school since September 2002. I opened Mackenzie Glen (MGPS) as a Tribes school in September 2002 and left in Junc 2006. Then I opened Moraine Hills (MHPS) in September 2006, where I am currently the principal. In both schools, I established an expectation that all teachers had to be Tribes trained in advance of the school opening. As well, secretaries, caretakers, and educational assistants agreed to take the training. This shared learning was a great team-building experience. Additionally, it provided us with an incredible opportunity to create a learning environment in which all the adults: a) had a common understanding of the Tribes Process; b) used a consistent language and approach through which to interact with the students; and c) implemented coherent expectations.
>
> In total, I have worked with the Tribes Process for nine years. The big challenge with any new initiative is that when you start, everyone is motivated, energized, and enthusiastic about implementing the innovation. Over time, the sustainability is the challenge. I have learned with Tribes and all new initiatives that to keep it alive, I must be the driving force. My leadership symbol is an animal with the head of a goose and the body of a border collie. As the goose, I establish the direction and lead towards the vision, and as the border collie, I focus on the sustainability challenge; specifically, all my efforts are focused on "nipping at the heels" and continuing to move everyone forward.
>
> In both schools, I learned early on that to keep moving forward and refining and improving our practice, I needed to model my expectations through my behaviour, the learning opportunities that I design for my staff, and the school-wide activities that model the Tribes Process, e.g., daily Appreciation Alerts, monthly staff meetings, school-wide cross-grade Tribes monthly assemblies, social activities for staff Tribes, and special events where students and staff work in their Tribes, i.e., Eco-Olympics.
>
> In both schools, I have used my staff meetings as my opportunity to be the teacher, with my staff as my students. All meetings are done in a community circle and every staff meeting begins with 30 minutes dedicated to a Tribes Learning Experience. Strategically, I begin the year with Inclusion activities so that school-wide we are all focused on this very critical stage of the Tribes Process. As the year progresses, I move to the all challenging Influence stage, again incorporating strategies from this stage at my staff meetings. And finally, I move to the Community stage and what that looks like in the classroom. As the staff (teachers, secretaries, caretakers, and educational assistants) is in Tribes, each is responsible to design and lead a Tribes Learning Experience at a staff

meeting. One of the things that I am constantly reviewing with my staff is that Tribes is not a passive process but an active one. In order to help our students build community within their classroom and to develop the collaborative skills that will enable them to work effectively in groups, we must explicitly teach these skills in the classroom and then reinforce their importance by consistently establishing a social goal along with a learning goal for all academic group work.

At monthly assemblies, students who practise the Four Agreements on a consistent basis are nominated by their teachers and are recognized with Agreement Awards. These certificates of achievement are a powerful way to highlight, celebrate, and motivate positive student behaviour. The Four Agreements and the Tribes Trail are painted on the gym walls and are a strong visual reminder to all students about these expectations within our school. All assemblies begin with a review of the Four Agreements/Tribes Trail and their importance in the success of our community.

Throughout the nine years of working with this process, I have witnessed such a positive impact on both schools' cultures. We continually receive positive feedback on the behaviours and attitudes of our students and the welcoming, warm environment throughout the school. We knew that what we were doing was having a positive impact through the feedback that we were receiving from parents, visitors, supply teachers, program providers, authors/speakers, etc., and our neighbouring secondary school. I started gathering testimonials from people as evidence that we had created a unique climate in our school. Listed below are several examples:

Supply Teachers:

"Moraine Hills stands out as a school with exceptional qualities. The staff members are always warm and supportive; the students are kind and respectful, and I feel welcomed as I enter each classroom. I feel that this may be due to the school's commitment to the Tribes process. I continually hear students mention the Tribes Agreements, and demonstrate them through their actions."

"This is to inform you that I felt very welcomed by wonderful staff and students. It was a pleasure to work in this friendly environment as a supply teacher. Thank you for giving me this opportunity. Looking forward to many more."

"I just wanted to let you know that I have had a very enjoyable time at your school today. Your staff and students were wonderful. This is my third year supply teaching at MGPS and my experience has always been positive. The students were all well-behaved, enthusiastic and stayed on task..."

"I have noticed that at MGPS the students at the various grade levels, particularly the Intermediates, are more polite, cooperative, helpful, and work better together as a group, than at other schools."

"Just a short note to commend you and your staff for making my stay a happy and healthy one. Everyone seems so energized and willing to help. Tribes works and I feel that this theory has been put to practice the best at MGPS. Everyone walks and talks the Trail."

Outside Groups and Presenters:

"The students here were great! They listened attentively and they were playing a part in everything I did. This was one of the best morning presentations I have had in a really long time. The students here are amazing. They were very respectful and wanted to be a part of what I was presenting. I am really excited about coming back soon. Thank you so much for having me here. I don't seem to know how to describe it, but there is something special here. I really enjoyed presenting here!"

"For both my presentations through Scientists in the School, I had a wonderful experience. Students demonstrated how they could work together in a positive and cooperative manner. This was consistent within all three classes with which I was involved. Each time I go to a school I use a process where, by the end of my session, students would be working cooperatively. At MGPS, this process was completely unnecessary for the students showed a real knowledge of working together to a common goal. Keep it up; you are heading in the right direction!"

Local High School:

"What are you doing there? Your students are different from the students who come here from the other five feeder schools. They are more respectful, polite, and work well in groups. Even when I come into your building, it feels different than the other schools."

Visitors, who were interested in learning more about Tribes, regularly commented on the feeling in the building. They felt it was tangible—a positive energy, a vitality in the building, where you felt welcomed. One group from Scotland commented that "We were very impressed by the implementation of the Tribes Process and its effect on developing relationships with your school!" Our partners at OISE [Ontario Institute for Studies in Education], the Doncrest Option, wrote: "I was in your school twice over the past two weeks and was so impressed with the teachers, the quality of instruction, the collegial environment, the activities, and the Tribes philosophy in action."

I considered these testimonials as data. Other data that I looked at included: 1) Staff attendance: the Board average for absence due to personal illness was 12 days per teacher; our average was 8/staff; and 2) Student behaviour: we had very little behaviour to deal with in the office. In both schools, we collected data on student incidents over time and it showed few suspensions and a small number of behavioural issues. Very little behaviour comes to the office as most is dealt with at the classroom level through the Tribes Process.

Interestingly, bullying, a form of power, disappeared in this York Region school. It is important to note that this particular school district supports its teachers and administrators learning Tribes. It now has approximately 4000 teachers who have completed the four-day program. Again, as mentioned earlier, not all those who take Tribes effectively implement it. Professional development, in and of itself, does not cause change. It is what we do after the professional development that determines the extent of the change.

School Two: York Region District School Board

These comments are from Marion Ahrens, currently seconded from York Region District School Board to work in the B.Ed. program and offer Tribes training for students at the Ontario Institute for Studies in Education (OISE) at the University of Toronto.

> My journey with Tribes began in my first year of teaching with my Grade 6 homeroom class. What really struck me about the students was how much respect they had for each other and how well they worked together. I also noticed that there was one girl in the class who would say "pass" if I asked her to share in class. The students did not react to this at all and I had seen posters in the school that said "the Right to Pass." So one day I gathered the courage to ask my students about this right to pass. What followed was a lively conversation by the class about what ended up being the Four Agreements. I recognized the language from the posters and asked a teacher on staff about them. What I discovered is that the school was a Tribes school when it opened and all of the teachers were Tribes trained. The students in my class had been in classrooms where the Tribes process was used for seven years. The fact that they wanted to teach me Tribes and were able to sustain the process even when the teacher did not know Tribes made me realize the true power of this process.
>
> I remember taking the Tribes training and being so excited to use it in my classroom. I became quite good at Inclusion and using the Four Agreements. This had positive results in my classroom, making it a nicer place to be. However, I did not realize the true potential and power of Tribes until I did the training again and truly understood the power of the Influence Stage. At the time, I was not good with conflict and would avoid it at all costs. Implementing Tribes taught not only my students but also me how to deal with conflict in more effective ways. I intentionally and explicitly taught my learners how to deal with conflict and make shared decisions. I gave them tools for dealing with conflict when working together and thereby empowered them to interact more effectively together. This is when my classroom went from being a nice place to be to also being a truly powerful place of learning. I was finally able to use cooperative learning strategies in more meaningful ways.

The impact the Tribes process had on my students was noticeable in many areas, one being classroom management. Although Tribes is not a solution to all classroom management issues, I found that it certainly made a big difference. Tribes allows students to accept and understand one another and this transforms what happens in the classroom. Throughout my career I always requested to have challenging students in my class (both academically and behaviour). When going through the Influence Stage of Tribes, not only did I learn so much about these students and what may be causing the "challenges" they would present, but the students learned about each other at the same time. I remember vividly one community circle where the sentence starter was "One thing I find hard is..." and one student who always entertained the class with his antics broke down and said, "Everything is hard for me! I have such trouble reading and writing and I always feel like everyone can do things better than me. I struggle so much with everything we do." The students were shocked, saying, "You always have a smile on your face and you are so funny we never knew you were having trouble." They rallied around him and for the next while made it their mission to help and support him both with his work but also his confidence. Another vivid memory is of a student who displayed many characteristics of a bully. Not only did I have to model how to treat this student and work with him on his choices, I also had to give the rest of the class strategies for dealing with him. This improved how he was able to work with others. What fascinated me was that some of the students, when given the choice of who to work with, actually chose this student and shared with me that they really wanted to help him grow as a student. Therefore, what I love about Tribes is that it allows classroom management to be proactive rather than just reactive. You create a culture in the classroom where students understand each other and are committed to the success of the whole learning community. Learners are given tools and strategies to deal with issues and, because both the academic goal of the lesson and the collaborative goals are made clear, students understand the importance not only of "what" is learned but also "how we learned it."

When Tribes is a shared commitment among all staff and administration, it becomes even more powerful. I worked at one school as a Literacy Teacher supporting staff from kindergarten to Grade 8 with their literacy programs. Knowing the impact Tribes had on my classroom, the principal and I decided to transform the school into a Tribes school. We began the journey as a staff planning what the first week of school would look like, where we introduced Tribes to the learners. Parents commented at Curriculum Night in September about the power of having their multi-aged children sitting at the dinner table excited to share that they had done the same activities that day. One of the most powerful things that the staff noticed about the school-wide implementation was that everyone (teachers and students) shared the same language when dealing with issues that arose in the classroom and on the playground. As a school we did activities to understand how the agreements would form the foundation of our school community.

The impact of using Tribes in my classroom was amazing. I have students to this day come back and visit me to tell me that the things I taught them about working together still help them in their lives now.

School Three: Edmonton Public School Board

These comments are from Judi Strang, a primary school teacher and now a consultant with Edmonton Public Schools, who also does Tribes Training.

I was a classroom teacher for 16 years before implementing the Tribes process in my classroom. My teaching experiences were mainly kindergarten and division one and based in city centre schools where the population is marginalized. I was an effective teacher with a good reputation among my peers and with the students' families. Before taking the Tribes course, I read articles about the Tribes process to determine if it would benefit me. I concluded that it would be a professional development opportunity that would extend and refine how I worked with my students. Interestingly, it caught me by surprise and led me to a new level of best practice that would not only positively influence my teaching practice but would bring about change in my school community and, in the long run, open new job opportunities both within and outside my school district.

In my kindergarten teaching experience, the Tribes process had a significant impact on the social skill development and management of behaviours in my classroom. Creating a positive environment with positive expectations for all is what Tribes ultimately teaches. Even my littlest learners were able to recite the four agreements and describe the meanings when resolving conflicts or appreciating one another. Instilling the agreements and promoting inclusion is key; it's a matter of the teaching staff and all school staff living the agreements within the classroom and school community to ensure that children see and hear the real-life application of the agreements in context along with discussion and participating in lessons.

During the basic course, I was provided with the strategies and knowledge to educate kids how to work together, resolve conflict, be successful and feel good about themselves.

There is nothing more rewarding than observing groups of five-year-olds in their classroom Tribes doing presentations. Group members have a role to play to ensure the success of their tribe.

It was a lot of hard work, consistency, and my trust in the Tribes process that made a difference in my classroom. The way I like to describe using Tribes in the classroom is that it is not only one more professional development session that you put on your "plate" to be an effective teacher...it is the plate.

School Four: Edmonton Public School Board

These comments are from Shannon Bennett-Pratt, a secondary English teacher with Edmonton Public Schools. Shannon is a full-time teacher and also does Tribes Training.

> I have been using Tribes for 10 years in my high school English and special needs classes. I also made the decision to become a Tribes trainer. Our population at our school is very multicultural and is also an entry point for new immigrants; as a result, having all students in the class feeling and believing they are included is important.
>
> There is a lot that happens during the year, so I will illustrate how I use Tribes to set the tone for my classroom at the beginning of each semester. The strategy I use is called Bubble Letter and I use it to build a sense of community. This pushes the inclusion level of Tribes (the first level you try to build). In class, students work on their own to first develop and then present in words and pictures information about themselves. The same evening I read through all of these and write down information with regards to the students. I then put the letters up on a wall—to stay for the duration of the semester. The next day I talk about the information and what I found was common to students or unique to students. They eagerly wait to hear about information that could be theirs and smile when I mention something that they have written. We then talk about why we did this strategy and what it has done for the classroom. This community building helps because students start to learn about others in the classroom and realize that they are not that different.
>
> During the first week of the semester, we also work through a looks like, sounds like, feels like chart for the four agreements. Once the Tribes four agreements are in place (the kids understand them and have had a chance to discuss them and experience them) I have fewer classroom management problems. Students often self-regulate their behaviour. For example, I have heard students say "I have a right to participate, so could you be quiet?" or "That is a put-down" if there has been some name calling. Students understand and appreciate how the agreements are like boundaries, and feel that they have some input and control in classroom behaviour. Interestingly, I also have fewer students coming late and better attendance than many of my colleagues at school. This is especially significant as I have a high population of at-risk and special needs students in my class.

Example of a Tribes Activity: Snowball

This is used for influence and a check for understanding. (Note that "influence" is one of the three levels of Tribes—the other two are "inclusion" and "community.") Students sit in a circle. Each student has a piece of paper. A math question is placed on the board. Students, working on their own, do as much of the problem as possible. When asked to stop, they crumple up their papers and do not write their names on them. When the teacher says, "One, two, three, snowball," they toss their "snowballs" into a container placed in the middle of the circle. Students then come up and get one. They sit down and read how this other student worked at the problem.

Next, they pair with a partner, share their two sheets and then together, using the two sheets and their own two efforts, they take another piece of paper and do as much as they can on the problem. Once again, they do the snowball when asked. One of the two students will get up and take a sheet done by two other students. They look it over and the teacher randomly selects a few students to put the solution on the "snowball" on the board. This is risk-free for those students, as it is not their work. This activity can work at most grade levels in most subject areas. Snowball is just one of about 125 safe and inclusive activities in the Tribes program and resources.

Connection to Classroom Management: How do you think Snowball works at enacting the concepts of success, safety, active participation, accountability, and novelty?

David and Roger Johnson: The Five Basic Elements

Like Tribes, the Five Basic Elements is also a four-day, 24-hour training program. This training is based on the Johnsons' research in classrooms over the last 40 years. Most of their work is gleaned from observing effective (and less effective) attempts at implementing cooperative learning. This work can be found in their *Cooperation in the Classroom,* often referred to as the "cooperative learning brown book" (Johnson, Johnson, & Johnson Holubec, 2008).

Where Tribes may be the foundation of effective group work, providing a way to create a safer, more inclusive learning environment, the Five Basic Elements may be considered the engine of effective group work. It helps teachers to understand why a group is functioning effectively or why it isn't, and how to begin to fix issues.

For the Johnsons, who have won international awards for their work, these five elements are essential to effective group work. If any one of these five elements is compromised, group work can become less effective.

1. **Individual accountability** simply means that everyone in the group must be accountable to participate. One cannot sit back and do nothing, nor take over and do everything—the teacher puts processes in place to make sure this does not happen.

2. **Promoting face-to-face interaction** refers both to the development of collaborative skills that encourage students to effectively engage with each other, as well as making sure students sit in such a way that they can easily see and interact with each other. This means the group size is two to four students. Once you have groups of five or more students, individuals can too easily become social loafers or fall through the cracks. The larger the number of students, the more time it takes for them all to talk.

3. **Teaching collaborative skills** implies teaching and inserting one, maybe two, skills the students should attend to as they work on their academic task. Social skills might be taking turns, using quiet voices, using each other's names, equal voice, voicing appreciation, and so on. Communications skills might be checking for clarification, attentive listening, paraphrasing, disagreeing with the idea not the person, and so on. Critical thinking skills would be suspending judgment, disagreeing agreeably, examining both sides of an argument, and considering all factors around an issue. Note that if students are not skilled at social skills, they will struggle with communication skills. They need both social and communication skills to enact critical thinking skills.

4. **Processing academic and collaborative skills** refers to having students discuss or reflect on how they did at accomplishing the academic task or objective, as well as on how well they did at enacting the specific collaborative skill.

5. **Employing one or more of nine types of Positive Interdependence** refers to nine ways teachers can increase the chances that students will work together, positively, to help each other learn (see Appendix D). The only one of the nine you must have is Goal Positive Interdependence. This refers to having a clear, meaningful group task—a task worth doing in groups. The other eight are optional; employ them judiciously and don't use them if you don't need them.

PMI Chart on the Five Basic Elements		
Pluses	**Minuses**	**Most Important**
Provides intensive/practical introductory training—information, modelling, practice is provided (theory, demonstration, practice)	No follow-up for those taking the training—transfer is minimal unless teachers come in teams or do it as a school staff; principal has to support it (no peer coaching)	Initial training in how to structure group work effectively and how to process academic and social learning; connects to assessment for learning
Provides teacher with key concepts (e.g., individual accountability, clear learning goals) that determine whether or not group work will function	Does not make the connection between social, communication, and critical thinking skills	Participants get an introduction to social theory, but must make further connections by integrating the Five Elements with other approaches on their own
Has an extensive research base	Does not provide a range of ways to structure groups, as does the work of Gibbs and Kagan	Assists the teacher to think more deeply about cooperative learning and the teacher's role prior to, setting up, during, and processing group work

Take a look at the rubric below and ask yourself how you would score. Your goal is to work toward consistently scoring Level 3 or 4 in each area.

Rubric for Teacher Self-Assessment of the Johnsons' Five Basic Elements of Effective Group Work				
Attribute	**Level 1**	**Level 2**	**Level 3**	**Level 4**
Individual accountability	Little or no evidence that students are all accountable	Emerging evidence that some students are accountable	Clear evidence that most students are accountable	Clear evidence that all students are accountable
Promoting face-to-face interaction	Students are not sitting in a way that promotes face-to-face interaction	Some students are sitting correctly; group size is too large (one or more groups has five or more students)	Most students are sitting appropriately; group size also appropriate (two to four per group)	All students are sitting appropriately; group size is appropriate (two to four per group)
Teaching collaborative skills	No evidence of a relevant skill being taught or introduced	Skill mentioned but not taught; skill not always appropriate to the task; at times too many skills mentioned	Skill taught and, for the most part, relates to the academic task; may mention one or two other skills but focuses on one	Skill taught meaningfully and relates to the academic task; teacher checks to make sure all students understand the skill

(continued)

Rubric for Teacher Self-Assessment of the Johnsons' Five Basic Elements of Effective Group Work				
Attribute	**Level 1**	**Level 2**	**Level 3**	**Level 4**
Processing academic and collaborative skills	Little or no evidence that students reflected on or processed their academic or social learning	Some evidence, but most processing is done by the teacher	Clear evidence that students reflected on or processed their academic and social learning	Clear evidence that students and teacher effectively processed their academic and social learning
Positive Interdependence (PI)	No evidence of PI; no clear goal stated; task may not be appropriate for group work	Some evidence of PI; goal stated but not as clearly or meaningfully as it could be; goal not discussed with students	Clear evidence of PI; goal stated, brief discussion with students; appropriate types of PI selected and applied	Clear evidence of PI; goal clearly stated and relevance discussed with students; appropriate type of PI selected and effectively applied

Connection to Classroom Management: In what ways do you see how effective attention to these five factors affects classroom management? How do these factors create problems? See Appendix D for an overview of how effective group work creates problems.

Social Studies Lesson on Goods and Services in a Community: A Sample Lesson Integrating the Work of Kagan, Gibbs, and the Johnsons

This lesson format is shown to have a positive effect on student learning (Hattie, 2012).

Academic Objective

Students will demonstrate their understanding of goods and services by first reflecting on a quick role play, and then completing a Concept Attainment lesson on goods and services using a Place Mat. They will identify where the idea of goods and services plays out in their lives.

Social Objective

Students will focus on the Tribes agreement of "attentive listening" when discussing with a partner and in their small cooperative groups. Students will demonstrate that they are attentively listening by taking turns talking, making eye contact with their partner, and making other positive gestures such as nodding. (Note: This skill has been taught and practised a number of times in previous lessons, so it is a review.)

Mental Set

Mrs. Davies from next door will come and want to borrow my video on fractions, and I will tell her that it will cost her $20. She will reply that she does not have $20, but she will do the photocopying for me for the fractions math test. I will agree and thank her.

Ask students to discuss with a partner what they thought just happened. Randomly call on students to share their ideas.

Stated Academic Objective

"Today for Social Studies we will be extending our understanding about two concepts that are found in a community and that you use all the time. We will start by doing a Concept Attainment activity on those two concepts."

Input/Modelling

"On the SMART Board you see two data sets. Side A represents one concept; side B represents the other. Focus on the roles A-side and B-side ideas play in a community. Put your ideas on your Place Mat. After we have done four pairs of ideas from the data sets, you will do a Round the Table."

Side A	Side B
You buy a skateboard	A dentist puts braces on your teeth
Someone sells you a car	The doctor fixes your broken arm
Your mom buys groceries for supper	A house fire is put out by firefighters
For your birthday you get a new book	Your business has a security guard

Checks for Understanding

"Do a Round the Table to see what the group thinks about the concepts represented on sides A and B. I will randomly call on one person from each group to share in about 90 seconds, so make sure you have all thought about what you are going to say for your group." After 90 seconds, randomly call on students to share but don't judge their ideas, just thank them for sharing.

"Below are three more A and B examples. Think to yourself, then discuss in your group: do they work with what you said? Make sure everyone gets a chance to share."

A	B
You buy a bike with your allowance	You babysit for friends
The furniture in your house	A neighbour walks your dog on Saturdays
Your mom wins a new computer	Your dad fixes your bike

"In the middle of your Place Mat put down what you think is meant by the ideas on the A side and the B side. Remember to listen attentively to each other's ideas. When you are finished, do a Walk About to compare your thinking with what other groups thought."

Have students stop for a moment and reflect on how well they did at listening attentively to others in their group and during the whole class sharing. Randomly call on several students to share their thoughts about what they saw.

Now give students these four cases (each person in the group takes one) and have them discuss whether they fit A, B, or both A and B.

1. You get the paper delivered to your house every morning.
2. You pick up a pizza for supper. (What if it was delivered?)
3. A person puts a new roof on your house.
4. Your grandmother makes you a birthday cake.

Introduce the idea of *goods and services*—discuss the terms as they relate to the A side and the B side. You may want to do a Venn diagram to show their relationship.

Closure/Reflection

Do a Milling to Music (or No Music). Have students discuss what is more important to a community—goods or services? Then have them discuss how the idea of goods and services plays out in their life. Ask students to reflect in their work journals how their family engages in the idea of goods and services by identifying what they think are the three main goods they purchase and the three main services they use.

Activity for Building Classroom Support for Effective Group Work

The value of fostering effective group dynamics can perhaps be confirmed with just a glance at the Employability Skills Profile from The Conference Board of Canada. Note how many of the expectations relate to working with others. These skills are critical for the future success of young people. Clearly, the chart suggests the next generation needs more than just competency in literacy and numeracy. What are you doing in your classroom to assist your students to acquire effective group skills?

EMPLOYABILITY SKILLS PROFILE: The Critical Skills Required of the Canadian Workforce		
Academic Skills	**Personal Management Skills**	**Teamwork Skills**
Those skills which provide the basic foundation to get, keep and progress on a job and to achieve the best results	The combination of skills, attitudes and behaviours required to get, keep and progress on a job and to achieve the best results	Those skills needed to work with others on a job and to achieve the best results
Canadian employers need a person who can: **Communicate** • Understand and speak the languages in which business is conducted • Listen to understand and learn • Read, comprehend and use written materials, including graphs, charts and displays • Write effectively in the languages in which business is conducted **Think** • Think critically and act logically to evaluate situations, solve problems and make decisions • Understand and solve problems involving mathematics and use the results • Use technology, instruments, tools and information systems effectively • Access and apply specialized knowledge from various fields (e.g., skilled trades, technology, physical sciences, arts and social sciences) **Learn** • Continue to learn for life	Canadian employers need a person who can demonstrate: **Positive Attitudes and Behaviours** • Self-esteem and confidence • Honesty, integrity and personal ethics • A positive attitude toward learning, growth and personal health • Initiative, energy and persistence to get the job done **Responsibility** • The ability to set goals and priorities in work and personal life • The ability to plan and manage time, money and other resources to achieve goals • Accountability for actions taken **Adaptability** • A positive attitude toward change • Recognition of and respect for people's diversity and individual differences • The ability to identify and suggest new ideas to get the job done—creativity	Canadian employers need a person who can: **Work with Others** • Understand and contribute to the organization's goals • Understand and work within the culture of the group • Plan and make decisions with others and support the outcomes • Respect the thoughts and opinions of others in the group • Exercise "give and take" to achieve group results • Seek a team approach as appropriate • Lead when appropriate, mobilizing the group for high performance

Source: The Conference Board of Canada

Most job ads ask for applicants to be skilled in communication and interpersonal skills, and be able to work with a team or with all stakeholders. We have never found an ad that calls for someone who can "sit in a row, work alone, and when stuck on a problem, put up their hand and wait for the boss to come around and help." We also never see job ads that say: "Wanted, a person who can only work with their best friends."

Analyzing Job Ads: A Cooperative Place Mat Activity

You may want to have students complete a Place Mat on job ads. Have students work in groups of four. Give each person two job ads to read. Have them write (individually) what their two job ads require from the applicant. Next, ask them to share their findings within the group (Round Table Share). Following the sharing, have students determine what each of the job ads have in common. It almost always comes down to interpersonal skills, communication skills, being part of a team, and computer skills. Have students discuss why these are standard in most job ads.

Consider the job ad excerpts below, both taken from the classified section of an Irish newspaper. Are skill requirements any different in your country?

Title: Manager—Accountancy Practice

The firm has a large client base spanning local business and the agricultural sector. The successful candidate will manage an experienced team of staff with.... They will also mentor and develop the existing team.

Title: Endoscopy Manager—Major Hospital

The successful candidate will work in close liaison with the consultants to provide a strategic approach to the development of endoscopy services and structures.

Will have excellent leadership and change management skills and experience.

Will have proven experience in leading, managing, and developing nursing staff.

A Brief Review of Cooperative Learning Structures and Programs

Kagan Structures

When using these structures, remember they can be a lot more complex than they appear. We find that weaving the Johnsons' Five Basic Elements into some of the structures increases their effectiveness, especially having students process how they did as a group on a particular collaborative skill.

Consideration: Most of the small group tactics will, at most, have a modest effect on student learning. This is *not* a problem—they are not designed to have large effects on student learning. When we watch teachers teach, they seldom push into the more complex structures of Academic Controversy, Team Analysis, Jigsaw, Teams Games Tournament, and Group Investigation.

Jeanne Gibbs's Tribes

When implementing Tribes, it is *much* easier if all teachers on staff are involved; some schools also involve the secretaries and custodial staff in the training. Denise McLafferty in the York Region District School Board stated that this was the sixth year of doing Tribes in their K to Grade 8 school and bullying had disappeared. The Medicine Hat School District recently provided the time for all teachers and principals (K to Grade 12) in their district to be certified in Tribes.

Consideration: Too many teachers do Tribes training and put up posters, play with it for a few days at the start of the year, and do virtually nothing else—they never go on the Tribes journey. This is typical if teachers are implementing Tribes on their own with no support or encouragement from other staff or, most important, from school administrators.

Johnsons' Five Basic Elements

The most important aspect of these elements is individual accountability and having a clear, meaningful task (Goal Positive Interdependence). When you do not have this aspect, you increase the chances of having management problems.

Consideration: There is a lot more to consider in the Johnsons' work than the Five Basic Elements. The other factors to take into account include the role of the teacher prior to, setting up, during, and processing the lesson; the role of competition; individual learning, and so on.

B.Ed. Initiatives to Support Cooperative Learning

In the following pages, we share how the Ontario Institute for Studies in Education (OISE) at the University of Toronto and Brock University are helping student teachers to learn how to create safer, more inclusive learning environments during their practicum. The Concept Map at the beginning of this chapter provides an overview of cooperative learning and where the programs of Brock University and OISE fit into the cooperative learning process.

University of Toronto—Ontario Institute for Studies in Education

The 65 students (who already have a four-year undergraduate degree) in the nine-month Doncrest Option of the Bachelor of Education program (one of 28 B.Ed. options at OISE) spend the first four days of their program getting certified in the Tribes program. The following week, they spend four days applying Johnsons' Five Basic Elements of effective group work. In addition, during those eight days, they experience various cooperative learning small group structures, some of which are found in the work of Spencer Kagan.

Two of the full-time instructors are also Tribes trainers; these two instructors provide the four days of training and ongoing support for the students. Another instructor (one of the authors of this book) has taken Tribes six times over eight years. He takes it each year with the B.Ed. students to more quickly build a relationship with them.

The B.Ed. program runs at Doncrest Elementary School, a kindergarten to Grade 8 school, as part of a university–school district partnership with the York Region District School Board. This school is one of approximately 200 schools involved in a systemic change initiative that focuses on instruction. Two components of the program at Doncrest involve the Johnsons' work on effective group work and Gibbs's work on Tribes.

The Doncrest students do their practicum in classrooms where their associate teachers have had similar training. This ensures student teachers and their associates have a common language. The York Region District School Board now has about 4000 teachers trained in Tribes. That said, not all teachers are implementing Tribes effectively or consistently. As stated previously, we often see classrooms where the overall implementation effort is minimal at best. In these cases, Tribes will not make a difference in the classroom.

The issue of poor implementation is similarly discussed by the Brock B.Ed. students. It must be noted that teachers do not intentionally decide to implement Tribes (or any innovation) ineffectively; it's simply that the classroom is incredibly complex and implementing new ideas is "messy."

Each year we ask our B.Ed. students to inform us about our program in terms of what to keep, what to rethink/rework, and what to remove. Each year, the students identify the Tribes process as key, reporting that it serves to bring them together as a cohort and fosters their support of one another throughout the year.

When we go out to observe our students, we notice how skilled they are at structuring groups and balancing independent work, small group work, and whole class work. The associate teachers typically tell us they learn a lot from our students about how to effectively enact group work. As well, we observe the minimal amount of time our students need to spend on dealing with issues related to classroom management—and that when such issues arise, they are resolved with the simple application of the low-key responses.

Brock University

Over the last six years, Gail Phillips (an assistant professor) has implemented the Tribes process as an integral part of her B.Ed. program. Gail spreads the four days of training over time; the first day takes place before the students' first practicum and the three remaining days happen before their second practicum. Her university students are in the Primary/Junior or Junior Intermediate streams and teach kindergarten to Grade 8 students in their practicum.

In 2010 Gail Phillips completed her Ph.D. on the long-term effects of Tribes from 2005 to 2009 (Phillips, 2011). Ninety-six of the 111 participants responded. Note that 87 percent of her students rated the importance of Tribes as 5 or 6 out of 6. A key reason students rate it high is that school districts now look for Tribes-trained teachers. The following comments from students drive home this point.

> "I took Tribes because I knew it was important within the school board and there was a big push towards it."

> "I took it because I thought it would help me in my future towards getting a job, and it did."

Moreover, feedback from students indicates that Phillips consistently "lives the process" of Tribes with her students.

> "In all honesty, we were doing a great deal of Tribes activities before the real training. You were openly saying that it was Tribes and it helped to create the community that we had."
>
> "We were already living it. You created it in the classroom... That's why our class was so good." (p. 92).

One of the comments that caused Phillips to think about the power of Tribes was that other instructors at Brock University would notice the impact of her approach, and make such remarks as, "Your B.Ed. students are different...they are so respectful..."

A student's comment summarizes their learning.

> I think that Tribes helped us to realize the importance of building a community with our students...that when kids feel safe and comfortable in their learning then they're going to be more open to share their ideas and explore their curiosity. If they don't have that feeling of trust and respect from their peers and know that they're attentively listening, if they don't have that, then they're not going to be willing to open up and learn, and to ask the questions that they want to ask. I think Tribes made us realize that you need to have that foundation before you can even get to the curriculum. (p. 93)

The students also note how the Tribes process helps them design more powerful learning environments.

> Tribes training gave me ideas for grouping students. I like to do group work, especially with my math. You never have that kid without a group. There is always a space for them... The grouping ideas worked really well with my general learning class as well...particularly with four students who were very introverted...now they want to work in groups. (p. 114)

Phillips's research reveals that students are disappointed when assigned to teachers, during their practicum, who fail to effectively and consistently implement Tribes, despite having taken the workshop.

The statement below indicates just how unskilled many educators are at the change process.

> This participant described a situation in which a new administrator made Tribes a major initiative for the school and insisted that all staff complete Tribes training. Those who were resistant or who saw it as a bandwagon were angry that they were being told to participate in the training and frustrated at a process that required them to "go out on a limb and take risks with people with whom they weren't comfortable." (p. 123)

Chapter 8 Conclusion

Creating a safe, respectful, inclusive environment throughout the school is critical. What gets in the way is the balkanization or individualization of school cultures—too many school and district staffs have failed to create learning organizations.

Having one or a few teachers working on creating this more powerful learning environment is better than nothing, but change happens over time. If students learn about Mind Maps or Venn diagrams in Grade 1, then the Grade 2 teachers are now at an advantage. And if the Grade 2 teachers do it, the Grade 3 teachers are at an advantage. We work with schools that do just that; they plan and identify when different innovations will be implemented so that their students get increasingly skilled as they move up through the grade levels. If you know about CBAM—Levels of Use (see Appendix E) then you will understand why this is so critical when it comes to assessing student learning. We would argue that educators who do not think and act on the incremental implementation of innovations are not acting ethically. Effective group work depends on sustained practice.

Clearly, if the idea of incremental implementation of innovations "plays up" within a school system, then the Grade 12 teachers are at an advantage. Unfortunately too many teachers do not want to work smart; they would rather simply work hard…not wise. Teaching is too complex, demanding, and important to *not* work smart.

What connection do you see between Tribes, effective group work, and the job ad below?

Executive Director, Medical Imaging
New collaborations are being forged within the regional health authority to optimize care and service. This multi-site partnership delivers integrated diagnostic programs and services and other specialty imaging procedures.

The role of Executive Director, Medical Imaging, requires proven leadership skills, an innovative mindset, business acumen, and strategic vision. In addition to a graduate degree in a related discipline, you must have 15–20 years experience in progressively senior leadership roles, ideally in complex, multi-site organizations. Proven networking and conflict resolution skills and experience managing complex service delivery systems are required to work with multiple stakeholders, successfully leading the senior management team and overseeing the direction, operations, and assessment of this rapidly evolving, innovative, and collaborative program.

School-Wide Responsibility for Student Behaviour

5 Key Areas of School-Wide Discipline

Faculties of Education
- Do they help or hinder?

New Teachers
- Where do we place them?

Less Effective Teachers
- How do they get this way?

Music and Second-Language Teachers
- How do we support them?

Guest Teachers
- How do we help them?

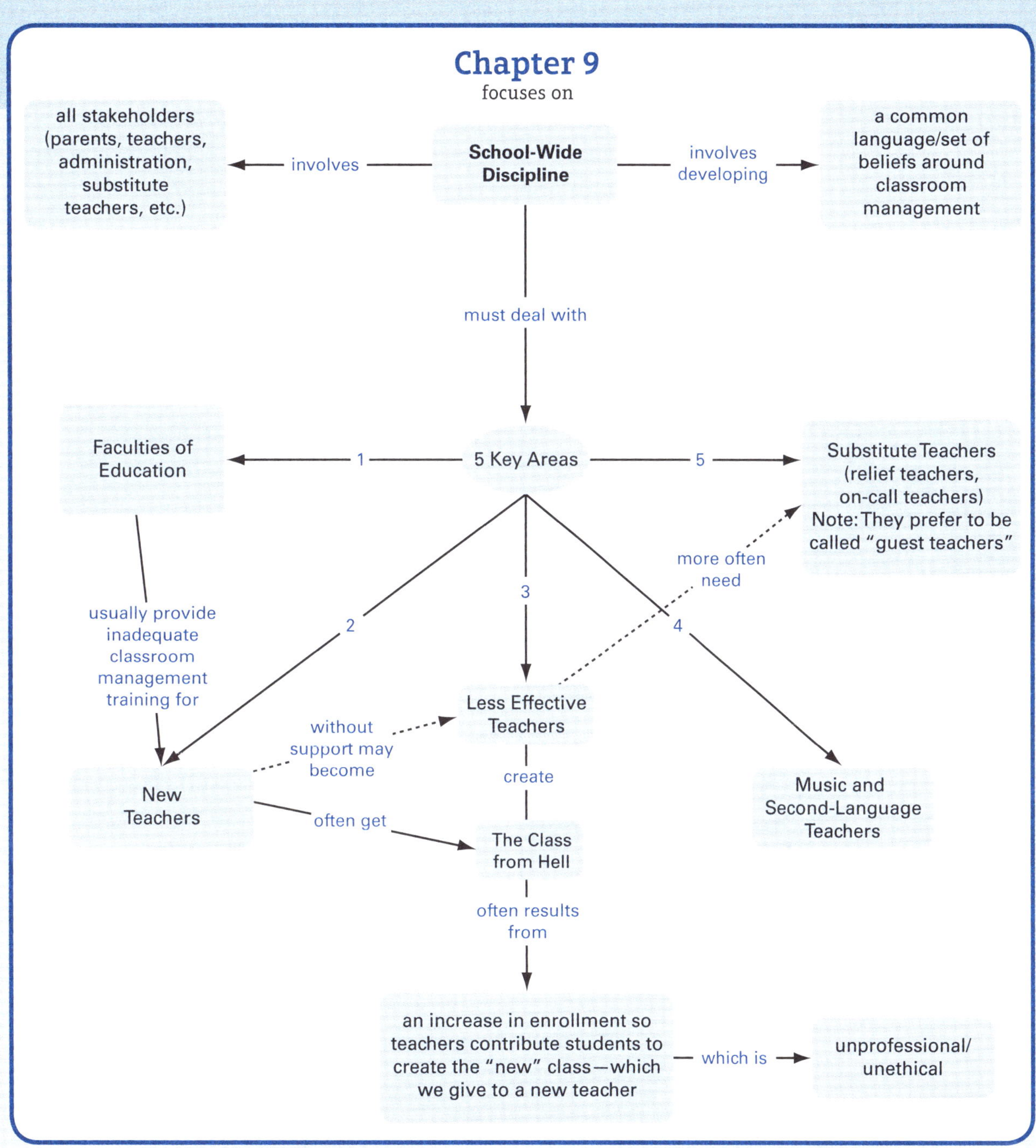
Chapter 9
focuses on
School-Wide Discipline
involves
all stakeholders (parents, teachers, administration, substitute teachers, etc.)
involves developing
a common language/set of beliefs around classroom management
must deal with
5 Key Areas
1
Faculties of Education
usually provide inadequate classroom management training for
New Teachers
2
3
Less Effective Teachers
4
Music and Second-Language Teachers
5
Substitute Teachers (relief teachers, on-call teachers) Note: They prefer to be called "guest teachers"
more often need
without support may become
often get
create
The Class from Hell
often results from
an increase in enrollment so teachers contribute students to create the "new" class—which we give to a new teacher
which is
unprofessional/ unethical

In this chapter, our focus shifts from the classroom to the school staff. We provide two surveys in Appendix F to help you identify how you and fellow staff members think about aspects of classroom management. We look at interconnected issues such as how ignoring the needs of new or less experienced teachers, teachers who struggle, music and second language teachers, and "guest" (substitute) teachers can lead, unwittingly, to the creation of the class "from hell." Finally, we offer suggestions for a school-wide discipline policy that will assist school administrators, teachers, and students to deal with power-related discipline issues immediately and most effectively.

Mrs. Mutner liked to go over a few of her rules on the first day of school.

To begin, most schools have in place some sort of policy to deal with classroom and school discipline problems, particularly to deal with frequent misbehaviours, including arriving late at school; fighting; wearing inappropriate clothing including hats, gang-related garb, or T-shirts with unacceptable advertising; bringing personal technology into classrooms; or having drugs or weapons on school property.

The challenge is to get teachers and administration to agree on what should be done and to be thoughtfully consistent in enacting a policy. The "missing think" is the failure or unwillingness of staff to develop and enact a collective effective response. Rules are not written for students; they are written for teachers. It is important to write them in such a way that they can be implemented and carried out in a consistent way across the variables of time, teachers, and students.

Complete the surveys in Appendix F. Ask yourself if your responses would mirror those of the staff at your school. From our experience, the answer is typically "no."

The Class from Hell—How We Create It...and How We Can Fix It

Spontaneous combustion is a reaction between two or more components that interact. Just like spontaneous combustion, a few factors must interact for the "class from hell" to first emerge, and then become a school-wide pain in the neck. The igniter of the combustion is usually the collective fault of staff. To understand such a class we must look first outside the school before shifting back to explore issues regarding new or inexperienced teachers, less effective teachers, and "guest" teachers.

1. Faculties of Education Provide Inadequate Training in Classroom Management

One of the authors of this text (Barrie) is a university instructor and has dealt with this issue for more than 25 years. The other author (Peter) has been sought out for his expertise on classroom management for 30 years by professors of B.Ed. programs. Peter was also responsible for designing and implementing a state-wide classroom management program in Western Australia over a six-year period.

The authors found that most university students don't have ongoing courses in classroom management as they move through their practicums. Student teachers get hired and placed in classrooms without having developed knowledge in this area. This concern is discussed in Duke's (1984, pp. 77–91) book *Teaching: The Imperiled Profession*. He presents research related to the question "How helpful is higher education?"

We have heard such comments from professors as, "Well, if you can teach you won't have classroom management problems" or "Doing classroom management before you actually start teaching is of little value." As authors, we have a combined experience of 75 years of teaching. We work with Faculties of Education and with school districts in a variety of countries, we work extensively with teachers who are at risk of losing their teaching positions, and as a result we can confirm that such thinking is flat-out wrong. Feedback from university students over the last 25 years confirms that classroom management coursework is extremely helpful during their practicum.

Solution: Faculties of Education must take more responsibility for equipping B.Ed. students with the skills to facilitate appropriate student behaviour, prevent misbehaviour, and respond to students who choose to misbehave. The Faculties must also have closer relationships with the school districts in which they place their students. University instructors need to dedicate more time to supervising their students during their placements. District staff need to make these demands to Faculties of Education and hold them responsible for providing those key skills!

For example, the 65 B.Ed. students in the Doncrest Option at OISE have a classroom management course prior to and after their practicum. They also have extensive learning in how to create more inclusive, safe classrooms; they are all certified in the four-day Tribes training in their first week of the B.Ed. program. When placed in their practicum, associate teachers are selected and matched to students. The associates have usually had similar training. As stated earlier, over 4000 teachers in the York Region District School Board are also Tribes trained. As well, the lesson planning process taught in their university classes parallels the district's lesson planning process. The practicum students and associate teachers have a common language.

2. Whom Do the Newest, Least Experienced Teachers Typically Teach?

The answer: The toughest class in the school, of course. What other profession puts their newest or least-experienced employees in the most difficult situations—law, medicine?

Research confirms that first-year teachers often get placed in the worst schools and get the worst class to teach and the worst classroom in which to teach. One of the first studies on this subject, conducted by Susan Rosenholtz (1985, 1989), found that 20 to 30 percent of the teachers she tracked did not return the second year; by the fifth year, another 20 to 30 percent had left. When she interviewed these teachers as to why they left, they gave three reasons:

1. No sense of efficacy about how to teach and motivate students.
2. Classroom management concerns.
3. Being alone in the school; no one to talk to.

Having staff and school administration work on a plan to help newer teachers will increase the chances that an inexperienced teacher doesn't end up with a classroom that is difficult to manage—a "class from hell."

Rosenholtz's (1989) book, *Teachers' Workplace,* shows what teachers, principals, and district administrators do in "stuck" (learning impoverished) schools compared to teachers, principals, and district administrators in "moving" (learning enriched) schools and school districts. (See Appendix H for a rubric on her work.)

Solution: Have a school policy, developed by staff, on integrating new teachers into your school. It is essential to set up safeguards against such occurrences as the following:

> A teacher in Australia won a position in a new school; he was considered highly effective in his previous school. Upon arriving in the new school, he was marginalized by staff, given the worst class, room, and assignments. It took him almost two years to get back to where he was in the previous school.

The author, who worked with this teacher as part of a project, discovered that staff had collectively set out to sabotage him because he was awarded the position over another teacher at the school.

Thankfully, we know of many highly effective principals who work diligently to support new and less experienced teachers. Those principals and their staff do everything possible to make sure less experienced teachers become successful. For example, the Halton Board of Education had one of the most powerful mentoring programs we've found. New teachers were assigned an experienced mentor who volunteered to be their support. The new teacher and mentor met at regularly scheduled times throughout the year, attended workshops together, and so on. This program was run by Gail Phillips, who went on to complete her Ph.D. in creating safe, inclusive learning environments (see Chapter 8). Partners in the Classroom, the new teacher mentor program in Halton, continued until it was replaced by the Ontario Ministry of Education's New Teacher Induction Program (NTIP). The Halton program was the first of its kind in Ontario and the ministry looked at the model when designing the NTIP program.

The Following Three Common Scenarios Increase the Chances of Creating a Class That Is Difficult to Control

a. Experienced teachers know a class from hell is coming their way.

Knowing a difficult class is coming, experienced teachers transfer to another grade or school to avoid this class—and of course, the new teacher gets this class. Because these students are already on a roll, they can really build up steam with the new teacher.

Solutions: If you are effective and your students respect you, and a difficult class is coming your way, then sit down with the current teacher and work together to begin putting in place expectations for these students during the year before they get to you. For example, support one or two students in your room. If they are misbehaving, one or two students can come and spend an hour, a half-day, or even a day or two with you in your class. This gives the struggling teacher a break.

Another solution is to have struggling students who will likely be in your classroom next year visit your current classroom. They will get a sense of what to expect. As well, older grade students can reassure visiting students that they will be supported in your class. By beginning to build relationships and establishing expectations and norms with coming students, students who attend your class the next year will be grounded in your approach to students and student learning.

b. Colleagues believe that new teachers must "pay their dues."

You have been teaching for a number of years, and you too had to teach the worst class when you started out, so you and other teachers on staff believe new teachers have to pay their dues. No one makes the move to change this norm. This new teacher is isolated and no one seems to care.

Solution: You have to change this norm. This is not how an effective professional person or organization thinks or acts, and new teachers need help to be successful. Where new, inexperienced teachers can't be placed in any other class, the staff should do everything possible to help them be successful with the class they get. Their class size should be reduced; they should be provided with in-class support and appropriate professional development. If a student misbehaves, that student should be sent to spend time in another teacher's class. Rarely will this action apply to more than three to four students in a class.

c. You have too many Grade 4 students, for example, and you have to create a new class.

A new teacher (often a first-year teacher) is hired to teach this newly created class. The other Grade 4 teachers each place students in the new class. They may not move in the most difficult students, but they do place the next level down, so now there's a class just ready for spontaneous combustion with the new teacher. Do you see how this practice creates a class that ends up out of control?

Solution: You have a professional obligation as school administrators and teachers to make sure this does not happen. If the teacher is new, or inexperienced, the class size should be reduced and the vast majority of students placed in this class should be respectful. It would be wise to bring in a supply teacher (guest teacher) and allow the original teacher to spend some time in the new class to help ensure a smooth transition for the new teacher. Students also do not like getting a new teacher a week into the school year. It is wise to involve the students in a discussion about why a new class is being created and solicit their thoughts and reactions.

Two Vignettes Involving First-Year Teachers

When one of the authors, Barrie, was in his second year of teaching, the school district he worked for in Edmonton, Alberta, block hired teachers. One teacher placed in his school was trained to be a French teacher; however, because all French positions were taken, she was assigned to teach science to students in Grades 7, 8, and 9. This teacher truly struggled; the students liked her but took advantage of her. She suffered a great deal of stress, so much that she developed a skin condition. She was a kind, first-year teacher who did not understand the content she had to teach—in a word, she was "muggable." The next year, she transferred to a different school, to teach French. When the author met her at a workshop that next year, she was really enjoying her teaching.

In another school district in Toronto, the author was asked, in mid-October, to support a first-year teacher—the *third* first-year teacher to work with this Grade 4 class. The author first went and observed her teaching. The next day, he taught the students for half a day himself to get a feel for the class. He had to work hard to get through the morning. When he asked the teacher how many students she would like to have removed from the class to allow her to teach, she took about 20 seconds and said, "Four." The author identified five.

The principal was brought in for a discussion about this class. This was a newly created Grade 4 class, put together because of an increase in enrollment. Each teacher contributed a few students to create this new class. To the school staff's credit, they did not put the most difficult students in this class; however, they did place the next level down. When I asked the principal if any teacher in the school would want to teach this class, she said "no." So the school had placed three new teachers, who were not familiar with the curriculum, to teach a group of students that experienced teachers on staff did not want to teach.

To solve the problem, we placed an inner-city consultant in the struggling teacher's class for a week to team-teach. The teacher was also given a two-day workshop on classroom management, which the consultant had taken. (The workshop was based on the ideas in this book.) We recruited three teachers in higher grades to take one or two students from her class when the teacher needed help. The students would stay for the day, or part of that day, to a maximum of three days. The consultant also worked with this teacher on Monday, Wednesday, and Friday after the workshop. On Tuesday and Thursday of the following week she dropped by periodically to see how it was going. The author saw that first-year teacher a few years later in a workshop he was giving, and she was still at that school and very much enjoying teaching.

The key issue in both of these situations is that these were school staff problems and the school staff had to rally around these first-year teachers—one did, one did not.

Districts should be held liable in a court of law for placing new teachers (without support) in situations that experienced teachers would struggle with. We find it difficult to believe that most districts and teacher unions have not created or pushed for a more responsible policy for the placement of new teachers.

3. The Teacher Is Not Effective

The teacher has no sense of humour and minimal enthusiasm, does not build a safe, inclusive environment, has a limited instructional repertoire, does not structure groups or frame questions effectively, and gives lessons that consistently lack meaning and interest for students. Students and parents complain, but the school administration, school district, and teacher's union do not work together constructively to

assist this teacher to improve or resign. These teachers have very low "mean scores."

Solution: This teacher needs a massive amount of support to change. One option is to bring in an experienced teacher to work with this struggling teacher, first full-time for several weeks, then three days a week for several weeks, then two days a week, and finally one day a week for two weeks. (This means the assisting teacher will need relief from a guest teacher.) If less-effective teachers decide not to accept this support, they should know that the union will be contacted about their decision and documentation will be started to have them improve or be removed.

The students who consistently misbehave (there will usually be three to five students) should be placed in an effective teacher's classroom (maximum one to two per class). Principals who lack the will, or the skills, to support struggling teachers should either reconsider their position, acquire the skills, or resign. Do you think districts that do not have a process to resolve these situations, or that lack the will to provide professional development or other solutions, should be open to lawsuits? Students are too important to be placed in the hands of "educators" who refuse to work at assisting struggling teachers to improve. If less competent teachers don't improve, they need to be removed or at least reassigned to duties outside the classroom. There are some excellent models for districts to consider and follow: Edmonton Public Schools, in Edmonton, Alberta, has a very effective process to support less effective teachers, a process worked out with the Alberta Teachers' Association.

A Vignette

One principal in a large Ontario school district asked to be placed at a more complex school. She was placed in a school where no principal had lasted more than a year in the previous 10 years. The staff was collectively dysfunctional, with a staff union representative who created wedges in any administrative effort to improve the school.

The previous principal left partway through the year and took early retirement. Five years later, the school had an emerging drama program organized by the union representative, a teacher who earlier had been documented for a dismissal. This teacher had asked to be transferred at the end of his first year; the principal told him that unfortunately, there was nothing she could write that would encourage anyone to hire him, that he was stuck with her and she with him. He would either improve or documentation would continue. When the principal was transferred five years later, this teacher gave her a hug, and said, "You made me a good teacher." He had become a teacher students liked, and was coaching students and putting on plays. Parents stopped phoning to complain. What did the principal do?

She did what educational change expert Michael Fullan said: "Don't waste time watering the rocks; over time rocks will move." She started with a few teachers whom she supported to become trained in Jeanne Gibbs's Tribes program, which is designed to create more respectful supportive environments. Within three years, all the staff took Tribes training.

This principal always ate lunch with the teachers—not in her office. She visited classrooms constantly to see if teachers needed anything; if they were agitated, she sent them to the staff room to take a break while she took over the class. If teachers were sick she sent them home and told them to take care of themselves. She modelled again and again that she cared. She washed all the washcloths and tea towels, she brought in cakes, she cleaned out old rooms that were dirty and dysfunctional, she encouraged the custodian to put more effort into cleaning the school—merging kindness with assertiveness. She washed the sport jerseys, folded them, and brought them back to school. She wore the staff down with repeated random acts of kindness. She did not tell teachers they were ineffective or that they needed to learn how to structure groups. She went to where they were and worked *with* them. This principal was highly skilled interpersonally—she modelled with teachers what the teachers needed to model with their students. She had the "will" and the "skill," even though the school district was ineffective at dealing with struggling teachers.

Her office was a place to which students (K to 8) wanted to come; they came in and read, lay on the couch if they were sick, came to eat if they felt lonely. The office was the students' room; teachers could send students down and the principal would let them sit and read or think until they were ready to chat about what was going on and to build a plan on how to get back into their class. Often they would just say, "I am okay now." And off they would go; nothing had to be said.

When early in the first year the school union representative came into her office shouting because she failed to recognize that taking his students from the class to the library constitutes supervision time (which it doesn't), she listened. When he finished ranting, she simply said, with tears in her eyes, "If you were trying to hurt my heart, you just did a really good job. Now you have to leave, and you can never come back into my office unless you can talk to me with the respect with which I am talking to you now." He left. That day, he had forgotten his lunch. The principal was in the staff room and offered him half of her sandwich. He accepted it. It was all about caring for students and teachers; making them believe that what they were doing was important. She stated that this teacher continues to stay in touch with her.

4. You Unwittingly Treat Music and Second-Language Teachers as If They Are Second-Class Citizens

In some schools, music and second-language teachers (for example, teachers of core French) are treated as if they are only there so that other teachers can get their spares. Music and core French are very complex subjects to teach, especially when it comes to classroom management. For example, every time there's an announcement, it's extremely difficult for music teachers to get the class refocused. We often see music classes that are 30 minutes long—that is as close to absurd as one can get. When students are learning core French, the teacher cannot employ some of the most powerful and complex instructional methods because the students' language skills don't allow the application of those methods.

In K to 8 programs, music and core French teachers also do not have as much time to build relationships with students as easily as a teacher that has the students all year (especially in elementary schools). Thirty students enter the room, and in 45 minutes or less they are replaced by another 30 students.

Solution: The staff and administration have to let the students in the school know that music and learning a second language such as French are important subjects in the school. Make sure some of the announcements are done in French—even if the school is not a French immersion school. Make sure all signs are in the languages that are offered. Have students perform the national anthem in different languages, record them, and play the recording over the PA system; play a different group or individual each week. Each class can take responsibility during the year.

You can't simply pay "lip service" to music and French. During the first two weeks, classroom teachers could give up their spare to go into the French and music classrooms and support those teachers. The principal and assistant principal should pop into the classes during the first month to let students know that music and French are important subjects in this school, and make sure students are behaving. During the third week, the teacher can simply pop in to ask if everything is okay—if there are misbehaving students, they need to be pulled out and asked to explain their choice to be disrespectful and to come up with a plan to resolve it. If the students don't resolve it, a consequence kicks in, such as having recess or lunch at different times or in different places than others in the school until they can come up with a plan to resolve the issues. Of course, a decision to change a student's recess or lunchtime must be discussed with parents. If this does not work after about three days, we suggest the student returns to a regular schedule and parents be involved in a discussion of a more formal plan of action.

5. Teachers Are Away and You Bring in a "Guest Teacher"

Teachers miss on average seven to 10 days a year. This is the problem: You bring in a supply, substitute, or on-call teacher—they prefer to be known as "guest teachers." But none of the teachers are taught how to treat a guest teacher. (See Appendix G for a sample lesson.) The research as far back as Conners (1927) and as recently as Cardon, Tippetts, and Smith (2003) reports on guest teachers' most common problems. These are listed in order below:

1. Can't interpret the lesson
2. Can't find things that are supposed to be there
3. Classroom management problems
4. Being treated like a second-class citizen by the staff in the school
5. Being called too late so when they get there the students are already disorderly

Our follow-up study with 300 guest teachers (in Edmonton Public Schools in Alberta) 50 years later found that guest teachers had the same five concerns, in the same order, as 1927.

Solution: This situation involves two approaches. The first is working professionally with the guest teachers; the second involves working with the staff in the school. Cardon (2002) quotes Conners's (1927, p. 79) recommendation that "A definite effort should be made to counteract the unfavourable opinion of the work of the substitute where such situation obtains. A judicious 'pointing out' of the necessity and value of such service should be made to the entire teaching staff. The enlistment of their efforts may well include provision for changing the viewpoint of pupils in similar fashion."

First Approach: Working with the Guest Teachers

In order to interpret the lesson, guest teachers need to have a similar language of teaching to that of the teachers they are supporting. The York Region District School Board has a common lesson planning process that can be easily adapted to any approach to teaching, and facilitates multiple instructional methods for differentiated instruction. This planning process is supported in Hattie's (2012) synthesis on the effects of instructional practices. In addition, this process is easily applied if the classroom teacher did not have time to leave a plan. (Some schools have teachers leave a three-day enrichment plan in case of an emergency.) If the district provides information, support, and workshops for guest teachers, those teachers will have a clear understanding of the processes used by the teachers they are replacing.

In the Thames Valley District School Board, professional development is provided for guest teachers on instructional and classroom management methods used by teachers in the district. This makes it easier for guest teachers to interpret the lessons left by classroom teachers. One of the authors has worked in both these districts to assist in developing this process.

To develop a common language, all districts should provide classroom management workshops for their guest teachers that parallel workshops provided to their full-time teachers.

The most sophisticated approach was applied in a district that, as a first step, identified the least number of supply teachers needed on any given day. Next, they invited their best teachers to become supply teacher consultants who would do enrichment and programming for teachers when they were away. The classroom teachers did not have to leave lesson plans; these supply teacher consultants knew the curriculum and went in and did enrichment lessons with students. The payoff was threefold. First, the students enjoyed having highly effective, engaging teachers. Second, classroom teachers knew that the guest teacher coming in was highly skilled, so this placed more responsibility on them to be prepared. Third, these consulting guest teachers were able to work around the district, see most schools, and become one of the pools for selection to administrative positions.

Second Approach: Working with Staff in the School

This approach shifts depending on whether it is an elementary, middle school, or secondary school. In K to 8 grades, some staffs take the time to teach a lesson on how to deal with guests in their classroom (which includes guest teachers). This lesson is taught the first week of the school year in all classrooms. This practice sets up expectations for the students, teachers, and school administration. (See Appendix G for a sample lesson.)

In the lesson, students are taught about their responsibility with a guest teacher. For example, they are to give the guest teacher a name tag. The name tags are premade and titled "Guest in Our School." A student is assigned to the guest teacher as a runner to get anything the teacher needs, such as photocopying, a book, or the principal. Students take turns being the runner during the year. When teachers go down the hall and see the Guest in Our School name tag, they take the time when appropriate to say hello and to welcome the guest teacher.

Some schools set their staff up in teams of four or five, so that if one of them is away, the other three or four make sure guest teachers get to the classroom and have everything they need. One teacher undertakes to pop in during the morning, and another in the afternoon, to ensure everything is fine. The administration also looks in once in the morning and once in the afternoon to check if the guest teacher has any needs. One teacher makes sure the guest teacher finds the lunchroom and is introduced to others. As well, in the staff room there is a board titled "Guest in Our School Today" with that teacher's name.

Having a simplified system for guest teachers is also a wise idea. For example, a simple handout that quickly informs the guest teacher of suggested Bump 1 skills and how to deal with an escalation is useful. Once the guest teacher has asked a student three times, over a reasonable amount of time, to stop an action, yet the student continues, that student is given a choice to behave appropriately, or to go to the office for the rest of the morning or afternoon. A student who is sent to the office twice in a day should be given an in-school suspension. The school administration should ask the student's parents to come to school to discuss and develop a plan for the student to get back into the classroom (if the guest teacher is to be there the next day). The principal should send a letter to parents at the beginning of the school year alerting them to this process. If parents are not supportive, however, contacting them may be unwise. In this case, treat the situation as an in-school suspension where the student is expected to develop a plan to get back into class. (See Appendix B for a sample form.)

Discipline Policies: Factors to Consider

This last section pulls together a few key factors to consider when establishing and enacting a discipline policy. These do not represent a panacea, but these elements increase the chances of your policy's success.

The first suggestion is to concentrate on what you can do to encourage appropriate behaviour—to prevent students from misbehaving. If you don't work at encouraging appropriate behaviour, your discipline policy will be an inert policy. Your policy is nested in what the staff collectively enact in the classroom. The higher the mean score of your staff (see Chapter 6, page 134), the greater the chances you can enact the policy. The larger the school, the more difficult this becomes.

Some of these ideas have already been presented. When teachers teach effectively and create safer, more inclusive environments, students are less likely to misbehave. And when they do, the situation is easier to resolve and students do not end up at the office.

Prevention—Easier

1. As a staff, focus on framing questions effectively so that students feel safer and are involved (see Chapter 7).
2. Introduce a program such as Mary Gordon's Roots of Empathy to encourage students to think beyond themselves; we have seen this also work in secondary schools.

The Roots of Empathy program was created in 1996 by Mary Gordon (a child advocate). It was first implemented in Toronto, Ontario. Gordon's rationale for creating the program was to create a kinder more empathetic society through working with kindergarten to Grade 8 students. (Note: It has also been implemented with older students.) Interestingly, one of the key impacts has been on the effect the program has on reducing bullying in schools. The key part of the program is the "teacher" who is an infant between the ages of 2 and 4 months. The infant is brought in by the mother and a trained Roots of Empathy facilitator. The "team" of infant, mother, and facilitator attend the class approximately nine times over the year. This provides the elementary students the opportunity to see the baby learn/evolve/interact with the mother. They also have the opportunity to interact with the mother and the infant.

In one secondary school in the Western Quebec School Board, the music teacher had the infant, mother, and facilitator team in the class and after the bell went and the students left, she saw one student, who was a troubled Grade 11 youth, holding and rocking the baby... only after all the other students had left the room. He came up to the teacher and asked: "Do you think that someone like me could be a good father some day?"

Roots of Empathy

Currently, over 2000 classrooms in different countries are involved with this program.

Prevention—More Complex

1. As a staff, focus on involving students (when appropriate) in group work. Keep group size small (two to four students). Take time to have students learn appropriate social, communication, and critical thinking skills. The more complex programs, such as those of the Johnsons and Tribes, are each four-day programs. For more information on cooperative learning, see Chapter 8.

2. To learn about effective group work, consider involving the staff in a program like Tribes. A number of schools in which we work have done so, and when the program is implemented effectively it results in a reduction of bullying, other student misbehaviours, and office visits. But remember, staff development is not the workshop, it is *what you do as a staff* after or between workshops. You don't become a great violinist simply because of lessons; the practice between lessons is what makes the difference.

   We have observed many teachers who take Tribes but do little implementation upon returning to their classrooms other than putting up Tribes posters and periodically reminding students of the Tribes agreements. Note that Tribes now has books for elementary, middle, and secondary school staffs. Make sure the workshop facilitator is experienced in your grade levels and has used the program with those grade levels.

3. Pay attention to Harry Potter—set up your school so that students feel they belong by having "houses." Students can get involved in chess tournaments between houses, intramural sports between houses, community projects run within and between houses. When one of the authors was in Mount Baker High School, in Cranbrook, British Columbia, every student and teacher was in the Alpha, Beta, Gamma, or Delta houses. We had cooperative competitions, did social work in the community, and more. We all felt we belonged.

4. Shift your program toward project-based or problem-based learning—make learning meaningful, interesting, and worth doing. Ask yourself, would you want to be a student in your classroom? Many different types of faculties at universities, including those of medicine, physics, and business, are moving away from the lecture format exclusively to teaching via group work that tackles real life problems and issues. Where programs do not promote relevance, variety, novelty, and student interest, students are more likely to rebel. And who can blame them? Most of us would rebel too.

Responding—Easier

1. Develop a common language and way of responding to students when they choose to misbehave. Look at the ideas in this book—Bumps 1 to 6.

2. Develop a handbook that provides a brief overview of the bumps for guest teachers or new teachers who have not had a chance to attend a workshop on classroom management.

Responding—More Complex

1. Develop strategies for the effective implementation of processes related to in-school suspensions, out-of-school suspensions, and expulsions. These responses are Bumps 8, 9, and 10, as discussed in our earlier book, *Classroom Management: A Thinking and Caring Approach* (1990). We don't explore these bumps in this book as the focus is on in-classroom responses to inappropriate behaviour.

2. Look into programs such as restorative justice designed for schools to respond to the more severe types of misbehaviour.

Interestingly, restorative justice processes or restorative practices predate Christ by about 2000 years. Both historically and currently, elements of this process are found in the First Nations cultures of North America. In England, the Laws of Ethelbert of Kent (c. 600 CE) included restitution schedules. The process is very logical—get the victim and the offender together, have a chat, take some responsibility for what happened, and restore a sense of balance between those two and the community. You can see how this process connects to what might happen in Bump 6 (The Informal Chat) and Bump 7 (The Formal Contract), and Bumps 8 and 9 (In-School and Out-of-School Suspensions).

From the perspective of today's school culture, restorative practices have been applied in schools since the early 1990s. Wrongdoing is seen as something that happens to an individual within a community. The restorative practice is enacted when a behaviour is harming others, or the property of others, to restore a sense of balance in the community. The process is designed to encourage a dialogue between the victim and offender. Australia was one of the first places to apply it in a large secondary school setting.

The rationale for attending to restorative practice is to create and maintain a supportive community where students feel a sense of safety and belonging. The basic need to belong of all humans was central to Alfred Adler's and Rudolf Dreikurs's work in the early to mid-1900s. They argued that if we cannot find ways to belong in a positive way, we will belong in a negative way—but we *will* find a way to belong. From an academic achievement perspective, social exclusion reduces intelligent thought (Baumeister, Twenge, & Nuss, 2002).

Currently, the process of restorative practices is one of the most well thought out ways for a school staff to deal with bullying in the school. An example of how this plays out in schools is illustrated in Belinda Hopkins's book, *Just Schools* (2004).

We would argue that a school staff who are enacting the Tribes process in their school are much better positioned to engage in the process of restorative practices. Tribes, like restorative justice, is a whole-school approach to creating a safer, more inclusive community, and it has a process for resolving conflict through dialogue. Restorative practices would simply extend the potential of Tribes to confront and resolve conflict.

Chapter 9 Conclusion

This chapter looked outside the classroom at the staff's responsibility in dealing with more complex issues such as teachers at risk, with new teachers, and with guest teachers. It also illustrated how we unwittingly create the "class from hell." To that end, university B.Ed. programs are too often also complicit in creating classroom management problems by not providing effective course work related to preventing and responding to students who choose to behave inappropriately.

As David and Roger Johnson argue in their approach to establish effective group work, we need to have students understand that they "sink or swim" together—this collaborative expectation for students most certainly applies to the staff in schools.

Teaching is incredibly complex, too complex for any one teacher to do on her own. Teachers need support. As stated earlier, every day 25 to 30 students enter the classroom with variables over which we have no control. These variables include different learning styles, intelligences, genders, lived experiences, race, and culture. Some students are experiencing a parental divorce; a few will experience their second or third parental divorce in a K to 12 experience. Research shows that one in six students in Canada lives in an at-risk environment. Some students will have learning challenges—some will have those challenges, and be gifted as well. And don't forget, some teachers also grew up with challenging variables, in at-risk environments.

CHAPTER 10

Research into the Thinking and Actions of Effective Teachers: A Historical Perspective

> *Almost any subject is studied with much more interest and intelligence by those who know something of its subject matter than by those who do not; and, conversely, that it is not profitable to study theory without some practical experience of the facts to which it relates.*
>
> **Sir Richard Winn Livingstone, *The Future in Education* (1944)**

A story is told about a university professor who had not been in a classroom for several decades. He was asked to visit a school to observe teachers teach. The professor went from class to class, taking notes, and at the end of the day met with the teachers he had observed. His opening remark, having cleared his throat, was thus: "This was a very interesting day. But I have a concern: my concern is that although what I observed is well and good in practice...will it work in theory?"

In this section, we briefly focus on several educators—some historical, some in practice—who have studied the subject of how teachers "manage" a class. Their work provides a snapshot of what effective teachers have done to encourage appropriate behaviour (and prevent inappropriate behaviour), and how they respond to students who choose to misbehave. A great deal of the research that remains relevant today has been conducted in the past 30 years. There are two excellent examples of this. One is Robert Marzano's 2003 text, *Classroom Management That Works: Researched-Based Strategies for Every Teacher.* In this text, Marzano summarizes 101 research studies related to classroom management. The other is John Hattie's (2012) *Visible Learning for Teachers: Maximizing Impact on Learning.* In this

text, Hattie's focus is on those instructional practices that most powerfully affect student learning.

As authors, we have studied and taken courses in many programs related to behaviour modification, assertive discipline, cooperative discipline, and so on. Although we understand and appreciate the works of theorists such as Alfred Adler, Rudolf Dreikurs, Carl Rogers, and Albert Ellis, as examples, we recognize that no one best approach exists. Clearly, we have to differentiate our classroom management efforts, just as we differentiate our instruction and assessment practices.

Interestingly, educators had acknowledged the concept of differentiation more than 100 years ago. Frederick Bolton, a director of the School of Education at the University of Iowa, included a chapter "Individual Variations and Differences" in his text *Principles of Education*, published in 1910. As you read Bolton's words, consider their similarity to Howard Gardner's work on multiple intelligences, formed some 70 years later.

> There are innumerable variations which are not so apparent and hence thought not to exist. Some persons burst forth into song with the most meager training, while others, with the best masters, could never carry a tune or discover discord; some are ready spellers, while many other are hopeless; some are born mathematicians, while others never can progress beyond the merest rudiments. One child exhibits mechanical genius, devising appliance for every sort of work, while another can never learn to put together the simplest contrivance;... one person picks up the pen and without training begins to produce literature, while another cannot chronicle accurately even the simplest event; one mounts the platform and charms the multitudes with his eloquence, while another is made mute in the presence of an audience. (p. 303)

In this book, we examine classroom management primarily through the lens of a humanist approach, rather than that of a behaviourist approach, because we believe that every student needs to feel a sense of belonging, and each student has an innate desire to be successful. A behaviourist approach at its simplest level considers behaviour as a direct response to a stimulus. As a consequence, its focus is on conditioning to ensure a predicted response to a problem. We are not convinced that such a singular focus can answer the complex needs of classrooms.

George Sugai

That said, in our work, we have employed behaviour modification with severely behaviourally challenged students and with teachers who struggled to improve their own behaviour. For insights into a thoughtful approach to a more positivist or behaviourist approach toward classroom management, we encourage you to research the work of George Sugai (2009), whose work has focused on effective applications of the principles of applied behaviour analysis and school-wide positive behaviour supports.

Historical Reflection on Teacher Thinking and Actions Related to Student Behaviour

One of the early texts on classroom management we discovered was by Ontario educators W.D.E. Matthews and M.W. Chalmers, titled *School and Classroom Management* (1959). Considering the date of publication, it is interesting to note that the authors already classified student behaviour based on the type of misbehaviour, dealt with the effects of the intersection of teacher and home on student behaviour, and emphasized the importance of relaxation and play: "Working at desks or tables is not natural for growing bodies" (p. 107). Their suggestions included the following:

- Do not preach, argue, nag, coax or complain—take some positive action.
- Avoid emotion in dealing with misbehaviour.
- Shun partiality in any form.
- Allow students some freedom of choice.
- Help students to analyze and think through their own situations.
- Provide interesting and appropriate work.
- Be cheerful and enthusiastic—nothing is more contagious.

One of the earliest multi-authored texts focusing on classroom management appears to be that edited by Daniel L. Duke in 1979 (reissued in 1982) titled, simply enough, *Classroom Management*. It includes 13 chapters by 20 experts in the field of classroom management.

In 1847, David P. Page wrote a book titled *Theory and Practice of Teaching: or, The Motives and Methods of Good School-Keeping*. In

the text, Page argues that "order" is the first essential for classroom happiness and success. He also argues that the best way to secure that happiness and success is through the teacher's personality. He also shares what most effective teachers quickly learn…that planning is critical. When students are "idle" and "unsure" of what to do, classroom management problems will emerge. Today, teacher personality, as well as the need to be organized and to have students actively engaged, are still considered key factors for maintaining an effective classroom.

Joseph Baldwin, in 1897, differentiated between teaching and the tactics of classroom management. He posited that teachers must demonstrate "variety in teaching but uniformity in tactics" (p. 151), arguing that we need to differentiate between situations that require judgment and creativity from those that do not require thoughtful action. He also argued that routines allow us to spend more time reasoning and being creative. Clearly, we see the connection between how we instruct—having a variety of instructional methods—and the need to establish routines. Tangentially, in 1917, Harry Eastman Bennett, in *School Efficiency: A Manual of Modern School Management*, stated, "If perfunctory matters are not reduced to routine, matters which require judgment will inevitably become perfunctory" (p. 207).

Page, Baldwin, and Bennett detailed the necessity of routines and a sense of order in the classroom. We also see in their works the emergence of the need to have a more extensive instructional repertoire and a growing focus on reasoning and creativity. In his 1901 book *Dickens as an Educator*, James L. Hughes examines comments made by Charles Dickens regarding the treatment of children and their education in the mid-1800s. Dickens studied with Friedrich Froebel, originator of the concept of kindergarten and indeed, Froebel's work was popularized by Dickens. It is fascinating how Dickens's ideas remain essential to our thinking today. Of Dickens's work, Hughes wrote:

"Dickens taught that loving sympathy is the highest qualification of a true teacher" (p. 4). "I remember very distinctly the visits made by Mr. Dickens to Madame Ronge's kindergarten. He always appeared to be deeply interested, and would sometimes stay during the whole session" (p. 9). He wrote about "the recognition of freedom as the truest process and highest aim of education...the importance of self activity...the need of child study, the effect of joyousness on the child's development, the benefits of play, the influence of nutrition, the idea of the community, the importance of imagination as a basis for intellectual growth...." He argued against "the sacrifice of power and life due to cramming, and the weakness of all educational systems and methods that regard fact-storing as the highest work of the teacher." (p. 11) Hughes quotes Dickens:

> When I was at school, one of seventy boys, I wonder by what secret understanding our attention began to wander...I wonder by what ingenuity we brought on that confused state of mind when sense became nonsense, when figures wouldn't work, when dead languages wouldn't construe, when live languages wouldn't be spoken, when memory wouldn't come, when dullness and vacancy wouldn't go. I cannot remember that we conspired to be sleepy after dinner, or that we ever particularly wanted to be stupid. (p. 10)

Hughes summarizes Dickens's criticism of corporal punishment:

> Corporal punishment, like all forms of coercion, robs the child of joyousness, and joyousness is one of the most essential elements in the true growth of a child... If in any school only one teacher relies on the rod as a stimulator to work and a restrainer of evil, her class is sure to be the most disorderly, the least co-operative, and the most defective in the original power of the school. (p. 83)

In 1897 John Millar, then deputy minister of education for the province of Ontario, wrote a book entitled *School Management and the Principles and Practice of Teaching*. The following 10 statements are from his book. Should they apply today?

1. If the pupil is continually directed, he fails to acquire the power of independent individual effort. As he advances, periods of effort entirely independent of supervision should be permitted. The centre of control should be gradually transferred from the teacher to each of his pupils. (p. 104)

2. In a school that is characterized by good discipline there is a high moral tone. The discipline is unobtrusive. It is kind. Love is supreme. Fear is not a controlling force. Justice reigns. Anger, vacillation, carelessness, and unreasonable demands are unknown. Courtesy, and self-control are shown by the teacher and the pupils catch his spirit.... (pp. 104–105)

3. Attractive surroundings help to make children love school, and lessen the task of securing attention. (p. 108)

4. The ends of discipline are no more secured when obedience results from intimidation, than from bribing or coaxing. (p. 104)
5. It requires the teacher's qualifications to train pupils to govern themselves. (p. 103)
6. The co-operation of the principal is essential to efficient control. (p. 106).
7. Harmony among teachers must be preserved in a school that has two or more teachers. A divided house cannot stand. Good discipline requires unity of action. (p. 107)
8. A troublesome boy may be managed if placed near those that are industrious. (p. 109)
9. Much of the restlessness of children is due to the need of bodily activity. (p. 112)
10. Easy control is out of the question when parents are so forgetful of the welfare of their children as to make before them disparaging remarks of the teacher's scholarship or professional attainments. (p. 108)

In 1917, John Dewey's *Democracy and Education* was first published. The book illustrated how the process of teaching and learning was a democratic social enterprise. Dewey argued, "the great danger which threatens school work is the absence of conditions which make possible a permeating social spirit" (pp. 415–416). Dewey invented what is known as the "problem method" (now called group investigation), which asked students to study common problems in life. Dewey argued that as part of this process, rules should be made and enforced by students as part of personalizing learning.

Dewey's work continues to have a major impact on how we teach, and problem-based learning has also become a respected process in universities. In effect, Dewey advocated the idea of cooperative learning, of effectively structuring groups. He also implied that when learning is of interest, students will monitor their own behaviour.

Research on Encouraging Appropriate Behaviour

Philip Cusick (1983) concludes that the primary concern of school staff is to contain the students who don't want to be there. David Cohen (1988) informs us that teaching and learning depend on a level of cooperation between teachers and students. He argues that without such cooperation, the teaching and learning process will not succeed. Given that education is compulsory, a certain percentage of students are forced to be in a place they are not interested in being in. Mary Kennedy (2010), in "Attribution Error and the Quest for Teacher Quality," reminds us that the problem is not simply one of motivation and cooperation. The issue is that students are still children or adolescents who have certain characteristics such as being immature, disorganized, and easily distracted. In addition, "they start school with no experience of sustained focused, purposeful work that is required for learning" (p. 595).

As adults, when we choose to attend workshops or courses, we typically opt to leave if we don't like the instruction. For us, the experience is much like going to a restaurant—if we like it, we return; if not, we don't. More important, we inform others of whether or not it is a good place to eat. In our public schools, students have to be there. We are (metaphorically) the only restaurant in town. Our students have no choice about the location or the menu. How would you behave if you had to eat the same meal, which you did not like, in the same restaurant that you deem gives you rotten service five days a week? It's likely you would be somewhat uncivil. Our guess is that students who find classroom learning meaningless, uninteresting, and unsafe will be similarly uncivil.

The extent to which students have relationships with other students has an impact on their sense of belonging. Having friends affects involvement in school-related activities, time spent on homework, and enjoyment at school, especially in adolescent years (Berndt & Keeffe, 1995; Steinberg, Dornbusch, & Brown, 1992). Interestingly, recent research shows that even for adults, getting along with colleagues at work makes a significant difference to well-being. In the May 2011 issue of *Health Psychology*, published by the American Psychological Association, an article entitled "Work-Based Predictors of Mortality: A 20 Year Follow-up of Healthy Employees" shows that individuals with a good peer support system at work are more likely to live longer than those without one.

The article lists ways to reduce stress: (1) use humour to deflect tensions; (2) respect diversity re race, ethnicity, gender, age, et cetera; (3) seek clarification if a problem erupts rather than arguing; (4) offer to help someone who seems overwhelmed; (5) work with others in a complementary fashion; if working on a team task, arrange the task so everyone is working to their strengths; (6) talk less, listen more. Clearly these six ideas are equally critical in kindergarten through to Grade 12 classrooms. Effective teachers have employed these same principles for decades.

Matthew Gladden's (2002) studies related to school violence show the key factor *against* the prevention of violence is poor implementation of the above ideas. His research shows that student bullying usually focuses on race/ethnicity, gender, or sexual orientation. In his 1999 study, 13 percent of students aged between 12 and 18 reported being harassed based on those factors over the previous six months. Tangentially, Gladden argues that safe schools are critical for quality educational opportunities. His work focused on two areas: prevention strategies and discipline strategies.

In the United States, during 2000, almost 90 percent of high schools reported having a required course that taught students social-cognitive skills, such as managing anger and conflict resolution techniques (p. 268). Unfortunately, the research shows that only about 20 percent of the learning was effectively implemented. To make a comparison, it is not the violin lesson that makes one an accomplished violinist; it is what one does between lessons. Likewise with most courses, the action of teachers and students outside the course is what makes the difference.

Research on Responding

The research on how to respond to classroom management situations sits on a continuum with humanist/constructivist ideas on one end and behaviourist/positivist ideas on the other. From our experience, there are pluses and minuses to both approaches, and the wise teacher understands how to borrow the best from both approaches. Researchers such as Kounin (e.g., 1977); Duke (e.g., 1979); Emmer and Evertson; and Brophy (e.g., 1983) were some of the most prolific educators researching topics related to classroom management. The work of Emmer and

Evertson appears in *Classroom Management for Middle and High School Teachers* (Emmer & Evertson, 2013); and *Classroom Management for Elementary Teachers* (Evertson & Emmer, 2013).

Jacob Kounin provided one of the first analyses of a teacher's classroom practice. He coined the terms *withitness, ripple effect, overlappingness,* and *winning over,* which were introduced in Chapter 6.

Those terms are conceptual; their effect is determined by the teacher's skill, behaviour, and choice of emotion.

Interestingly, in the 1941 *Encyclopedia of Educational Research*, there is no mention of classroom management. While this encyclopedia does include delinquent behaviour and the role of the home as a possible factor in such behaviour, classroom management is not an identified area of inquiry. The 1969 *Encyclopedia of Educational Research* devotes six pages to "behaviour problems," with most of the discussion focused on prevention. In the 1986 *Handbook of Research on Teaching*, a 32-page chapter is devoted to classroom organization and management. In addition, the idea of classroom management appears in other sections throughout the handbook. This initial push to understand classroom management was undoubtedly fuelled by the work of the above researchers in the 1970s and 1980s. However, there is no section on classroom management and organization in the more recent edition of the *Handbook of Research on Teaching* (Richardson, 2001). Instead, the focus is on teaching and issues related to the teaching and learning process.

The behaviourist approach to student misbehaviour plays out in the research of Becker, Engelmann, and Thomas (e.g., 1975), Douglas Carnine (e.g., 1976), and Lewis and Sugai (e.g., 1999). George Sugai's work is currently used in many classrooms in the United States and Canada. Perhaps one of the most pervasive structured programs centred on a behaviourist approach is that of Lee and Marlene Canter's Assertive Discipline. Based on assertiveness training and applied behavioural analysis, Assertive Discipline promotes a teacher-in-charge classroom environment that operates on defined, stated classroom rules. It has moved somewhat from its authoritarian roots in the 1970s to become a more democratic approach where decision making, for example, is shared between teacher and student.

As mentioned earlier, in this text we take a more humanist view, in line with the approaches of Dinkmeyer and McKay in their books

The Parent's Handbook: Systematic Training for Effective Parenting and *Systematic Training for Effective Teaching*. Those texts are based on the work of Alfred Adler et al. (1967), Rudolf Dreikurs (1968), and William Glasser (e.g., 1969). Interestingly, Adler, Dreikurs, and Glasser were all medical doctors interested in understanding and responding to inappropriate behaviour. Their ideas endure, as evidenced by Linda Albert's *Cooperative Discipline* (2002), a text that remains current, and is also based on the work of these three doctors.

Gladden (2002), whose work on violence was mentioned above, also researched discipline strategies related to dealing with bullying behaviour in schools. He shows that, as logic would dictate, school staffs need fair and consistent rules. Consequences must be responsive to the event. We similarly emphasize in this text that a response must match the inappropriate behaviour and be felt to be reasoned rather than punitive. That said, from our experience, having rules is not the solution; the challenge is to enact them consistently. As Gladden notes, "sound discipline policies do not ensure sound discipline practices" (p. 269). School staffs need consistent enactment in classrooms, hallways, lunchrooms, and so on. A great many books on bullying are available, including, for example, Terrence Webster-Doyle's 1997 book *Why Is Everyone Always Picking on Me: A Guide to Handling Bullies.* This Benjamin Franklin Award–winning book is accessible and practical. It is based on three steps: (1) take an interest in stopping the bullying; (2) learn to understand why people bully; and (3) develop non-violent skills to deal with bullies. We would add that students must be able to identify the essential attributes of bullying so that they can recognize bullying when it happens.

Paulo Freire, in his book *Pedagogy of Indignation*, argues for the concept of "praxis"—the intersection of thought and action. He maintains that thinking in the absence of action, and action in the absence of thinking, are both untenable situations. Freire's work focused on the resolution of conflict and power struggles on a massive scale in Brazil, his home country, where he was exiled for his belief that the poor need to be literate and to have a voice. Interestingly, when students feel they have a voice in deciding what consequences will play out, they are more likely to understand the consequence as logical and reasoned, which decreases the chances that the consequence will lead to an escalation of student misbehaviour. This idea of merging thought and action is clearly described in James Dillon's (2012) new book about bullying.

Chapter 10 Conclusion

Dating back to the 1800s and before, many thinkers and educators have researched and written on issues related to student behaviour with a focus on deeper understanding of more progressive, thoughtful, caring ways to encourage appropriate behaviour and to respond to students when they act inappropriately.

We clearly see the complexity of the issue—the diversity of students, the pressures in their lives, and the demands of the educational system. We know that creating powerful learning environments is dependent on factors such as the teachers' knowledge about and passion for their subject, their knowledge of assessment, their instructional repertoire, and their skills to prevent and respond to student behaviour. Those factors play out with the variables over which we have little control (multiple intelligences, gender, ethnicity, and so on), which create that diversity. What other profession is as complex, demanding, and important as teaching? If we do not make it interesting and fun, the students will do it for us—and usually at our expense.

Bumps 7 to 10

In our 1990 book *Classroom Management: A Thinking and Caring Approach*, we discuss four additional bumps, or escalations. Those four are briefly described below.

The key factor to remember with Bumps 7, 8, 9, and 10 is that these are out-of-class responses that involve others (combinations of assistant principal, principal, parents, guidance counsellor, social worker, and so on). They also imply the student is now in a position to determine what happens. The student makes the decision to shift to each of these escalations—his or her behaviour determines what happens. That said, at all times the student is treated with respect and understands that he or she is "wanted" in the school.

(Note: As a staff you have to make sure that you are not the reason the student is in this situation. If your classes are boring, have no meaning, are of no interest to these students, are not safe, and so on, then it is less likely that Bumps 7, 8, 9, and 10 will work. If you are the "only restaurant in town" and the food is not tasty, the same meal is served every day, and the service is poor but people have to eat at your restaurant, then you can expect them to complain.)

Bump 7: The Formal Contract

The formal contract is similar to the informal chat; the key difference is that a consequence is now invoked and it involves school administration and one or more parents or guardians. The situation is explained in terms of what has happened to this point, and what the staff has done to work at solving the problem. This is where it is helpful to explain how Bumps 1 to 6 have been applied—that as a staff you can show a responsible history of interventions that show your respect for the student.

The consequences can be invoked at school and/or at home. Consequences can refer to earning the right to attend school trips and to use the computer or watch TV.

Bump 8: In-School Suspension

In-school suspension can be one of the consequences of the formal contract. In-school suspensions are basically time outs. They provide the opportunity for the student to think about what has happened and what he or she is going to do to resolve the issue. The student may be required to complete a plan of what he or she will do on returning to the classroom. The student must clearly understand that personal behaviour is what got him or her to this point.

The in-school suspension can mean that the student is suspended to another class (we suggest a higher grade with a teacher who is highly respected) or to a room in or around the office where the student is monitored. We suggest that initially the student comes into the room and does nothing; students enjoy this for about 10 minutes and then they start to get bored. Remember, you want them to *want* to go back to class. If the suspension room is more exciting than the classroom, you will have a problem. You can see that this goes back to your mean score—the extent to which you have won students over or the extent to which they respect you as a teacher and a human being.

Bump 9: Out-of-School Suspension

This move is where the student sees a tunnel with a light at the end of it, namely, the decision the student makes to get expelled from school. Work to have students understand that their behaviour will decide whether or not they enter the tunnel and how fast they move through it. It is important to remind such students that the reason this is happening is that their behaviour is making it difficult for the teacher to create an effective learning environment for the rest of the class. They must sense you like them but cannot accept their behaviour.

What makes out-of-school suspensions difficult is that you need the support of the parents. Unfortunately, parents in these situations are often part of the problem and will not position themselves to follow through on what is decided should happen at home. This is where you live or die on how hard you have tried as a staff to work with parents over the years their children have been in your school. For a lot of parents of at-risk students, the school is seen as a place where they were not successful, and they are very hesitant to show up for these meetings. Schools that implement programs to build up students' sense of self (for example, schools that have successfully implemented Tribes school-wide) are less likely to end up in these situations. This is one way that the school can reap what it sows. In one school in Medicine Hat, Alberta, where the staff is working to implement Tribes from kindergarten to Grade 6, bullying and suspensions have virtually disappeared. The district is now providing Tribes training for kindergarten through Grade 12 at the request of K to 12 teachers.

Bump 10: Expulsion

Expulsion is the final escalation, and here you have to refer to school board policy on how it plays out. The key is to demonstrate how you worked with this student and the student's parents or guardians over time. If you can show how you have worked with Bumps 1 to 9—and how at all phases you were respectful and thoughtful with the student—then students will sense they had a voice in the decision. It was not done to them; they did it to themselves. A plan also has to be in place for what happens now, including the conditions under which the student could earn his or her way back into the school.

Sample Personal Plans

Personal Plan

Name ______________________ Teacher ______________________

Date ______________________ Time In ______________________

Time Out ______________________

(Note: This allows you to track the number of minutes a student is in the office.)

Why I made the decision to leave the room.

What needs to happen in order that the problem is solved?

Signed ____

Teacher response:
- ❑ (1) matter resolved
- ❑ (2) request further administrator involvement
- ❑ (3) additional action taken (e.g., call parents)

Who Is the Problem?

A principal shared this vignette with us.

A grade one student was in the sandbox in the playground; he was throwing sand. The teacher on supervision, a bigger man, came up and loudly asked, "What do you think you are doing?" The student put his head down. The teacher repeated, "I asked you what you think you are doing?" The student got up and walked away. The teacher, not accepting this, followed the student and took him by the arm to the office. When the principal asked the student what happened, the student said, "I was twying to use my thrategy to solve the pwoblem, but the pwoblem followed me."

Office and Parent Notification of Misbehaviour

Student: ____________________________

Homeroom Teacher: __________________

Date: ______________________________ Office Intervention: Y ____ N ____

A Note to Parents:

Students need to cooperate in class, so that everyone can learn. Your son's or daughter's behaviour interfered with the learning in our classroom.

1. Please read the notes below.
2. Please discuss them with your child. You may contact the homeroom teacher, too.
3. Please sign and return this form.

The teacher will keep this form on file for the rest of the school year. If your son's or daughter's behaviour continues or becomes more serious, the principal may ask you to meet with the teacher.

Thank you for your cooperation.

Type of Misbehaviour

Persistent despite several recent reminders and, therefore, interpreted as defiance:

_____ homework/assignments incomplete
_____ lateness
_____ materials, books not in class
_____ hat worn in school
_____ inappropriate dress
_____ loitering in hallways
_____ other: ____
_____ combination of the above (as specified)

Incidents of a serious nature:
_____ putdown of others
_____ physical altercation
_____ disrespect toward teachers/insolence
_____ graffiti
_____ abuse of others' property
_____ other: ____
____
____
____

Student's Description of Misbehaviour:

(*continued*)

Student's Suggestions for Preventing This Misbehaviour in the Future:

1. ______________________________

2. ______________________________

3. ______________________________

Student's Signature: ______________________________

Additional Teacher Comments Regarding the Misbehaviour:

Teacher's Signature: ______________________________

Parent's Comments:

Parent's Signature: ______________________________

Date: ______________________________

Designed by John Mazurek

Bloom's Taxonomy

Bloom's Taxonomy (Bloom, Krathwohl, & Massia) was first published in 1956. It provided a way of thinking about the cognitive domain in the design of learning situations. The taxonomy was recently revised to switch the top two levels of thinking (which was a good idea). The new taxonomy is identified below. Note that we prefer the original term *Synthesis* over the new term *Creating/Designing*. Synthesis is a more precise term; it means to put things together in a new way. Designing and creating are more amorphous concepts; one can design and create and not put things together in a new way.

The key thing to consider is that students prefer to operate at the higher, more complex levels of thinking; students also remember information longer when they operate at the more complex levels. You can see how this relates to classroom management: when students are more motivated to learn and are more successful, they are less likely to misbehave. Also, when teachers use the instructional skill of wait time, they must consider the complexity of thinking—the more complex thinking is required, the more time students need to think before responding publicly.

- Creating/Designing (previously Synthesis)
- Evaluation
- Analysis
- Application
- Comprehension/Understanding
- Recall/Remembering (previously Knowledge)

Note: Beware of confusing *levels* of thinking with *types* of thinking. Types of thinking can often fit at multiple levels. When teachers use Bloom's charts of verbs, those verbs are types of thinking. For example, we always see the verb *identify* under Recall/Remembering. That is fine, if the task is to identify the parts of a flower. What if it is "Identify the number one reason why Canada entered the war in Afghanistan"? That is Evaluation. What if it is "Identify the similarities and differences between a republic and a democracy"? That is Analysis. Whether you are deconstructing educational outcomes and objectives or creating your own, you cannot escape dealing with levels and types of thinking.

How Effective Group Work Creates Problems

In this appendix, we illustrate how the Johnsons' Five Basic Elements intentionally create problems. Teachers must understand that when students are put in groups—especially when they first begin the journey of developing the skills to work in groups—there will be conflict. Effective group work and conflict are like ice cream to the cone. Michael Fullan, an expert on educational change, argues that smooth early use of group work is a sure sign that you are not implementing it correctly.

Individual Accountability

Individual accountability is a critical attribute of effective group work. As soon as students realize that they are not accountable and will not be held accountable, they will begin hitchhiking off the efforts of others: they become social loafers. Like electrons, students will take the path of least resistance.

As soon as students who are used to not having to work, who are not used to being responsible learners, are put in a situation where they actually have to work, they will push back. Also, others will speak up when the group processes how they functioned together, letting the group members know how they felt about their participation and the participation of the group. This is why group structures like Place Mat work; it is difficult to escape, as others can see you doing or not doing your work. The downside of Place Mat is that it can make the situation unsafe; often, you would be wise to cut the Place Mat up and have students do it individually first and then come together as a group, tape it together, and share their work.

Face-to-Face Interaction

Face-to-face interaction refers to having students sit in such a way that they can see each other when they are talking. David and Roger Johnson use the phrase "face-to-face, eye-to-eye, and knee-to-knee." Here you are working at how you structure your groups, the size of the groups, and who works with whom. You can see the issue of friendship groups—students like to work with their friends because they can predict how they will be treated. The problem is that in real life, one does not go to work with one's best friends; that may happen, but it is not a condition of employment. The condition of employment is that you learn to work with whoever is there. When you start to put students in teacher-structured groups or groups based on random assignment, you are putting them in situations that are outside of their comfort zone.

When you go into classrooms where the teacher has been working on effective group work for a long time (especially in schools where the school staff works on effective group work), students easily move from group to group and have no issues with working with whoever is in the group.

Teaching Collaborative Skills

At first students think to themselves that this is, for example, English class or History class, and why do we have to learn about equal voice and attentive listening? When you take the time to discuss the importance of attentive listening and where in life it plays out (for example, on a date), they slowly begin to see its relevance.

That said, students will often push back when you begin the journey of developing a repertoire of social skills, communication skills, and critical thinking skills. If you attempt to have students play with the critical thinking skill of examining both sides of an issue and they don't have the social skill of cqual voice and the communication skill of attentive listening, you will have problems. Less complex skills drive more complex skills. We see this issue played out in secondary schools when teachers move into the area of critical thinking. High school students seldom have the social and communication skills to pull off the process of critical thinking.

Processing the Academic Task and Collaborative Task

This component of effective group work relates to assessment *for* learning and *as* learning. The students are giving themselves and each other feedback on how well they achieved the task assigned. When students first start to work in groups, they often don't all do their share, or one or two students take over and don't let others be involved. Those issues will come out in the feedback, and you need a process to resolve them. Community Circle from Tribes is one excellent way to begin a dialogue to reflect on and begin resolving these issues. Don't panic about these issues; this is exactly what happens when you and your students begin to implement effective group work. If you refer to Appendix E on CBAM, you will see that when you first start, you are a mechanical user and this level is rife with conflict. The change literature refers to this stage as the implementation dip.

Positive Interdependence

As a concept, Positive Interdependence has been around since the 1950s. It refers to what teachers and students can do to increase the chances that group work is successful, and that students each care about each other's learning. The Johnsons refer to this idea as "we sink or swim together." Each of the nine types of Positive Interdependence creates its own problem.

1. **Goal Positive Interdependence:** This refers to the objective of the lesson—the academic and social learning. When the academic task is not clear, meaningful, and worth doing in a group, you will have problems. We have found that if we as teachers fail to structurally include interest and meaning, students will structure interest into the task for us—and usually at our expense.

2. **Role Positive Interdependence:** Roles, by design, give each student a responsibility during the group work (for example, the reader, the writer, the material manager). The problem emerges when students are assigned a role they do not want. If you've not taken the time to teach these roles, you will compound the problem. We suggest you be very careful when using roles. We don't use them unless we absolutely need them. We find roles of the

moment are more effective. For example: "Person B, would you please come up and get the cards? Person A, please take out a pen or pencil." Then at the end of the lesson: "Could person C please put the cards back on the table?" One key thing to stay away from is predetermining the person who reports. If you have the reporter as a role, you can forget about individual accountability; the only person who panics to get it done is the designated reporter. Better to say, "I will randomly call on one of you to share your group's work. Murphy's Law tells me you will be asked, so make sure you can all explain the work."

3. **Sequence Positive Interdependence:** Whenever you use sequence, you run the risk of creating a situation where students have to deal with the problem, "What do I do if I have nothing to do?" In most cases with Sequence Positive Interdependence, while one person is doing his or her part, the others are waiting; it is the waiting time that creates the time for off-task behaviour. Best to make sure you have something planned for them to do while they are waiting for their turn in the sequence.

4. **Incentive Positive Interdependence:** Nothing gets students more excited than when they get something for the work they do—especially if competition is involved. Incentive Positive Interdependence refers to something each group receives for completing a task successfully. The problem can occur when one or two people in the group do not do their work or fool around so that the others in the group do not get the incentive. Expect calls from parents.

5. **Outside Force Positive Interdependence:** This refers to the group working to beat a standard, or a time, or other groups. When a prize is awarded to the group that gets the highest mean score in the quiz, you set up a "We are the winners, you are the losers" situation. If you do not take the time to talk about how one behaves when one wins and when one loses, expect to have a lot of conflict on this one.

6. **Simulation Positive Interdependence:** Simulation Positive Interdependence is very complex and is actually an instructional strategy unto itself. Role play and simulations have a powerful impact on student learning. The problem is that when students are acting something out (for example, how food moves from the mouth to the anus and each student has a body part), you have the problem of Sequence Positive Interdependence. They will also argue over who gets what role in the simulation. When you do Simulation

Positive Interdependence correctly, you will, by default, hit most if not all nine types of Positive Interdependence.

7. **Identity Positive Interdependence:** This refers to the group building a common identity, and it's often the boys who can be the problem. When they decide to come up with a team name and one person wants to be the Toronto Maple Leafs and the other the Blood Hounds...well, you know what boys can be like.

8. **Environmental Positive Interdependence:** This refers to creating an environment that by default has students sitting together. Having a group of students sit around a hula hoop or around a scale to do their science experiment creates "you're in my space" problems. This is why you want to keep your groups small (two to four students). We suggest groups of two for kindergarten to Grade 2 students.

9. **Resource Positive Interdependence:** When students have to share resources, they will often need the same item at the same time. (Younger students sharing crayons may both need red at the same time!) The problem is having the skills to be patient and to understand what the concept and process of sharing looks like and sounds like.

APPENDIX E

Concerns Based Adoption Model (CBAM)

One way that teachers self-assess how well they attend to the essential attributes of an innovation is by using rubrics. Another way is to self-assess the *level of skill* that a teacher models with an innovation. This form of assessment is particularly critical to the impact of any innovation—in this case, the impact of cooperative learning. Levels of skill relate to the Levels of Use of an innovation, a concept developed by Susan Loucks-Horsley that is part of a larger framework developed by Hall and Hord (2006), known as the Concerns Based Adoption Model (CBAM).

Levels of Use measures teachers' and students' skill shift at eight levels, shown in the table below. The first three levels describe nonuse of the innovation, and the last five describe increasingly skilled use.

Levels of Use of an Innovation	
1. Nonuser	You are not using the innovation, but you may have heard of it.
2. Orientating	You are interested, and you are seeking out more information.
3. Preparing	You are getting ready to apply the innovation for the first time.
4. Mechanical	You are applying the innovation in your classroom, but your application is clunky.
5. Routine	You have applied the innovation for enough time that it is working smoothly.
6. Refined	You are extending how you apply the innovation into new areas.
7. Integrative	You are connecting the innovation to other innovations.
8. Refocusing	You are searching for other innovations.

Source: Hord & Hall (2006).

Hord, Hall, and Loucks-Horsley have researched the Levels of Use model over the last 35 years, and their research shows that, until teachers and students reach the Routine level of use, the innovation has little effect on student learning. For the fundamental work on Levels of Use, see Loucks, Newlove, and Hall, 1975.

In a conversation with Susan Loucks-Horsley approximately 10 years ago, she mentioned that, in their research on instructional methods in secondary school science classrooms, they rarely found teachers even at the Mechanical level of use in any instructional innovation. From a change perspective, students and the teacher at the Mechanical level are in the *implementation dip*; things are actually getting worse rather than better. Therefore, if teachers or researchers attempt to assess the impact of an innovation such as cooperative learning on student learning without first assessing the teachers' and students' level of use of this innovation, they will not accurately assess the innovation's impact.

The Levels of Use framework and related research provide a precise and thorough approach to analyzing and assessing the evolving skill level of teachers as they implement innovations. More important, the Levels of Use also apply to students.

Interestingly, from our experience with the implementation of instructional innovations, each level of use engenders another implementation dip. The dips don't go away; they simply become progressively more complex.

On the next page is a rubric that illustrates how three of the Levels of Use (Mechanical, Routine, and Refined) relate to the Five Basic Elements of Effective Group Work. How many teachers do you think are Routine or higher users of cooperative learning? What would it take to get from the Mechanical to the Routine and Refined levels?

How Levels of Use Relate to the Five Basic Elements in Cooperative Learning		
Mechanical	**Routine**	**Refined**
Teacher has notes reminding how and when to apply the Five Basic Elements.	Teacher may have a few notes to refer to, but for the most part, smoothly plays with the Five Basic Elements.	Teacher does not need notes; clearly and effectively applies the Five Basic Elements.
Accountability not as high as it should be. Not all students are involved; others may be taking over.	Most students are accountable. Periodically, one or two students take over and do more.	All students, most of the time, are accountable and actively involved.
Discussion of the academic goal happens, but is not as meaningful to students as it could be. Students find it somewhat confusing.	The academic goal is discussed and is, for the most part, meaningful. Students expect this to happen, but still need to be reminded. A narrow range of collaborative skills is used.	The academic goal is discussed, is meaningful and of interest, and is clearly worth doing in a group. Students do it naturally. A wide range of appropriate collaborative skills is used.
Students are not very skilled at processing their academic and social task.	Most students can process the academic and social task, although the social task is sometimes not processed.	Students skilfully process their academic and collaborative tasks.
Students have few skills to confront and resolve conflict. Students struggle to work with some other students.	Students are beginning to deal with their own conflicts but may need help at times. Students can work with most students in the class.	Few conflicts; if they occur, students usually deal with them. Students easily work with all students in the class.
Teacher does not merge Five Basic Elements with other instructional methods.	Teacher is beginning to connect the Five Basic Elements to other instructional methods, but only to less complex methods.	Teacher, when appropriate, easily and effectively integrates the Five Basic Elements into other instructional methods, including into more complex strategies.

Staff Surveys

Reaching Agreement About Defining Inappropriate Behaviours

Please rate the following inappropriate behaviours on a scale of 1 to 10. With 1 being "no big deal" and 10 being "a real big deal." Circle your answers and when finished, compare your responses with several of your colleagues.

1. A student is chewing gum in your class.
   1 2 3 4 5 6 7 8 9 10
2. A student walks into class wearing a hat.
   1 2 3 4 5 6 7 8 9 10
3. A student enters class wearing a T-shirt that is sexist and extremely suggestive.
   1 2 3 4 5 6 7 8 9 10
4. A student calls out an answer when he was not supposed to call out.
   1 2 3 4 5 6 7 8 9 10
5. A student is running down the hall to the library.
   1 2 3 4 5 6 7 8 9 10
6. A student makes a verbal put-down of another student in class.
   1 2 3 4 5 6 7 8 9 10
7. A student talks back to you in front of other students.
   1 2 3 4 5 6 7 8 9 10
8. A student consistently comes late to your class.
   1 2 3 4 5 6 7 8 9 10
9. A student rocks in her chair in the class.
   1 2 3 4 5 6 7 8 9 10

The overwhelming response we get when we discuss teachers' thinking is, "We need more information. We can't make an appropriate response unless we know more about the student and how often it has happened." What this illustrates is the difficulty in establishing a common view of acceptable behaviour. Each is individually and situationally specific.

Assessing Your School-Wide Discipline Process

The following activity is designed to determine whether or not you have a clearly articulated and effectively implemented discipline process.

Task: As individuals, please respond to the following questions.

1. Do you clearly understand the circumstances under which you can send students to the office?
   1 2 3 4 5
   no somewhat yes
2. Do you clearly understand what happens to students when they are sent to the office?
   1 2 3 4 5
   no somewhat yes
3. Are you satisfied with your school's procedures related to students coming late to class?
   1 2 3 4 5
   no somewhat yes
4. Are parents aware of your school's discipline procedures?
   1 2 3 4 5
   no somewhat yes
5. Do you have an effective process for the school staff to resolve conflicts related to school discipline issues?
   1 2 3 4 5
   no somewhat yes
6. Does your school staff have a set of common beliefs related to how to respond to student behaviour?
   1 2 3 4 5
   no somewhat yes
7. If you have a school-wide discipline process, does most of your school staff work at effectively implementing it?
   1 2 3 4 5
   no somewhat yes
8. Are the roles and responsibilities of teachers and administrators clearly defined?
   1 2 3 4 5
   no somewhat yes
9. Is there a process in place whereby teachers can discuss classroom behaviour problems and receive non-critical collegial advice?
   1 2 3 4 5
   no somewhat yes
10. Is the administration perceived as being supportive?
    1 2 3 4 5
    no somewhat yes

Sample Lesson for Guest Teachers

The lesson below employs Madeline Hunter's Lesson Design strategy as an organizer. See Hattie's (2012) research on the effect this organizer has on student learning. Modify the lesson based on the age of your students.

Mental Set: Have students think to themselves about what comes to their minds when someone says "guest." Have them do a Think-Pair-Share and then randomly call on them to share their thinking.

Objective and Purpose 1: Share that today students will be exploring their thinking about who would be considered guests in the school and how guests should be treated. Tell them that at the end of the lesson they will have to discuss why they think this lesson is relevant to this class and to this school.

Transition: Put students into groups of three. Use teacher-selected groups or random assignment to groups—friendship groups are not a good idea.

Input 1: "In your groups of three, brainstorm on your piece of paper all the people who would be considered guests in our school. Person C, you are the recorder, but you also have to put down ideas. You have about 60 seconds to see how many you can identify."

At the end of 60 seconds, have students do a 45-second Walk About to see if anyone had ideas different from theirs. When asked to return to their groups at the end of 45 seconds, students add any additional people that would be considered guests.

Input 2: "Discuss in your groups of three how people tend to treat those who are guests and why they get treated that way." Let students know that they will be randomly called on to share their ideas. Record their ideas on the white board.

Objective and Purpose 2: Now have students focus on the idea of substitute/on-call/supply teachers as guests, to have them understand why such teachers are guests and to develop a plan for how they will treat them when they arrive in their classroom.

Input 3: Now say: "Think to yourself, please do not share, I will just call on some of you to share. In what ways are supply teachers or on-call teachers like guests in our classroom?" Give students 10 seconds wait time and randomly call on students to share. Once three to five have shared, invite others to share any additional ideas. Put their ideas on the board.

Input 4: Have students identify why it is difficult to be a supply teacher or an on-call teacher. Have them discuss in their groups, and randomly call on students to share.

Application of Ideas: Now have students create a Place Mat and have each person come up with a series of things they could do as a class to make sure the guest teacher has a "good day" in their class. Do a Round the Table Share and have students put the top three ideas in the middle of the Place Mat (give them about four minutes for that activity). When they have identified the top three, do a One Stray the Rest Stay to share and pick up any new ideas (this usually takes about three minutes). Then have them post their Place Mats on the wall and do a Gallery Tour. Once they have done the tour (this takes about two minutes), have each group come up with a plan for how they can make sure the guest teacher has a good day—they can use ideas from all the Place Mats. Have them do a plan from the start to the end of the school day. Tell them that when a guest teacher comes, they will have to implement their plan. They will put their group name in a hat and have a name drawn to see whose plan is used first.

Alternatively, you can come up with one class plan rather than implementing each group's plan.

Closure/Check for Understanding: Have students do a plus minus interesting (PMI) analysis on guest teachers. Have them do a Snow Ball on why this lesson was relevant to the class. Do the Snowball in a Community Circle and have students go around the table reading the idea on their piece of paper. Have them volunteer any comments they would like to make before the lesson finishes.

Learning Enriched and Learning Impoverished Schools

Susan Rosenholtz's (1989) study on teachers and administrators in 78 schools identified two learning cultures that she labelled "learning enriched (moving)" and "learning impoverished (stuck)." The terms moving and stuck are important; they imply that as educators we are capable of moving into and out of these learning cultures. Below is a CBAM rubric related to some of the key factors that favour learning enriched schools. Rosenholtz's work paved the way to the current work with professional learning communities.

	Mechanical—stuck	Routine—beginning	Refined—moving
Norms of Continuous Learning	A few teachers have an emerging belief that teachers must continuously learn; still too many teachers believe they do not need to be lifelong learners.	Some to most teachers sense that they must continually refine their practice.	Most to all teachers are working to continually refine their practice.
Collaborative Culture/Collective Responsibility	A few teachers are beginning to work together and sense they are collectively responsible to maximize student learning.	Some to most teachers are working to create a collaborative culture where they sense they are collectively responsible to maximize student learning.	Most to all teachers are sustaining their work to collectively collaborate in taking responsibility to maximize student learning.
Shared Goals	A few teachers are beginning to work toward a common focus.	Some to most teachers are working toward a common focus.	Most to all teachers are working more intensely to create a common focus.

	Mechanical—stuck	Routine—beginning	Refined—moving
Teacher Efficacy	Some teachers are working toward building a sense of efficacy to impact student learning and resolve problems.	Most teachers are well on their way to collectively working toward building a sense of efficacy to impact student learning and resolve problems.	Most to all teachers are collectively and continuously working toward building a sense of efficacy to impact student learning and resolve problems.
Mutual Support	A few teachers are taking time to provide support to each other.	Some to most teachers are taking time to provide support to each other.	Most to all teachers are taking time to provide support to each other.
Higher Student Achievement	Students are still not demonstrating improved student learning compared to other schools with similar students.	Some to most students are demonstrating improved student learning compared to other schools with similar students.	Most to all students are demonstrating improved student learning compared to other schools with similar students.

A 2012 Vignette on a Learning Enriched School

Interestingly, in stuck schools the principals were unsure of their knowledge and had personal concerns: they protected their turf and rejected even the smallest attempts teachers made to resolve classroom and school problems; teachers were met with intimidation and distance; teachers learned they were in this alone. This connects to Leithwood, Mascall, and Strauss's (2009) work, which showed that the second most powerful predictor of student achievement was the involvement of the principal in supporting teachers' refinement and extension of their instructional practices.

"[T]he hallmark of any successful organization is a shared sense among its members about what they are trying to accomplish" (Rosenholtz, 1989, p. 13). Key here is the idea of members: we are in this together.

Related to classroom management, you can see that students are more likely to stay focused on learning when they are in schools where teachers work collectively to design a collaborative supportive learning environment. What follows is a brief description of one learning enriched (moving) school. One of the authors is involved with this school and worked with these educators the day before the start of the 2012 academic year (June 1). Compare what these teachers and administrators do to make a difference in student academic and social learning with what you do in your school.

This kindergarten to Grade 12 school is in the second poorest socioeconomic area in Los Angeles, California. Approximately 95 percent of the students are Hispanic.

- Students are in school 200 days of the year (in the United States 175 days is typical).
- On the day before the start of each academic year, teachers begin with a workshop to focus their efforts.
- The school works in partnership with California State University to research their efforts.
- Teachers are on a one-year contract (which they wanted).
- All teachers support each other in their efforts to impact student learning.
- The school has connections to China and teachers take in students from China.
- Students graduate being able to speak English, Spanish, and Cantonese.
- One hundred percent of the students graduate.

Description of Instructional Methods Discussed in the Text

Academic Controversy

This more complex cooperative learning strategy is the work of David and Roger Johnson. It involves students sitting in small groups (usually four to six). Each group of four to six is then divided in half, with each half exploring opposite sides of an issue (such as, "Be it resolved that all large cities should have zoos"). The topic relates to something they have been studying. This process is similar to debating. As part of the process, students apply the social, communication, and critical thinking skills necessary to present and argue their case. The key difference between a debate and Academic Controversy is that in the Academic Controversy students get a chance to plan and present both sides of the issue—they do the pro and con of the argument.

Concept Attainment

This inductive thinking strategy pushes the analysis level of thinking. It was designed by Jerome Bruner, and it is basically the process parents employ to have their own children grasp concepts. Parents show children examples: "Yes, that is a truck." "No, that is not a truck—that is a car." Given that everything you can put a label on is an example of a concept (except most proper nouns), you can see that almost all concepts can be taught using this process. It is considered a constructivist approach to teaching and learning as the student has to determine the common attributes from the examples shown. At times the data set will involve words, pictures, objects, role plays, vignettes, or a combination of those options.

Concept Formation

This inductive thinking strategy pushes analysis. It was developed by Hilda Taba, and is basically the process employed to develop language. The strategy has students classify objects they collect or that they are presented with into groups based on common attributes. We put things together because that group of things has something in common, and give it a label and a definition—for example, "chair" or "truck" or "love" or "democracy." This strategy is similar to Concept Attainment, but in Concept Formation, the students have to classify the data.

Corners

This is a small-group structure that facilitates students taking a stand or a position or identifying a perception on an issue. You can use three or four (five if necessary) places for students to move. The teacher asks a question, students have time to think, and then when signalled they move directly to that corner or designated place in the classroom. Students then find a partner or group of three and discuss why they selected this position (make sure everyone gets a chance to talk). Then randomly select students to share what they discussed. Often you can use: Strongly Agree; Somewhat Agree, Somewhat Disagree, Strongly Disagree—for example, if you were deciding on whether or not we should have nuclear power. Or you can use three types of math—Geometry, Algebra, and Calculus—and students have to decide which one is most valuable and be prepared to defend their stance. This process also connects to data management; you can graph the responses on the white board.

Gallery Tour

This cooperative tactic involves students learning from the efforts of others; often, it can be applied as assessment *as* learning—where students compare and contrast their efforts with the efforts of others. With Gallery Tour, students put their work up on the wall, as in a gallery, and then move around the room and look at the work of the other students. Usually, half the class will stand by their work as other students move around the room—those students staying with their work explain what they did, key idea, and so on, and the other students ask them questions that they have formed. After an appropriate period of time, students switch roles. Of course this implies that students have taken time to understand different kinds of questions that could be asked. Students who are nine or ten years and older should be able to apply aspects of Bloom's Taxonomy to assist in forming questions; they should also think of different types of open- and closed-ended questions they could ask.

For example, when students finish their Mind Maps or Concept Maps or Time Line, they can put them up on the wall and share their efforts with other students.

Possible questions:

1. If you could do this again, what would you do differently?
2. Which do you think helps you more, Mind Maps or Concept Maps?
3. What parts of your Mind Map do you think will be on the final exam?
4. Do you like doing Mind Maps?
5. Why didn't you use cross-links on your Mind Map?

You can see that Gallery Tour has elements of a Ghost Walk. The key difference is that in a Gallery Tour, students stop and discuss their efforts. Also, Gallery Tour occurs near the end of the students' efforts, whereas Ghost Walk usually occurs during the work to provide a perspective on where they should be or to act as a check for understanding.

Ghost Walk

This tactic involves having students get up from their individual or small-group work and walk around to get a sense of what other students or groups are doing. Often children are slow to start or get bogged down; this exercise provides an opportunity for them to check for understanding or to see how they are doing compared to others.

We usually give students about 45 seconds to a minute to walk around the class. They are not to talk—just to take note of what others are doing. We usually remind the boys to try to not "walk through people" in their quest to be ghosts. If you let students know in advance you will be doing a Ghost Walk, it increases accountability in that they know that others will be coming around to see what they or their group are doing.

We also remind students that in the real world, people watch what you do. Whether you are a plumber or a prime minister, you are visible. We ask them if teachers are visible beyond their students. We also ask them if teachers should lock their doors, put paper over the windows, and not let people come in to watch them teach. Students think that teachers are too private and will ask: "Why don't teachers watch each other teach? Everyone watches hockey players and basketball players, and when you work at McDonald's everyone watches you." Interesting.

Graffiti

This cooperative learning structure is akin to group brainstorming. Students connect with the name as it represents what often happens on the buildings in their community. The structure is a great way to start phase 1 of Taba's Concept Formation strategy that involves generating the data, and that sets up phase 2, classifying the data. From there, students can do Ranking Ladders, Venn diagrams, Word Webs, Fish Bone Diagrams, Mind Maps, and Concept Maps.

Students sit in groups of three or four and they are given a topic in the middle of a piece of chart paper. They are then asked to write down everything they know about that topic, or the top three or four or five ideas on that topic. When directed to do so, they get up and have a specified amount of time to put their ideas on as many other sheets as possible. As an alternative, if you think the students may not be able to handle moving around randomly, you can have them collectively move from group to group or simply pass the paper around. That said, students usually prefer to get up and randomly move. If you think a student may write something inappropriate, give them each coloured markers, but give that student a specific colour. Remind students that they are not to talk while they move around; also tell them not to read other students' ideas. If two or three or more write the same idea, that tells that group when they return that it is likely an important idea. When the students return to their groups, they then start a process to deal with the data.

For example, in one high school English class, the teacher, Kathy Green, had her students identify everything they knew about each of the characters in *Romeo and Juliet*. Each piece of chart paper had a different character. When the group returned, they had to pick out their top 10 ideas, rank them using specific criteria, and then individually write a character sketch on that character.

In an elementary math class, students went around putting different math problems on other groups' Graffiti sheet. When each group returned, the teacher quickly went around and circled the problems with a felt pen, putting the problems into groups of three or four (you can differentiate this activity by having the sharper students do a few more than the children who struggle). The students then worked on solving the questions in their circles.

Group Investigation

This complex cooperative learning strategy was first conceptualized by John Dewey and then turned more into a specific strategy by Herbert Thelan. This strategy has students initially form questions around a topic, then if necessary condense them into a set of key questions that require answers on a particular issue. This is not a report on a topic; it is about exploring an issue such as "Why is it that members of Parliament get away with such bad behaviour when they should be modelling how students are being asked to debate issues in school?" or "Why is it that our school is not doing anything to deal with bullying?" Students then sign up for the question they want to answer, and as a group of two, three, or four they go about finding that information. They meet with other groups during this time to share how they are doing and to begin to plan how they will get together to present their final report, where each of the groups presents their data.

Jigsaw

This complex cooperative learning strategy was developed by Elliot Aronson. The process is used to have students learn a piece of information and then teach that piece of information to the group. Jigsaw is a lot more complex than it looks. It has three phases. In phase 1, students work alone and read through their material. In phase 2, they shift to expert groups to develop a deeper understanding of the information and to decide how to teach that information to their group members. In phase 3, they return to their home group and teach that information. Groups of three work best; groups of four get a bit too big. Note that the students have to be very skilled in social skills, such as equal voice, taking turns, and being polite; communication skills, such as attentive listening, probing for clarification, and disagreeing agreeably; and critical thinking skills like suspending judgment.

Lesson Design

This advanced organizer strategy is considered one of the top four frameworks for creating lessons developed in the last 50 years. We argue it is by far the best of the four. See Chapter 6 in *Beyond Monet: The Artful Science of Instructional Integration* (Bennett & Rolheiser, 2001) for more in-depth information.

Lesson Design is an instructional strategy created by Madeline Hunter (born in Saskatchewan) as a result of her research into the process of effective teaching. She found these seven components were played out in most lessons of effective teachers, though not always in the same order.

- **Mental Set or Anticipatory Set:** This component is akin to the "hook" or introduction to a lesson. It has three attributes—it links to the past learning of students, it relates to the objective, and it involves all students. I also suggest you make it interesting and meaningful.
- **Sharing the Objective and Purpose:** This is an instructional skill that often occurs near the start of the lesson; however, it can also evolve in the Closure—the end of the lesson. The students are involved in understanding what they will be learning and why it is important.
- **Input:** This component refers to the information to be learned that relates to and supports the objective. This is where the teacher also attends to issues such as multiple intelligences and learning styles, and so on.

- **Modelling:** Modelling refers to the visual, auditory, or tactile representation of the idea to be learned. It must contain all the attributes of the concept being modelled and students should engage in describing those attributes. The model must relate to the objective.
- **Checking for Understanding:** This component refers to what a teacher does to make sure students grasp what was told or shown prior to applying what they learned. It should involve all students and relate to or support the objective. This is one of the most misused concepts in classroom instruction. The rubric below describes four levels of checking for understanding during the lesson. Thinking of what you do in your classroom, at what level would your students put you?

Level 1	Level 2	Level 3	Level 4
Teacher explains or demonstrates, then states: "Now, does everyone understand what I did? Are you sure? No questions? Okay good, let's move on." All you know for sure is that the teacher understands.	Teacher explains or demonstrates, then asks for someone to explain what he or she did. One or two students share with the class and then the teacher asks: "Now, does everyone understand what they said? Are you sure? Okay good, let's move on." All you know for sure is that the teacher and those one or two students understand.	Teacher explains or demonstrates, then has students think to themselves and then share with a partner. The teacher then asks for students to share what they discussed with the class; some students volunteer. The teacher now asks: "Does everyone understand? Are you sure? Okay good, let's move on." Now you know they all had a chance to check, and if your groups are structured effectively they all may understand. But you still only know that the teacher and those students who shared understand.	Teacher explains or demonstrates, then has students think to themselves and then share with a partner. The teacher then randomly asks for students who are high performing, average performing, and low performing to share with the class. The teacher often randomly asks students to paraphrase what another student said. The teacher states: "Great, let's move on." Now you know they all had a chance to check, and if your groups are structured effectively they all may understand. You also know the strongest to weakest students understand so that the chances that they all understand are increased.

- **Practice:** This component is divided into Guided and Independent Practice. Guided means the students have access to someone to assist them; Independent means they work on their own without much support.
- **Closure:** This component involves students summarizing the key components of the lesson. The summary relates to or supports the objective, and all students are involved. Note: This component is not part of Hunter's original Lesson Design strategy.

Milling to Music

This small-group structure, found in Jeanne Gibbs's Tribes program, is used to get students to share information, to get multiple perspectives on an idea, and to extend their thinking by listening to multiple voices.

The teacher makes a request or asks a question. Students stand and, when the music starts, randomly and quietly walk around the room. When the music stops, they put themselves into groups of two, three, or four. (The teacher usually tells them in advance the size of the group they are to form when the music stops.) Students then share their thinking related to the question or request. When the music starts, they again walk and repeat the process, responding to the same or a different question or request.

Place Mat

This small-group tactic involves having students working in groups of two, three, or four on a piece of paper. Regular-sized paper is fine; sometimes you may need something as large as chart paper. Students divide the paper up so that they each have a place to write, as well as a place in the centre or top to summarize their ideas. Different configurations can be used. Some teachers now cut up the Place Mat so students can first work on their own; they then come back and paste it together and share. Having students work on their own first provides time for the teacher to make sure all students understand before coming back to their group to share.

PMI (Plus Minus Interesting)

Edward de Bono

This thinking structure was designed by Edward de Bono. It is one of 60 tactics for critical thinking from his CoRT program. We often find it useful to shift the *I* from meaning interesting to either important or intelligent.

Positive Interdependence

This is one of the Five Basic Elements of effective group work as developed through the research of David and Roger Johnson. Positive Interdependence refers to students understanding that they "sink or swim" together, that they are all responsible for helping each other learn. The following are nine ways to encourage this responsibility.

- **Goal:** Make sure students have a clear, meaningful task or learning objective.
- **Role:** When appropriate, divide the task up so each student has a role in completing it.
- **Sequence:** Analyze the task, have each person take a part, and then put the parts together.
- **Incentive:** Each group, upon successfully completing the task, receives something.
- **Outside Force:** Something external, like time or a minimal standard; must be met.
- **Simulation:** Students act out a situation—note this needs Role Positive Interdependence.
- **Identity:** Students come up with a group name, logo, or way of signifying their group.
- **Environmental:** The environment is structured so students have to work in a defined area.
- **Resources:** Limit the resources so students are forced to share and work together.

Teams Games Tournament (TGT)

In the strategy of TGT by De Vries, the original approach involves having questions written on a card with answers on the back of that card that students were required to answer in a tournament situation (much like Trivial Pursuit). One of the authors (Barrie) ran into a first-year teacher years ago in Colorado, and she suggested using playing cards where you typed the question on the computer so you could edit, revise, and share. A much better idea.

- **Materials:** Question Sheet, Answer Sheet, Recording Sheet, Deck of Playing Cards. If 24 questions, then take out the Ace to 6 of each suit

(Ace = 1) and put the rest of the deck away. Place six questions under Spades, six under Clubs, six under Hearts, and six under Diamonds. Do the same with the answer sheet, six answers under each suit—so suit, question number, and answer number match.

- **Process:** Students study in home teams of six and letter off AA, BB, and CC so that the six students assist each other learn the key ideas. Structure the groups so that you have a higher, average, and lower performing student in each group and each pair has a stronger and less strong student. If you have a group of seven, two students can act as one. Once the study time is over, they then move to tournament teams. Each pair of students competes against a pair of students from another group (so the tournament group size is four). In the middle are the shuffled playing cards, the answer and question sheet for each suit, and a recording sheet for their answers.

One pair is designated the teacher at the start (they take the answer sheet); the other pair is the student to start (they take the question sheet). The student pair now draws a card—if they draw the 4 of Hearts, they read the question out loud, discuss the answer, and then try to answer that question (they take turns answering, but always discuss first). If they get it right, they get a check mark on the sheet. Some teachers award points according to the number on the card. So, if they draw the 6 of Hearts and get it right, they get six points. They rotate after each question. Cards are used only once. At the end, they add up their score and return to their home group where they add the three scores together. Any group that gets more than a target you've decided on gets their homework cut in half or gets to hear a joke. One of the authors (Barrie) saw a teacher bring in a cake and tell the students the winning team gets the cake—she wrote it on the board, but did not put a period after the sentence. When the winning team was announced, she added, "…to cut up into equal pieces and give to the rest of the class, and the last six pieces are yours." She then reminded them of the importance editing one's work.

Tribes Agreements

There are four: Attentive Listening, Mutual Respect, Appreciation Statements, and Right to Pass (when appropriate).

Value Lines

This structure is also found in the work of Jeanne Gibbs in her Tribes program. It pushes the evaluation level of Bloom's Taxonomy. You can use a piece of masking tape or just an imaginary line to record students' positions. Students place themselves on the line between the two positions of an issue. They then share with others close by in a Think-Pair-Share format why they selected that point on the line. Students are then randomly called on to share with the class; their ideas can be recorded. It is wise to have students think about where they will stand and why they selected that position prior to getting up and placing themselves on the Value Line. If you use tape, students can sign their name. You can debate the issue using Academic Controversy, then they can come back to the tape and sign their name again—you can have them measure the shift and you could calculate the mean shift in their thinking. You can also have them stand at three, four, or five points on the line and form a body graph, which you can then draw on the white board (Strongly Agree, Somewhat Agree, Somewhat Disagree, Strongly Disagree, Undecided).

REFERENCES

Adler, A., Ansbacher, H. L., & Ansbacher, R. R. (1967). *The individual psychology of Alfred Adler.* New York, NY: Harper Torchbooks.

Albert, L. (2002). *Cooperative discipline* (3rd ed.). Shoreview, MN: AGS Publishing.

Baldwin, J. (2008). *School management and school methods.* Charleston, SC: BiblioBazaar. (Original work published 1897).

Baumeister, R. F., Twenge, J. M., & Nuss, C. (2002). Effects of social exclusion on cognitive processes: Anticipated aloneness reduces intelligent thought. *Journal of Personality and Social Psychology, 83*, 817–827.

Becker, W. C., Engelmann, S., & Thomas, D. R. (1975). *Teaching 1: Classroom management* (2nd ed.). Chicago, IL: Science Research Associates.

Bennett, B. (2002). Instructionally intelligent…socially smart. *Orbit, 32*(4), 1–5.

Bennett, B. (2010). *Graphic intelligence: Playing with assessment possibilities.* Toronto, ON: Bookation.

Bennett, B., & Rolheiser, C. (2001). *Beyond Monet: The artful science of instructional integration.* Toronto, ON: Bookation.

Bennett, B., Rolheiser, C., & Stevahn, L. (1991). *Cooperative learning: Where heart meets mind.* Toronto, ON: Educational Connections.

Bennett, B., & Smilanich P. (1990). *Classroom management: A thinking and caring approach.* Toronto, ON: Bookation.

Bennett, H. E. (2008). *School efficiency: A manual of modern school management.* Charleston, SC: BiblioBazaar. (Original work published 1917).

Berndt, T. J., & Keeffe, K. (1995). Friends' influence on adolescents' adjustment to school. *Child Development 66,* 1312–1339.

Bloom, B. S., Krathwohl D. R., & Massia, B. B. (1956). *Taxonomy of educational objectives.* White Plains, NY: Longman.

Bolton, F. (1910). *Principles of education.* New York, NY: Charles Scribner and Sons.

Brendtro, L. K., Brokenleg, M., & Van Bockern, S. (1990). *Reclaiming youth at risk: Our hope for the future.* Bloomington, IN: National Educational Service.

Brophy, J. (1983). Classroom management and organization. *The Elementary School Journal, 83*(4), 265–285.

Canter, L., & Canter, M. (2001). *Assertive discipline: Positive behavior management for today's classroom.* Bloomington, IN: Solution Tree Press.

Canter, L., & Hausner, L. (2009). *Homework without tears.* New York, NY: Harper Collins.

Cardon, P. W. (2002). A qualitative study of the perceptions of substitute teaching quality. *SubJournal: For Personnel Responsible for Substitute Teaching, 3*(2), 29–45.

Cardon, P. W., Tippetts, Z., & Smith, G. G. (2003). The effectiveness of substitute teacher training: The effects of a Utah study. *ERS Spectrum: Journal of Research and Information, 21*(1), 40–46.

Carnine, D. (1976). Effects of two teacher-presentation rates on off-task behavior, answering correctly, and participation. *Journal of Applied Behavior Analysis, 9*(2), 199–206.

Cohen, D. K. (1988). *Teaching practice: Plus ça change* (Issue Paper 88–3). East Lansing, MI: National Center for Research on Teacher Education, Michigan State University.

Conners, F. H. (1927). *The substitute teacher service in the public schools* (Unpublished doctoral dissertation). Ohio State University, Columbus, OH.

Cummings, C. (1987). *Plan to teach.* Teaching Incorporated.

Cusick, P. (1983). *The egalitarian ideal of the American high school: Studies of three schools.* New York, NY: Longman.

de Bono, E. (1992). *Serious creativity: Using the power of lateral thinking to create new ideas.* New York, NY: HarperCollins Publishers.

Deci, E., & Ryan, R. M. (2008). Facilitating optimal motivation and psychological well-being across life's domains. *Canadian Psychology*, *49*(1), 14–23.

Dewey, J. (1917). *Democracy and education: An introduction to the philosophy of education.* New York, NY: Macmillan.

Dillon, J. (2012). *No place for bullying: Leadership for schools that care for every student.* Thousand Oaks, CA: Corwin.

Dinkmeyer, D., Sr., McKay, G. D., & Dinkmeyer, D., Jr. (1980). *Systematic training for effective teaching: STET.* Circle Pines, MN: American Guidance Service.

Dinkmeyer, D., Sr., McKay, G. D., & Dinkmeyer, D., Jr. (1997). *The parent's handbook*: *Systematic training for effective parenting.* Bowling Green, KY: STEP Publishers.

Dreikurs, R. (1968). *Psychology in the classroom: A manual for teachers* (2nd ed.). New York, NY: Harper and Row.

Dreikurs, R., Cassel, P., & Dreikurs Ferguson, E. (2004). *Discipline without tears: How to reduce conflict and establish cooperation in the classroom* (rev. ed.). Hoboken, NJ: Wiley.

Dreikurs, R., Grunwald, B. B., & Pepper, F. C. (1998). *Maintaining sanity in the classroom: Classroom management techniques* (2nd ed.). Levittown, PA: Taylor & Francis.

Duke, D. L. (1979). *Classroom management.* Chicago, IL: University of Chicago Press.

Duke, D. L. (1984). *Teaching: The imperiled profession.* Albany, NY: State University of New York Press.

Ebel, R. L. (Ed.). (1969). *Encyclopedia of educational research.* New York, NY: Macmillan.

Ellis, A. K. (2001). *Teaching, learning, & assessment together: The reflective classroom.* Larchmont, NY: Eye on Education.

Ellis, A. K. (2005). *Research on educational innovations* (4th ed.). Larchmont, NY: Eye on Education.

Ellis, R. (1952). *Educational psychology: A problem approach.* New York, NY: Macmillan.

Emmer, E. T., & Evertson, C. M. (2013). *Classroom management for middle and high school teachers* (9th ed.). Upper Saddle River, NJ: Pearson.

Evertson, C. M. (1985). Training teachers in classroom management: An experimental study in secondary school classrooms. *The Journal of Educational Research, 79*(1), 51–58.

Evertson, C. M., & Emmer, E. T. (2013). *Classroom management for elementary teachers* (9th ed.). Upper Saddle River, NJ: Pearson.

Evertson, C. M., & Weinstein, C. S. (2006). *Handbook of classroom management: Research, practice and contemporary issues.* Mahwah, NJ: Lawrence Erlbaum.

Freire, P. (1970). *Pedagogy of the oppressed.* (M. Bergman Ramos, Trans.). New York, NY: Herder & Herder. (Original work published 1968).

Freire, P. (2004). *Pedagogy of indignation.* Boulder, CO: Paradigm Books.

Fullan, M. (2002). Socially smart...instructionally intelligent. *Orbit, 32*(4), 50–52.

Fullan, M. (2011). *Choosing the wrong drivers for whole system reform.* Melbourne, Victoria, AU: Centre for Strategic Education.

Gardner, H. (1983). *Frames of mind: The theory of multiple intelligences.* New York, NY: Basic Books.

Gardner, H. (1989). *To open minds.* New York, NY: Basic Books.

Gibbs, J. (2001). *Discovering gifts in middle school: Learning in a caring culture called Tribes.* Cloverdale, CA: CenterSource Systems.

Gibbs, J. (2001). *Tribes: A new way of learning and being together.* Cloverdale, CA: CenterSource Systems.

Gibbs, J. (2006). *Reaching all by creating Tribes learning communities.* Cloverdale, CA: CenterSource Systems.

Gibbs, J. (2007). *Guiding your school community to live a culture of caring and learning: The process is called Tribes.* Cloverdale, CA: CenterSource Systems.

Gibbs, J., & Ushijima, T. (2008). *Engaging all by creating high school learning communities.* Cloverdale: CA: CenterSource Systems.

Ginott, H. G. (2009). *Between parent and child.* New York, NY: Random House.

Gladden, M. (2002). Reducing school violence: Strengthening student programs and addressing the role of school organizations. *Review of Research in Education, 26*(1), 263–299.

Glasser, W. (1969). *Schools without failure.* New York, NY: Harper & Row.

Glasser, W. (1985). *Control theory: A new explanation of how we control our lives.* New York NY; HarperCollins.

Glasser, W. (1998). *Choice theory in the classroom* (rev. ed.). New York, NY: HarperCollins.

Glasser, W. (1999). *Choice theory: A new psychology of personal freedom.* New York, NY: HarperCollins.

Golding, W. (1999). *Lord of the flies.* New York, NY: Penguin Books.

Habermas, J. (1984 & 1987). *The theory of communicative action* (Vols. 1–2). (T. McCarthy, Trans.). Boston, MA: Beacon Press. (Original work published 1981).

Hall, G. E., & Hord, S. M. (2006). *Implementing change: Patterns, principles, and potholes* (2nd ed.). New York, NY: Allyn and Bacon.

Hall, G. E., & Hord, S. M. (2011). *Implementing change: Patterns, principles, and potholes* (3rd ed.). Upper Saddle River, NJ: Pearson.

Hattie, J. (2009). *Visible learning: A synthesis of over 800 meta-analyses relating to achievement.* New York, NY: Routledge.

Hattie, J. (2012). *Visible learning for teachers: Maximizing impact on learning.* New York, NY: Routledge.

Hopkins, B. (2004). *Just schools: A whole school approach to restorative justice.* London, UK: Jessica Kingsley Publishers.

Hughes, J. L. (1901). *Dickens as an educator.* London, UK: Edward Arnold.

Hunter, M. C. (1976). *Rx improved instruction: Take 10 staff meetings as directed.* El Segundo, CA: TIP Publications.

Immen, W. (2011, January 28). Defusing the uncivil workplace. *The Globe and Mail.*

Ing, C. (2006). *The expert blind spot.* (Master's thesis). Ontario Institute for Studies in Education, University of Toronto.

Johnson, D. W. & Johnson, R. T. (1989). *Cooperation and competition: Theory and research.* Edina, MI: Interaction Book Company.

Johnson, D. W., & Johnson, R. T. (1999). *Learning together and alone: Cooperative, competitive, and individualistic learning.* Edina, MN: Interaction Book Company.

Johnson, D. W., & Johnson, R. T. (2006). Conflict resolution, peer mediation, and peace making. In C. M Evertson & C. S. Weinstein (Eds.), *Handbook of classroom management: Research, practice and contemporary issues* (pp. 803–832). Mahwah, NJ: Lawrence Erlbaum.

Johnson D. W., Johnson, R. T., & Johnson Holubec, E. (2008). *Cooperation in the classroom* (8th ed.). Edina, MN: Interaction Book Company.

Johnson, S. M., Berg, J. H., & Donaldson, M. L. (2005). *Who stays in teaching and why: A review of the literature on teacher retention.* Cambridge, MA: The Project on the Next Generation of Teachers, Harvard Graduate School of Education.

Kagan, M., & Kagan, S. (1993). *Advanced cooperative learning: Playing with elements.* San Juan Capistrano, CA: Kagan Cooperative Learning.

Kagan, S. (1994). *Cooperative learning.* San Juan Capistrano, CA: Kagan Cooperative Learning.

Kagan, S., & Kagan, M. (2009). *Kagan cooperative learning* (2nd ed.). San Clemente, CA: Kagan Publishing.

Kennedy, M. (2010). Attribution error and the quest for teacher quality. *Educational Researcher, 39*(8), 591–598.

Kounin, J. S. (1977). *Discipline and group management in classrooms* (2nd ed.). Huntington, NY: R. E. Krieger.

LeDoux, J. E. (1996). *The emotional brain: The mysterious underpinnings of emotional life.* New York, NY: Touchstone.

Leithwood, K., Mascall, B., & Strauss, T. (Eds.). (2009). *Distributed leadership according to the evidence.* New York, NY: Routledge.

Léger, D. (1992). *Maxine's tree.* Victoria, BC: Orca Books.

Lewis, T. J., & Sugai, G. (1999). Effective behavior support: A systems approach to proactive school-wide management. *Focus on Exceptional Children, 31*(6), 1–24.

Little, J .W. (1982). Norms of collegiality and experimentation. *American Educational Research Journal, 19*(3), 325–340.

Little, J. W. (1990a). The "mentor" factor phenomenon and the social organization of teaching. In C. Cazden (Ed.), *Review of Research in Education, 16,* 297–351.

Little, J. W. (1990b). The persistence of privacy: Autonomy and initiative in teachers' professional relations. *Teachers College Record, 91*(4), 509–536.

Loucks, S. F., Newlove, B. W., & Hall, G. E. (1975). *Measuring levels of use of the innovation: A manual for trainers, interviewers, and raters.* Austin, TX: Southwest Educational Development Laboratory.

Louis, K., & Miles, M. (1990). *Improving the urban high school: What works and why.* New York, NY: Teachers College Press.

Lyman, F. (1981). The responsive classroom discussion: The inclusion of all students. *Mainstreaming Digest.* College Park, MD: University of Maryland.

Marzano, R. (2003). *Classroom management that works: Researched-based strategies for every teacher.* Alexandria, VA: ASCD.

Matthews, W. D. E., & Chalmers, M.W. (1959). *School and classroom management.* London, UK: Dent.

Millar, J. (1897). *School management and the principles and practice of teaching.* Toronto, ON: William Briggs.

Moffit, T. E., Caspi, T., & Taylor A. (2010). How common are common mental disorders? Evidence that lifetime prevalence rates are doubled by prospective rather than retrospective ascertainment. *Psychological Medicine, 40*(6), 899–909.

Monroe, W. S. (Ed.). (1941). *Encyclopedia of educational research.* New York, NY: Macmillan.

Monroe, W. S., & Ebel, R. L. (Eds.). (1969). *Encyclopedia of educational research.* New York, NY: Macmillan.

Naftulin, D. H., Ware, J. E., & Donnelly, F. A. (1973). The Doctor Fox lecture: A paradigm of educational seduction. *Journal of Medical Education, 48*(7), 630–635.

Nathan, M. J., & Petrosino, A. (2003). The expert blind spot among preservice teachers. *American Educational Research Journal, 40*(4), 905–928.

Page, D. P. (2009). *Theory and practice of teaching: Or, the motives and methods of good school-keeping.* Charleston, SC: BiblioBazaar. (Original work published 1847).

Palmer, J. A., Bresler, L., & Cooper, D. E. (Eds.). (2001). *Fifty modern thinkers on education: From Piaget to the present.* London, UK: Routledge.

Perkins, D. (1994). *Knowledge as design: A handbook for critical and creative discussion across the curriculum.* Hillsdale, NJ: Lawrence Erlbaum.

Perkins, D. (1995). *Outsmarting IQ: The emerging science of learnable intelligence.* New York, NY: Free Press.

Pearson, C., & Porath, C. (2009). *The cost of bad behavior: How incivility is damaging your business.* New York, NY: Penguin.

Phillips, G. (2011). *The effects of Tribes training in a beginning-teacher-education program* (Unpublished doctoral dissertation). Ontario Institute for Studies in Education at the University of Toronto, Toronto, ON.

Piaget, J., & Inhelder, B. (2000). *The psychology of the child* (2nd ed.). (H. Weaver, Trans.). New York, NY: Basic Books. (Original work published 1966).

Reati, J., & Hamilton, V. (2010). *Bullying awareness: Reclaiming our schools bullying prevention program.* Retrieved from http://www.bullyingawareness.ca/bullying-awareness-reclaiming-our-schools/teacher-and-support-staff-resource-package

Richardson, V. (Ed.). (2001). *Handbook of research on teaching* (4th ed.). Washington, DC: American Educational Research Association.

Rogers, C., & Freiberg, H. J. (1994). *Freedom to learn* (3rd ed.). Upper Saddle River, NJ: Prentice Hall.

Rosenholtz, S. (1985). Effective schools: Interpreting the evidence. *American Journal of Education, 93*(3), 352–388.

Rosenholtz, S. (1989). *Teachers' workplace: The social organization of schools.* New York, NY: Longman.

Rowe, M. B. (1972). *Wait-time and rewards as instructional variables: Their influence on language, logic, and fate control* [PDF document]. Retrieved from http://www.eric.ed.gov/ERICWebPortal/detail?accno=ED061103

Rowe, M. B. (1974). Reflections on wait time: Some methodological issues. *Journal of Research in Science Teaching, 11*(3), 263–279.

Rowe, M. B. (1986). Wait time: Slowing down may be a way of speeding up! *Journal of Teacher Education, 37*(1), 43–50.

Ryan, T., & Kariuki, M. (2011). A two-year comparative analysis of cyberbullying perceptions of Canadian (Ontario) pre-service educators. *Journal of the Research Center for Educational Technology (RCET),* 7(2), 100–111.

Seashore-Louis, K., & Miles, M. (1991). Managing reform: Lessons from urban high schools. *School Effectiveness and School Improvement, 2*(2), 75–96.

Selye, H. (1984). *The stress of life.* New York, NY: McGraw-Hill.

Shanker, S. (2013). *Calm, alert, and learning: Classroom strategies for self-regulation.* Toronto, ON: Pearson.

Shirom, A., Toker, S., Alkaly, Y., Jacobson, O., & Balicer, R. (2011). Work-based predictors of mortality: A 20 year follow-up of healthy employees. *Health Psychology, 30*(3), 268–275.

Skinner, B. F. (1968). *The technology of teaching.* New York, NY: Appleton-Century-Crofts.

Slavin, R. E. (1995). *Cooperative learning: Theory, research, and practice* (2nd ed.). Boston, MA: Allyn and Bacon.

Slavin, R. E., Hurley, E. A., & Chamberlin, A. (2001). *Cooperative learning and achievement: Research, theory and practice.* Needham Heights, Boston, MA: Allyn and Bacon.

Soar, R. S., & Soar, R. M. (1979). Emotional climate and management. In P. Peterson & H. Walberg (Eds.), *Research on teaching: Concepts, findings and implications* (pp. 97–119). Berkeley, CA: McCutchan.

Soar, R. S., & Soar, R. M. (1987). Classroom climate. In M. J. Dunkin (Ed.), *The international encyclopedia of teaching and teacher education* (pp. 336–342). New York, NY: Pergamon.

Stanley, E. (2006). *The deliverance of dancing bears.* San Diego, CA: Kane Miller.

Steinberg, L., Dornbusch, S., & Brown, B. (1992). Ethnic differences in adolescent achievement: An ecological perspective. *American Psychologist, 47,* 723–729.

Sugai, G. (2009). What is school-wide positive behavioral interventions & supports? [PDF document]. Retrieved from www.pbis.org/school/what_is_swpbs.aspx

Sugai, G., Horner, R. H., Fixson, D., & Blasé, K. (2010). Developing systems-level capacity for RTL implementation: Current efforts and future directions. In T. A. Glover & S. Vaughn (Eds.), *Response to interventions: Empowering all students to learn: A critical account of the science and practice* (pp. 286–309). New York, NY: Guilford.

Taba, H. (1966). *Teaching strategies and cognitive functioning in elementary school children.* San Francisco, CA: San Francisco State College.

Taba, H., Durkin, M. C., Fraenkel, J. R., & McNaughton, A. H. (1971). *A teacher's handbook to elementary social studies: An inductive approach* (2nd ed.). Reading, MA: Addison-Wesley.

Tobin, K. (1987). The role of wait time in higher cognitive level learning. *Review of Educational Research 57,* 69–95.

Vygotsky, L. S., & Kozulin, A. (1986). *Thought and language* (rev. ed.). (Hanfmann, E., & Vakar, G., Trans.). Cambridge, MA: MIT Press.

Wagner, J. (1980). *John Brown, Rose and the midnight cat.* London, UK: Puffin.

Webster-Doyle, T. (1997). *Why is everyone always picking on me: A guide to handling bullies.* Berkeley, CA: North Atlantic Books.

Williams, R., & Ware, J. (1976). Validity of student ratings of instruction under different incentive conditions: A further study of the Dr. Fox effect. *Journal of Educational Psychology, 68*, 48–56.

Wittrock, M. C. (Ed.). (1986). *Handbook of research on teaching: A project of The American Educational Research Association* (3rd ed.). New York, NY: Macmillan.

INDEX

CREDITS

9: (cartoon) HERMAN © (1979) Jim Unger. Reprinted by permission of Universal Uclick for UFS. All rights reserved; **18:** (cartoon) VISU*TronX*; **22:** (cartoon) CALVIN AND HOBBES © (1994) Watterson. Dist. By UNIVERSAL UCLICK. Reprinted with permission. All rights reserved; **24:** (cartoon) VISU*TronX*; **25:** (cartoon) VISU*TronX*; **26:** (poem) Vera Tourangeau. Poem: Why Does My Mother Want to Die? Page 13. Book: *Miss, It Hurts*; **27:** (cartoon) VISU*TronX*; **40:** (cartoon) HERMAN © (1979) Jim Unger. Reprinted by permission of Universal Uclick for UFS. All rights reserved; **64:** (cartoon) CALVIN AND HOBBES © (1992) Watterson. Dist. By UNIVERSAL UCLICK. Reprinted with permission. All rights reserved; **88:** (cartoon) CALVIN AND HOBBES © (1994) Watterson. Dist. By UNIVERSAL UCLICK. Reprinted with permission. All rights reserved; **92:** (cartoon) VISU*TronX*; **137:** (cartoon) CLOSE TO HOME © (1997) John McPherson. Reprinted with permission of UNIVERSAL UCLICK. All rights reserved; **140:** (cartoon) CLOSE TO HOME © (1993) John McPherson. Reprinted with permission of UNIVERSAL UCLICK. All rights reserved; **143:** (cartoon) VISU*TronX*; **150:** (cartoon) HERMAN © (1979) Jim Unger. Reprinted by permission of Universal Uclick for UFS. All rights reserved; **152:** (cartoon) CALVIN AND HOBBES © (1994) Watterson. Dist. By UNIVERSAL UCLICK. Reprinted with permission. All rights reserved; **163:** (photo) Courtesy of Barrie Bennett; **180:** (chart) The Conference Board of Canada; **190:** (cartoon) CLOSE TO HOME © (1993) John McPherson. Reprinted with permission of UNIVERSAL UCLICK. All rights reserved; **231:** (table) HALL, GENE E., HORD, SHIRLEY M., IMPLEMENTING CHANGE: PATTERNS, PRINCIPLES AND POTHOLES, 2nd Ed., ©2006. Reprinted and electronically reproduced by permission of Pearson Education, Inc., Upper Saddle River, New Jersey.